JOURNEY INTO BARBARY

WYNDHAM LEWIS

JOURNEY INTO BARBARY

MOROCCO WRITINGS
AND DRAWINGS

EDITED BY C. J. FOX

BLACK SPARROW PRESS
SANTA BARBARA 1983

JOURNEY INTO BARBARY: MOROCCO WRITINGS AND DRAWINGS OF WYNDHAM LEWIS. Copyright © 1983 by the Estate of Mrs. G. A. Wyndham Lewis by permission of the Wyndham Lewis Memorial Trust.

INTRODUCTION and NOTES. Copyright © 1983 by C. J. Fox.

LIBRARY OF CONGRESS CATALOGING IN PUBLICATION DATA

Lewis, Wyndham, 1882-1957.
    Journey into Barbary.

    Bibliography: p.
    1. Morocco—Description and travel. 2. Lewis, Wyndham, 1882-1957—Journeys—Morocco. 3. Authors, English—20th century—Biography. I. Fox, C. J. (Cyril James), 1931-   .
II. Title.
DT310.L43   1982   916.4'044   82-20784
ISBN 0-87685-520-6 (deluxe)
ISBN 0-87685-519-2
ISBN 0-87685-518-4 (pbk.)

This book is dedicated
to
Froanna
who also made the journey

ACKNOWLEDGEMENTS

For use of all Wyndham Lewis materials in this volume, acknowledgement is made to the Wyndham Lewis Memorial Trust, holder of the copyright.

The excerpts from *Kasbahs and Souks,* from Lewis's letter to Grayson and Grayson and the letter to Lewis from *The Geographical Magazine* are published with the permission of the Department of Rare Books at Cornell University, Ithaca, New York. Donald D. Eddy, head of the Department, and Susan Lovenburg were extremely cooperative in providing access and guidance to the vast Lewis archive at Cornell.

The opportunity provided by the Poetry/Rare Books Collection of the University Libraries, State University of New York at Buffalo, for an examination of the typescript of *Filibusters in Barbary* in its possession yielded invaluable results, for which thanks go to the Curator, Robert J. Bertholf. The typescript is cited with the Collection's permission.

Helpful editorial suggestions came from Paul Edwards, Bernard and Pierrette Lafourcade, Walter Michel, Omar S. Pound and George Short. The editor expresses thanks to them, to Henry A. O'Callaghan, and to Reuters Limited which provided a sabbatical leave for research.

On the pictorial side, grateful acknowledgements are due to John Cullis, D. H. Gault, Omar S. Pound, Walter Michel and Pier Van der Kruk, together with the Herbert F. Johnson Museum of Art at Cornell, which possesses a rich collection of Lewis drawings. Dr. James F. O'Roark of Santa Barbara, California, provided reproduction proofs for drawings otherwise unavailable, and Mac Campeaunu photographed the pictures which could be located in England. The maps were drawn by Nicholas John.

CJF

TABLE OF CONTENTS

FILIBUSTERS IN BARBARY
(Record of a Visit to the Sous)

Part One: London to Casa

Part Two: Rio de Oro

KASBAHS AND SOUKS

EDITOR'S INTRODUCTION

Wyndham Lewis, writer and painter, went to Morocco in the spring of 1931 and stayed there well into the summer of that year. He travelled from London via Paris to southern France, then from Marseilles by Mediterranean packet to Alicante in Spain and Oran, Algeria. From there he went south to Tlemcen and across into Morocco to Oujda and Fez, then to Marrakech (Lewis's spelling) by way of Casablanca. From Marrakech, Lewis journeyed to the southwestern town of Agadir and on into the *bled,* or semi-wilderness, of the Sous area, with its great forts—the Kasbahs—built by the Berbers at Animiter, Tagontaft and other sites dominating the valleys of the Atlas Mountains. Finally he reached a thin line of beleaguered French military outposts. Beyond that lay the Rio de Oro, the vast stretch of Western Sahara wasteland—ostensibly controlled by Spain but where in truth, given the fierceness of the marauding nomads, "no European [could] pass without immediate death or capture," as Lewis put it.

From this expedition into Morocco, the westernmost part of the Berber homeland known to tradition as Barbary, came a travel book, *Filibusters in Barbary,* published in 1932; a second book, called *Kasbahs and Souks* but never published; two articles drawn from that work, and a considerable number of drawings which exemplify the inventive and elegant side of Lewis the painter. All these facets of Lewis's "Record of a Visit to the Sous" are well represented in this new collection which should not only provide an account, in words and pictures, of Barbary and its people as seen by an artist of highly unconventional vision, but also demonstrate the contrast between his ways of transmuting experience as writer and painter. In addition the collection reveals Lewis in what for him is a highly unusual frame of mind— exuding admiration for a particular people, occasionally to the point of eulogy. What enthralled Lewis about the Berbers, when he otherwise scorned mankind as stereotyped into groups, was their vigour, tenacity, bravery, earthy artistic flair and two qualities often associated with himself: a penchant for the peripatetic life and an attitude of aggressive alertness to the machinations of circumjacent humanity. His Moroccan writings and paintings can be regarded as a tribute, sometimes laced with the sardonic to be sure, to the people he called "the Norsemen of the African steppes." His admiration is especially evident in the excerpts from *Kasbahs and Souks* now published for the first time.

Readers seeking further ideological and biographical perspectives on Lewis's Morocco trip might want to consult my article "The Forgotten *Filibusters in Barbary*" in *Wyndham Lewis: a Revaluation* (ed. Jeffrey Meyers, Athlone Press, London, 1980). Here, it can be recorded that Lewis—long fascinated by the exotic global vistas to be found in Hakluyt, Doughty, Prescott and Burton—set off for distant parts himself after almost a decade of intensive literary work. A stream of controversial books had been launched by this self-styled "Enemy" of orthodoxy, ranging from philosophy and fiction to sociology and political polemic. The book which did most to undermine his reputation, *Hitler,* had appeared shortly before his departure (he refers to it obliquely in the eighth chapter of *Filibusters in Barbary*), and he was involved in much wrangling with publishers and others. Morocco must have seemed an ideally remote region of escape from the hard labour and worries of a Luther-like figure, as he saw himself, hemmed in at his working redoubt in Ossington Street, Kensington, by a host of powerful antagonists. But fascination with the Moroccan scene soon took over from the merely negative exhilaration of escape, as is vividly shown by the literary and visual results of his explorations and researches. And, though doubtless delighted to be far removed from personal and professional crises, he in no sense put behind him the deep crisis through which the Western world at large was then passing.

As Lewis set off for Barbary, the West was wallowing in the Great Depression. This and the attendant political disasters overtaking Europe and America in 1931, along with the evolution up to that time of Morocco itself, loom large in the pages of *Filibusters in Barbary* and its companion writings, and Lewis's numerous allusions to them call for some historical scene-setting at this point. America, for instance, was still little more than halfway through the unfortunate presidency of Herbert Hoover. The light-hearted controversies of the Twenties over such issues as the anti-alcoholic Eighteenth Amendment had given way to anguish over the growing armies of nomadic unemployed and the plight of workers like the coalminers of Kentucky whom Theodore Dreiser (as Lewis notes in *Filibusters in Barbary*) outspokenly championed with revelations of their appalling conditions. In Europe, memories of the great 1914-18 war lingered on, though the last Kaiser of Germany had long since been banished to Dutch exile in Doorn. The Weimar Republic in 1931 was degenerating into the nightmare of street battles between the Far Right and Far Left as the Nazis thrust for the power they were to win two years later. In Spain, the monarchy in the person of Alfonso XIII had just been supplanted by the Republic under the likes of Zamora, Lerroux and Prieto (itself to be obliterated in the Civil War that lay five years on). In France, the Third Republic of such figures as Aristide Briand and Edouard Herriot and the bourgeois Radicals of the Bonnet Rouge circle was being attacked by the Action Française and other vociferous rightists who denounced it as, among other evil things, a front for dubious financiers like Oustric. Though the Republic was entering its last, turbulent decade, the French overseas were seemingly consolidating their hold on Morocco and other colonies in the Maghreb (Northwest Africa), as well as in neighbouring Mauritania. Farther south, they held parts of that huge band of territory spanning the breadth of the continent and named by medieval Arab historians the Soudan.

France formally assumed control of Morocco in 1912, some 850 years after Yousseff ben Tachefin and his Berber warriors swept up from the south in a great puritanical crusade, establishing Marrakech and founding the Almoravid dynasty, with a kingdom stretching from Algiers in the east to Catalonia in the northwest. As Lewis notes, successive dynasties, the Almohades and Merinides among them, came into existence as a result of similar whirlwind movements of purgation and rejuvenation among the fanatically Islamic tribes of the southern and eastern regions of Morocco, periodically galvanized by self-styled messiahs known as Mahdis. But even before the Saadian dynasty was established in the Sixteenth Century, Moroccan history had become entwined with that of Europe beyond Iberia. British commercial contacts began in 1551 with the first voyage to Barbary of "a tall ship called the Lion of London, whereof went as captaine Master Thomas Wyndham."

With the steady growth of European power, the outside world obtruded increasingly on the materially backward land of Morocco, the so-called Cherifian Empire. By the late Nineteenth Century, the system of "capitulations," under which the nationals of various European countries—the "Roumis" or Nazarenes, the frequently despised foreigners—enjoyed extraterritorial rights, had become an institution. By the 1890s, the power of the central government, the Maghzen, was so eroded that the authority of the regional chieftains in the Berber southlands had assumed national significance. The Seigneurs de l'Atlas, the "great lords of the Atlas," became so influential that one of their number, the legendary El Hadj Thami Glaoui, was able to play a crucial role in the overthrow of a notoriously fickle Sultan. Meanwhile the power of France in the country had been growing rapidly, and the fallen monarch's successor proved to be the obliging Moroccan signatory of the 1912 treaty which inaugurated the French "Protectorate." Apart from Spain, with its nominal holding in the Rio de Oro and sovereignty over the mountainous northern region of Morocco known as the Riff, the only European power to assert itself seriously in this French-dominated area of Barbary was the Germany of Kaiser Wilhelm II. The dramatic appearance of the German gunboat *Panther* off Agadir in 1911 reflected among other things the audacious commercial drive of such Teutonic magnates as the Mannesmann Brothers, as Lewis notes. After the downfall of Imperial Germany, the French in Morocco were left with no European challengers except for swarms of petty intriguers in the form of the gun-running, racketeering "filibusters" of Lewis's title.

Under Marshal Lyautey, first Resident-General of the Protectorate, the French quickly tackled the task of "pacifying" the native population, just as in ancient times the Roman power centred at Volubilis (a name recalled by Lewis) had campaigned against rebel tribesmen who swept down from the Atlas Mountains on frontier settlements of the Empire. Louis Hubert Gonzalve Lyautey (1854-1934)—formerly with the French colonial forces in Madagascar, protégé of Galliéni who commanded the French military establishment in Indochina, and disciple of the Royalist leader de Mun and of the novelist and critic de Vogüé—sought to exercise control over his new and difficult domain partly through the "Great Lords," whose power waxed accordingly. But in 1925, Lyautey resigned. The position of this Roman-style imperialist (a figure rather idealized by Lewis as a sort of hero of Right-wing Romance) had been undermined, so one gathers from *Filibusters in Barbary,* by European business schemers who had no time for the Marshal's strategy of wooing the southern Caïds with promises of safeguards against the incursions of profiteering *colons.* Lyautey's position was further weakened by the rebellion of the pioneer Moroccan nationalist Abd el-Krim in the Spanish-controlled Riff. Lyautey sailed for home in the liner *Anfa* and, according to his friends, was tendered a wholly demeaning non-welcome by his ungrateful Republican masters.

It was with revolt apparently still seething in the Riff and with the French kept busy dealing with Berber dissidence in southern Morocco that Lewis (accompanied by his wife, though this is not acknowledged in his "Record") arrived from London. The French Protectorate had, as it happened, 25 years to run before Morocco regained its independence. To most Westerners, the country perhaps was known if at all as a "Desert Song" land of Sheiks, bandits, the Foreign Legion, P. C. Wren's novel, *Beau Geste*, the Goums and the daredevils of the French

Aéropostale service pioneering new routes between Europe and South America high over the *ergs*—the great drifting sand-dunes—of the desolate Rio de Oro. The silent film era of Valentino was over but Lewis was to stumble on two bands of movie-makers, one led at Marrakech by the American director Rex Ingram, whom we find comically pilloried in a chapter of *Filibusters in Barbary* called "Faking a Sheik."

Even before Lewis embarked for Morocco, the country was well represented in British travel literature. R. B. Cunninghame Graham—Scottish nationalist, revolutionary and adventurer—had published the best-known English-language travel book on Morocco, *Mogreb-el-Acksa,* in 1898. Shortly before Lewis's arrival, the novelist Richard Hughes, whose *A High Wind in Jamaica* appeared in 1928, took up residence in Tangier and was to produce stories based on wanderings through Morocco. Two other Britons, the physician Arthur Leared and the historian-ethnologist Budgett Meakin, wrote studies of the country which, together with works by such French scholars as Gautier, Montagne and Basset, were to furnish major sources for Lewis in the wide background reading he did for his journey.

From the start, Lewis saw the Berbers—the majority population in rural areas—as ethnically separate from the Arabs. Today certain authorities deny this, insisting that the only difference lies in language. If Lewis, on this as on so many other issues, now seems decidedly unorthodox, he is not alone. There are signs that Berber culture, and particularly the distinctive architecture he admired so much, is winning recognition among some contemporary scholars. They view it as representing a tradition different from Arab culture even if, in the words of one such expert, it remains no less impregnated with Islam. "Obviously there can be no question of endangering the coexistence of the people of the Maghreb," writes one expert, Chérifa Ben Achour, on the occasion of a 1980 exhibition of art from the High Atlas held at the Musée de Grenoble. "It is simply a question of understanding and recognizing the distinctiveness of a community that has little opportunity to express itself." Politically speaking, it is interesting to note that, just as during Lewis's visit the Berber "Blue Men" of the Rio de Oro were violently at odds with the central authorities in Morocco, recent years have seen further warfare waged by equally independent-minded fighters—the Polisario Front—in that same area, against rule from Rabat.

Such are the backgrounds to Lewis's foray into Morocco. The measure of his intense interest in the scene is the fact that he wrote not one but two books about it. The second, dealing specifically with Berber life as reflected in the Kasbahs and rural Souks—the mountain castles and market centres—of the South, was to be embellished with drawings and diagrams by the author. Much of the typescript was lost in the chaotic circumstances of Lewis's life. But part of it survives, with corrections and revisions in his hand, at the Cornell University archive of his papers. The work was never published in its entirety because, possibly, it was too specialized, indeed pedantically so in places. Lewis's general troubles with publishers and reviewers (most of the critics gave *Filibusters in Barbary* a cool reception) may have been another factor. But Lewis extracted from his typescript the material for two articles which did appear, "What Are the Berbers?" and "The Kasbahs of the Atlas." The surviving unpublished chapters are mainly interesting for their rollicking evocation of the violent life of the Berbers in their southern wilderness ("The Lotus Land of the Bravo," as Lewis picturesquely called it) and for the analogies drawn between the structure of social life in the Barbary badlands and conditions in the Western world. The excerpts printed here deal with these themes and serve to round out the arguments of *Filibusters in Barbary* and the other material published previously.

The published travel book—original tentative title *Filibusters of Rio de Oro (Record of a Visit to Barbary)*—was to have included an envoi and a bibliography, neither of which finally materialized. But two chapters on the film troupes Lewis encountered in Fez and Marrakech were added at such a late stage that they do not appear in the typescript of the book in the Lewis collection at the State University of New York, Buffalo. Lewis was, to the last moment, saving these for an entirely separate work. He made still another eleventh hour decision in withdrawing from *Filibusters in Barbary* two chapters intended for the book and in fact included in the Buffalo typescript. Instead these sections finally went into the novel *Snooty Baronet* (1932) where they appear in revised form as chapters VII and VIII. They deal with a visit to the poet Roy Campbell in the south of France, Campbell appearing as "Rob Seaforth" in the *Filibusters* typescript and "Rob McPhail" in *Snooty*.

Such mixing of the fictional and "real" in the original typescript of *Filibusters in Barbary* survives into the published book (for example, the name of Borzo, the Italian hotel-keeper at Agadir, evolves from Ponzo and a number of other earlier variants). *Filibusters in Barbary* gives the impression of being not so much a travelogue as a spirited venture in semi-fiction, a working up of vivid satirical "impressions" in a way that, ironically, Lewis's old literary antagonist Ford Madox Ford would have approved. It might be because *Filibusters in Barbary* inhabited that limbo-region between the documentary "real" and the fictional—rather like the early prose sketches of Lewis's "Wild Body" period—that some of the actual circumstances of the Morocco trip, including the presence of Mrs Lewis, were glossed over.

But the book was not so fictional, in the eyes of the English courts, as to rule out the possibility of at least one of the characters ridiculed in its pages being identified. The result for the English edition, published by the London firm of Grayson and Grayson, was a suit in libel based on passages in Part Two, Chapter V, which were alleged to have concerned one Major T. C. Macfie. Lewis protested that he had not intentionally referred to Major Macfie anywhere in his text but Grayson and Grayson agreed to withdraw the book from circulation and pay Macfie compensatory fees. As a result, the London edition is now one of the rarest items of Lewisiana, though the American editions issued by Robert McBride of New York and the National Travel Club were free of these complications.

A letter to his London publisher, dated February 10, 1934, in which Lewis attacked the decision to pay compensation and withdraw *Filibusters in Barbary,* also provides a forceful defence of the book. It was, he asserted, part of a deadly serious "antiseptic mission" by a writer who had already demonstrated his sweeping satirical intentions, long before going to Morocco. Referring at one point to the contemporary political scandal in France involving that mysteriously influential underworld moneymonger, Serge Stavisky, Lewis tells his publisher:

> When we last met I outlined the questions at issue in my book—questions of great moment, as it appears to me: it was an aspect of my composition that had, apparently, impressed itself imperfectly upon your mind. Let me now recapitulate for you what I then said, more or less. Let us take the figure of the "obese groceress," encountered upon the *paquebot* from Marseilles to Oran, and upon the delineation of which your reader at that time (Pat Curwen) complimented me, you may remember, as did you also. That was exceedingly good fun you thought (and I was glad to hear it). But it must surely have occurred to you that it was something more than irresponsible fun.
>
> "And this obese groceress wallowing in the profitable squalors of the Third Republic became symbolic, perched up in that way upon the *passerelle* of the Algerian Packet. It was a Statue of Liberty. A century and a half after the tumbrels and the guillotine, here stood this bogus butter-and-egg marchioness—this enthroned charlady—being borne in triumph towards a land won for the Third Republic by the great Lyautey—a Christmas Present for a régime which could find no better way to thank him for his gift than to dismiss him at last, with an insult-

ing recall, allowing him to leave the shores of Africa anonymously, in the first Packet at hand, much like the one we travelled in—less honoured than this inflated daughter of the democratic bureaucracy, whose husband got the pip in his buttonhole from Herriot, probably, for two decades of dirty work!"

The picturesque ridicule that I called upon, in the pages of *Filibusters in Barbary,* to assist me in my antiseptic mission—throwing into the most comic, unromantic and unattractive light possible—the least flattering language I could command—the types selected, in this cosmopolitan colony of France, to show the unsatisfactory operation at a distance of a crooked political system—this picturesque ridicule was, that I should have thought is obvious enough, a *satiric* enterprise, and not the mere horseplay of a fun-maker. Indeed my other books, I should have imagined, would have been sufficient to suggest that this was the case!

In general the Moroccan scene as described in *Filibusters in Barbary* reveals the existence of a conflict between the colonizing, the Roman, impulses of the French Nation—of which impulses Lyautey is the archetype—and the irresponsible, commercial and capitalistic, interests. It is the old cleavage between the French army and the more honourable of the French professorial classes, upon the one hand, the crooked radical lawyer politicians of the Third Republic upon the other—the ephemeral instruments of irresponsible finance about whose doings I daresay you have recently been reading in the papers. Stavisky, it appears, had amongst other things, interested himself in contraband activities in Morocco. I mention all this because those are in fact the *backgrounds*—sociologic and political—of any account of Morocco that is more than a mere tourist's guide book.

A solemn purpose, then, behind all the anecdotal hilarity. But, by contrast, Lewis's Morocco drawings were done in a very different spirit, representing a fanciful, purely visual savouring of the landscape, architecture and people. Some were used as illustrations for a magazine serialization of *Filibusters in Barbary* and for one of the articles taken from *Kasbahs and Souks,* and no doubt these and others would have adorned the books if circumstances had allowed. (The American editions of *Filibusters in Barbary* were illustrated but only with stock photographs not of Lewis's making.) The drawings, however, are not mere illustrations in the conventional sense, though they complement the text closely and are reproduced in this collection as near as possible to the literary descriptions Lewis gives of the same or similar subject-matter. They are in fact autonomous works which, when juxtaposed with their literary counterparts, show how closely Lewis came to fulfilling the ideal he set himself as a practitioner of two arts: "that this double life, to be successful, has in truth to be thoroughgoingly *double*—one mode must not merge in, or encroach upon, the other." (Some mutual encroachment was inevitable, not least because Lewis's prose was such a visual means of expression. And the reader is aware of a painterly presence in, for instance, the erudite reference in a chapter of *Filibusters* called "A Child of Don Quixote" to an obscure drawing of the generously eyebrowed Anglo-Catholic, Charles Gore, then Bishop of Oxford.)

This new volume includes most of *Filibusters in Barbary*. The relatively few excisions were made to highlight the narrative and descriptive side of the book where Lewis's talent operates to best effect. Most of "What Are the Berbers?" and all of "The Kasbahs of the Atlas" (both articles published in 1933) are printed here in the context of the excerpts from the unpublished sections of *Kasbahs and Souks*. The collection ends with a sort of postscript, parts of a newspaper article by Lewis lamenting the lack of support in the West for the Berbers against the final, brutally direct, stage of French "pacification" of the remote Moroccan tribes. Throughout the book, omitted matter is signified by [. . . .]. Any matter inserted in the text is bracketed.

Eight of the reproductions illustrating this book come from photographs of the original pictures, located in private and public collections. The unlocated seven, which bear no collection designation in the list of drawings in the back of the book, were among the pictures chosen to accompany the magazine articles, and their reproduction here is based on either printer's proofs or the published illustrations.

FILIBUSTERS IN BARBARY

(Record of a Visit to the Sous)

EDITOR'S NOTE

The basic text for this section was taken from the London edition of *Filibusters in Barbary,* with some corrections and, very occasionally, the insertion of an explanatory footnote where a reference might be wholly obscure to present-day readers. (All footnotes are the editor's.)

Lewis's highly original system of capitalization, used in the British edition, is diluted so as to avoid confusion. In the late Twenties, as an indication of his view that considerations of nationality were given undue importance in the Twentieth Century world and possibly influenced by French style, Lewis took to "uncapping" the words "English," "German", "French," etc., when these were used as adjectives. But he was inconsistent in this and gradually abandoned the practice. He maintained, however, his unconventional capitalizing of what he deemed to be important nouns and, to some extent, his equally unorthodox non-capitalization of certain other words ("Communist," for instance, which he took to denote a general revolutionary ferment rather than a particular party). This collection retains some of these latter idiosyncrasies. It also retains Lewis's avoidance of commas, where this actually serves his purpose of more effectively conveying the rhythms of speech.

In most cases, the text preserves Lewis's spelling of place-names. He adheres, for example, to "Mauretania," as favoured by Meakin, and often to French rather than English transliteration, as in "Marrakech." Lewis went so far as to suggest that the sound of many of the placenames had no exact equivalent in any European language and he settled on a system that seemed to him most faithful to the originals.

Omitted from this printing of *Filibusters in Barbary* are about half each of chapters VI and VII in Part One, passages wholly devoted to details on the makeup of population effectively indicated elsewhere in the collection; a portion of Chapter XII given over to topical controversy; two sections of Part Two, Chapter VII, dealing with the minutiae of contemporary dispute over French policy on Morocco; a portion of Part Two, Chapter VIII, consisting of lengthy quotations from, and paraphrasings of, Cunninghame Graham's *Mogreb-el-Acksa;* half of Part Two, Chapter X, comprising an inquiry into rivalries among local tribes; and detailed historical background in Chapter XVII, which is rendered somewhat superfluous by the more cogent account in subsequent pages of the historical fate that befell the southern Berbers.

The English edition of *Filibusters* shows litle sign of publisher's editorial attention while some, at least, of the editing in the American was apparently done without Lewis's involvement.

PART ONE

LONDON TO CASA

AUTHOR'S FOREWORD

Headed for the High Atlas, then the Sous, and the Rio de Oro—tickets bought, hurriedly I sold my goods, "liquidated" my belongings, sold my barrels, upon which stood my lamps, put in store my books. The "Luther of Ossington Street" (as the naughty, naughty post-Ninetyish old and young kittens call him) left that ultra-Lutheran spot, he kicked the dust of moralist and immoralist England off his un-Lutheran feet, determined for a while to exchange it against the red dust of the Sand-Wind of the Rio de Oro! I said I would go back to the tent for a while. I promised myself that I would forget this squalid quagmire of an oasis, over-moist London. Thoroughly unanchored, all trim in the rear, ready for anything (even slander after demise) with a *loupe*, water and oil colours, wood and clay palettes, razors for pencils, inks, insecticide, an *Arabic Without Tears*, a *Berber for the British*, and a *Fool-proof Tifinar*, a map of the Sahara and one of the High, Middle and Anti-Atlas—*Stovarsel* against dysentery, a Kodak (an unfortunate purchase)—unaccompanied, I set out.

Departure in the heroic style: though of course it was unsaluted that I left; shrouded in anonymity I "stole silently away" (in fact quite like the proverbial Arab, having struck my tent first—and in order, as it happened, to go out in search of that proverbial Bedouin). The sedentary habits of six years of work had begun, I confess, to weary me. Then the atmosphere of our dying European society is to me profoundly depressing. Some relief is necessary from the daily spectacle of those expiring Lions and Eagles, who obviously will never recover from the death-blows they dealt each other (foolish beasts and birds) from 1914 to 1918, and all the money they owe our dreary old chums the Bankers for that expensive encounter. I thought I would not take the beaten track to Russia (where all those go as a rule who require a "breather" after too prolonged immersion in the fumes and fogs of "capitalism") but to a less controversial spot.

Perhaps nothing short of the greatest desert in the world, or its proximity, would answer the case. Yes, the Kalahari or Gobi would be too little! Also, most luckily, the biggest on earth is also the nearest. I said to myself that I would go to the highest mountains in Africa and look down upon the mirages of the great electric desert, then: perhaps, I would come round behind the mountains, this side of them, and enter this enormous waste from the West, at its Atlantic extremity, rather than approach it via Biskra, or the "loop" Beni Abbes–Timimoun–Guardaïa—with all the stupefying squalor of Anglo-American tourism about one, poisoning the wells and casting its Baedekered blight.

I was in Morocco all the summer: I got a footing in the High Atlas without any difficulty. But the latter part of the programme indicated above, namely, to enter the Sahara at its western end, was, I discovered, impracticable. You would have to go as far south as Dakar, in Senegal, it turned out, and so to Timbuctoo, and thence up to the Touat Palm Path, to approach the Sahara from the Atlantic. Odd as it may sound, it is in fact impossible to enter the Sahara from the West. The Occidental Sahara is *verboten* as far as the Paleface is concerned. No European, I discovered to my extreme astonishment, is able to set foot upon these forbidden sands and steppes. The finest of all the *ksars*,[1] those at the foot of the Moroccan Atlas, are unapproachable. The Rio de Oro is a closed book. There is over a thousand miles or more of quite unknown desert—*erg*, mountain, steppe, with towns, *ksars*, oases. No European has ever been able so far to penetrate it. One rapidly crossed this region in 1850. This was, it would seem, the only European who has done so. His name was Léopold Panet. He started from St.-Louis-du-Sénégal. Wounded and robbed of everything, he succeeded in reaching Mogador. And then last year, in 1930, a young Frenchman made a feverish raid into it from the North to a depth of a few hundred miles. He lies buried in the citadel of Agadir. "Voir Smara et mourir!" is more or less his epitaph.

As to the Palm Gardens, and, it is reported, beautifully, built Saharan *ksars* east of this ancient Kingdom of Tazerwalt, we have two or three meagre accounts of that, none recent. Foucauld, disguised as a Jew, hid in one or two of them for a few weeks. Then there was Rohlfs. But it is really the most unknown part of the Globe.

Upon the edge of this vast and perilous western desert I halted. Who would not? And the following book which I have called *Filibusters in Barbary* is an account of what I learnt in Southern Morocco, short of this impassible line of "dissidence," as it is called by the French. Beyond those desertic marches, where "Rio de Oro" begins, and the French Zone ends, no European can pass without immediate death or capture, and if the latter, there are, it seems, fantastic ransoms accompanying that.

---

[1] Fortified villages.

CHAPTER I

A CONVENTIONAL FAREWELL

England had its watercart on at full blast as I left; there had been no sun for ten months—if you ceased to allow the Briton to wet his inside with a little bitter hops he would at once give up the unequal fight. England, my England! I gasped, my face streaming with rain. Shall I return; or, like so many of your sons, become from henceforth an exile? I wished frankly to escape for ever from this expiring Octopus, that held me to it by my mother-tongue (unless America can be said to share, with England, that advantage over me).

My first stop was in Paris: that was a short stop, as all stops in Paris should be. There I provided myself with a quantity of books and maps. I always desire the fullest information regarding any habitation or work of man, strange to me, which I propose to approach and interrogate. I was about to visit the country of Jugurtha and of Masinissa, so I began reading about these persons[1]—before I set foot in Maghreb I knew more about the inhabitants of, say, the hinterland of Tetouan than they know themselves—though I never have been to Tetouan, and only came to read about it because the Gomara are a sort of "Soussi," strangely "Berberophonic" in the midst of Arabic-speaking tribes. But as a result of this preliminary preparation, I knew long before I put my legs across its back or had ever clapped eyes on it, that the ass of which the Berbers make such an extensive use is of Egyptian origin, and that the Berbers got to know of these valuable little animals through the Libyans, the people occupying the steppes west of the valley of the Nile. The wild ass, its ancestor, is still to be found in the North-East of Africa; that I knew too. Then, when I reached it, I was able to recognize in Maghreb which manner of goat alone in fact belongs to it—the skinny one namely, with very long black hair, like tufts from its master's head, apparently not interesting to the dairyman; whereas I knew that the Maltese, Spanish, and Angora goats (which I recognized at once) were new-comers.—This will suffice to give you an idea of the extent of my reading before I landed at Oran. It may be wrong, but that is the way it interests me to enter a

---

[1] Kings of ancient North Africa.

country. I stepped on shore in Algeria better documented than most guides, although I had never so much as seen an Arab before, except in France selling carpets.

Paris I left within twenty-four hours. That Mecca of the high-brow globe-trotter is down on its luck, progressively it has had its life squeezed out of it by the Machine-Age and is at its last gasp as a pleasure-city; Berlin could beat it if it were not for Hitler. For a day the express train dashed on through the rain, hail and fog. Avignon was reached at length, and the sun sprang forth and shone. It was April, for two years I had not seen the sky properly; so at Avignon I got out and looked up. There at least was the proper sunlit sky. I will not describe it: there it was, however, blue and well, after the sick, moist countries. Avignon, or a little before it, is where travelling south the sky can first be encountered. You don't often see it as far north as Rheims. All Heidsick or Ayala[1] must, of course, come from somewhere else: they have to stick to the old names—there was sun there once.

The climate of Europe is changing. Indeed the climate of the world is doing so. In New York, taxi-drivers (great observers of the weather, of necessity) informed me—that was three years ago—that ten years before that there were always heavy snowfalls in the winter in New York State. For several years they had seen no snow. The seasons in New York, in short, are now less differentiated. But in Morocco they say, on the other hand, the climate has become European (European in the old, superseded sense of seasonal)—"Now we have your European seasons," as one *Vieux Morocain* said to me, with some pride, as if it were a result of the French Protectorate.

However, having struggled with a strong locomotive out of the zone of the rain-storms, I alighted at Avignon. From that city, still everything brightly lighted, I went on to Marseilles.

---

[1] Champagne.

27

CHAPTER II

MARSEILLES GOES JAPANESE

Marseilles was full of Japanese Jack-tars. There were three slate-coloured warships in port, hung with tiny Japanese washing, like a million sheets of notepaper, at the bottom of the port. What a strange appearance the Japanese present in this particular disguise! How un-nautical! Thousands passed up and down in parties. They were not only extremely slight and small, but in every respect looked like the merest children. Looking in their timid mask-like faces, noticing their disciplined behaviour, one was compelled to think of something like a Celestial Reformatory out for a constitutional, with its mild warders. Why had these good children been put in the Reformatory? Perhaps for confessing that they had secretly desired to possess a blossom off a cherry-tree which was taboo! In addition to such immaturity, they displayed an uncanny listlessness.

Boats full of little children, dressed up as Jack-tars, continued to be sent ashore. They pervaded the town like an army of phantom dolls. In all directions, a little stiff, they drifted, interested in nothing, their arms hanging lifeless at their sides. A few miniature officers, bandy-legged and grasping toy-cutlasses of filigreed brass, transfixed in attitudes of studied naval decorum, gazed in different directions. These were waiting to catch trams, or had drawn up ponderously to orient themselves. The exaggerated Europeanism of the Cannebière, with its shabby uninteresting South-French republican *populo*, of swarming shoppers and factory workers, absorbed these packets of Japanese with difficulty.

Before this I had not realized how youthful in the mass a great nation could remain—or was it become? Here were swarms of small creatures in tutelage. They were authentic Peter Pans, it could not be doubted. An "old Asiatic race" we should call them. But if you think of an average able-seaman of the British Warfleet you see that he would look like a hoary elder, of a more primitive stock, compared to any given specimen of this Far-Eastern nursery afloat—trained, paradoxically, to handle torpedoes, and fire Thirteen-Inch Artillery.

Next afternoon I went on board the packet for Oran, in Algeria.

After seeing about my cabin, I returned to the main deck, and stood looking at a Japanese battleship—with the festoons of tiny pants and vests of the Japanese children-ratings and the long pencils of their slate-blue guns—just the same size as if they had all been giants, or British Blue-Jackets, that manned them. Once or twice I turned over in my mind the opinions of the average townbred routine-man regarding what are for us the distant places of the earth. I just put myself the question, for form's sake—why was I going out to discover the Grand Style at first-hand, upon the spot, to interrogate or enjoy it in the flesh, or in the dark carapace of famous mountains? Such things can be imagined. All experience teaches us the extreme difficulty of experiencing in the flesh the enjoyments of the mind, when it dreams of what is strange to it.

All I could reply to that secular argument, of the *plus ça change* order, in the face of the displacement I was about to make, was first that I am restless by nature. I prefer moving about it seems. Secondly, in England we exist so much in the midst of the reverse of all that is satisfyingly life-size, naked and simple, so much in fact in contact with what is undersized and so *everymanishly* mean (far too *menschlich*, in the German of Nietzsche) that one might cease to believe in its existence if one did not go and resume contact with natural things from time to time, to forget how men have dwarfed it to their own stature, especially under the guidance of the Democratic Idea. To whom must I excuse myself for preferring the Sand-Wind to the fogs of Anglo-Saxony (some mental, some physical)? I spat into the waters of the port when I came to the *Democratic Idea,* and went below to the bar.

CHAPTER III

HIGH TABLE

(*The Ship to Africa*)

I was going to Oran, which is the Mediterranean port for French Morocco. You pass two nights at sea, you stop for an hour at Alicante in Spain. No international tourists ever go by this packet, I was told: it is the route used by officials and officers going on leave and returning to duty. After nightfall there was a dense haze, it grew into a regular fog as we proceeded. The ship's siren roared and boomed, with twenty-second intervals. At dinner a surprising pandemonium occurred: the sepulchral bellow of the Radio (Toulouse Station, I imagine) mingled with the siren, and then a gramophone was brought into action. It all sounded like Radio, complete with atmospherics and groans of the abyss. But it may have been all gramophone—done with knitting-needles and cracked disks, it was impossible really to say which.

In consequence of some of the combination of sounds involved, an uproar resulted that was in its kind unique. The *Valse triste* of Sibelius for instance and the siren in sinister chorus were a particularly disturbing number. At moments the discord became so startling that even the colonial passengers seemed to notice it slightly. For my own part I was seized upon once or twice by an indescribable panic. There was something frantic and deliberate in the cacophonous attack, taken in conjunction with the stolidity of the ship's guests—the decorous colonialism of them. Some communist demon of the mist must have conspired with the ship's staff—doubtless "Reds" to a man, how could they be otherwise!—to afflict with disarray the dinner-hour rites of this imperial packet.

During *It Happened,* the sixth number on the programme, the steward rushing from the pantry with a pagoda of fresh plates and dishes, succumbed to a slight irregularity in the movement of the ship. The heavy ship's china cascaded to the floor, where it crashed to pieces at the same time as the thunder of the siren broke out again—and the siren was the most full-blooded, I think, that any boat of that tonnage can ever have carried in its funnel, reminiscent of those apocalyptic voices possessed by some undersized inoffensive men, to startle a

street or electrify a railway-carriage, when they ask for a match.

Should we at this moment have rammed a vessel transporting luna-
tics from say Corsica to Brest (or vice-versa)—then, I felt, a certain
satisfying logic, a cause and effect of sorts, would have been introduced into this irrational, gratuitous disorder—but as it was, wild but
squalid, and merely ridiculously bereft of all sweet sense.

The *Programme* (whether Radio or Gramophone as I have said I do
not know) was as follows—I put it in my pocket before leaving the
table.

PROGRAMME

1. Si j'étais Roi (Ouverture 1ère partie).
2.   do.   do. (do.   2ème partie).
3. Carmen (Sur la place).
4.   do.   (Que cherchez-vous?).
5. Song of the Dawn.
6. It Happened.
7. Valse triste (Sibelius).
8. Sérénade. Vol du Bourdon.
9. Nelly Waltz.

2ème partie
1. Comte Luxembourg (Je vous aime).
2. La Veuve joyeuse (Heure exquise).
3. Léonore, No. 3 (Ouverture).
4.   do.   do (do.   )
5. Manon (Avez-vous peur).
6.   do.   (do.   )
7. Whatever You Are.
8. Just Imagine.
9. Paillasse (Pauvre Paillasse).

But the first-class dining-saloon afforded one a first furtive glimpse
of the domestic side of Colonialism. All Colonialism must be much the
same. There was a table at the upper end of the saloon, that was the
"high table," as it were. Not being French, a place was reserved for me
at an inferior table, where I messed with a German governess whose
destination was Alicante.

There were very few passengers on the boat, at the "high table"
there were only four—a middle-aged civilian and his wife, a young
officer and his wife. Later they were joined by the captain—with as
much gold braid as a Commodore of the White Star Fleet. The two

colonial couples stood up when this dignitary entered—with a stern look, because there was a fog.

During the two days' trip the wife of the colonial official made her appearance in a succession of the most surprising costumes. Upon the second night this wardrobe culminated in a massive white silk dressing-gown—which was Roman, which was senatorial. It recalled the contemporary illustrations in the Alcan Edition of the works of Guy de Maupassant. She took the floor upon this Mediterranean ferry with the air of a typically gross operatic empress, impersonating a Wagnerian goddess. There was a Second Empire fringe, a particular corseted embonpoint, an unquestioning, and unquestionable feminity—all of which were redolent (for that is the word) of the rounded bourgeoisdom of a recently vanished period of French history: the "Victorianism of the French" in fact. How long could this imposing woman possibly have been in Morocco (or in Oran) in order to have preserved so intact all this impressive provincialism, this mellow Gallic light of the France that knew Boulanger, or Sarah Bernhardt *jeune*—before the "Revolution Dreyfusienne"?

This was a great woman, but *très femme*, as befitted the lady of a French colonial mandarin. Confidences of a rather intimate and sickly order, as it were, spontaneously flowered, under the stimulation of the captain's wine. The big queen among colonial women tenderly went through a little act, a dove-act, with her blushing coco, at her side, for the benefit of the young honeymoonish couple, the young staff-officer, who looked on *attendri* of course. A colonial idyll of "the generations," Cupid omnipresent, ambushed in the frowsy curtains of the Packet!

This great old Daughter of Empire (French style) was plainly the ornamental half of a great little minor administrator of sorts, probably a cantonal Post and Telegraphic Chief, or perhaps the *Sous-directeur* of The National Office of Combustible Liquids. He might have been the Town Clerk and treasurer of Oran itself, or the *Intendant* of the Salt Régie of the Tell. That she really was the wife of a little Somebody, ashore, was confirmed later in Oran itself, for, escorted with great ceremony by several obsequious persons, I observed her sail up and settle, three days after that, in a conspicuous place in the main café of the town—the Continental, which had an immense, dark and tented terrace, the largest café terrace I have ever encountered.

During this first triumphal, but turbulent, evening on board, as the Queen of High Table, senior colonial lady present, she played her part to perfection. When the pandemonium all about her was at its height, she was graciously, and I think wittily, conversing—just as if

these hideous discordant explosions had been arranged in her honour (a little barbaric, but well-meant!) and as if in fact they had been
the invariable accompaniment of this delicious journey back to the
quasi-proconsular splendours of her official life beyond the seas.

When the steward hurled all the plates at her feet, while the strains
of "It Happened!" smote her ear, and the Siren rushed in and shat-
tered her ear-drum as if resolved to finish her off, she merely gave a
whimsical side-glance at the crockery, and seemed (ever so slightly,
but with a matchless graciousness) to incline her head in the direction
of the resourceful menial. Next moment she had obviously forgotten
his existence—although to be forgotten, even, by such a lady would be
an experience that the less favoured might well envy.

Someone said about Talleyrand that he was such a perfectly
polished gentleman that, should you approach him stealthily from
behind, while he was conversing, and kick him hard in the bottom, he
would not show by the displacement of so much as a muscle of his face
that he was conscious of what had occurred—except perhaps for giving a slight jerk. That I was reminded of this story does not mean that
the sons and daughters of France at the High Table of the Packet
could in any particular recall such an exquisite figure as that of Talleyrand. (Indeed I am sorry that I mentioned that Frenchman of the
Ancien Régime at all, in the same breath with this company. It was
undoubtedly a grave fault of taste.)

There was no British standoffishness or snobbish shyness however
about this colonial elegance. The graciousness of the premier lady was
a democratic condescension. Even our humble estate was not forgotten. The following morning, as we were finishing breakfast, the Sile-
sian governess and I, this great White Queen sailed over from the
High Table and, to the obvious alarm of the little wizened flower of
East Prussia, addressed a few gracious words to her. It was the condescension of the victorious victim to the vanquished victor, so to
speak. The lady "Hun" laughed afterwards, slyly, as the "Hun" will.
But she would often be spoken to after that, for an appreciable
number of minutes or seconds, in passing, and made at home on the
Packet—the great freemasonry of the *Frauenzimmer*—I turned away
when it occurred, as a gentleman will avert his head when passing a
door marked DAMES.

In the night the fog lifted. Next day was fine and cool. I never
ascended myself to what I suppose is called the "Hurricane Deck" or is
it only "the Bridge"? It is upmost of all—the Officers' Quarters were
there and the captain when he wished the ship to go a little quicker, or
slower, or to left or right, as the case might be, rang a bell on a sort of

35

elevated verandah. There were cabins on a little deck just below the verandah. There all the officers in turn, and there were a good few, might be observed playing with a brightly-polished instrument of the navigator's art. I dare say it was a patent sextant, secured on "appro." Evidently it was new, and they all played with it in turn. That evening—dressed as a lady-motorist of the earliest days of the internal-combustion engine (with a dash of the Victorian yachts-woman, something Liptonesque, R.Y.S., and smelling of Cowes, I. of W.) the great official's lady was up on the Hurricane Deck. Whatever it might be at ordinary times, it became a Hurricane Deck at least the moment she trod it. Buffeted by a mild breeze—she allowed her spot-less garments to billow out gently behind—her arms described arcs which embraced the horizon. And this obese groceress wallowing in the profitable squalors of the Third Republic became symbolic, perched up in that way upon the *passerelle* of the Algerian Packet. It was a Statue of Liberty. A century and a half after the tumbrels and the guillotine, here stood this bogus butter-and-egg marchioness— this enthroned charlady—being borne in triumph towards a land won for the Third Republic by the great Lyautey—a Christmas Present for a régime which could find no better way to thank him for his gift than to dismiss him at last, with an insulting recall, allowing him to leave the shores of Africa anonymously, in the first Packet at hand, much like the one we travelled in—less honoured than this inflated daugh-ter of the democratic bureaucracy, whose husband got the pip in his buttonhole from Herriot, probably, for two decades of dirty work!— So thought I privately at least to myself, as I watched this gutter-empress, surrounded by the gold-braided officers' corps of this glor-ified ferry.—And then one ran back into the cabin and brought out the gilded instrument. Our old female friend took it as the Queen of England takes anything that is offered her for inspection, anywhere that she goes, held it up and squinted through it, sat down and placed it upon her knees, asking the most amazingly well-informed ques-tions, one could see at a glance. And I noticed they were all playing with it still when the gong went for dinner.

Upon the first night out the captain would slip away from time to time—the Siren called him—everyone understood! Duty necessitated the abrupt abandonment of a half-finished mouthful—*the captain's place is the bridge!* Was there not a dense fog? He did not excuse himself—as we saw him go the bureaucrat stuck out his jaw and nar-rowed his eyes (it was a Man's World after all!) but the ladies under-stood as well. Anyone could plainly see that they understood per-fectly: it was not their *wish* that the captain should say "excuse me" like a perfect gentleman every time. They in fact respected him for putting the Boat, so to speak, above the Soup Tureen.

But upon this second night as ever the captain was able to give his undivided attention to his distinguished passengers. The Great Woman was very tender with her "coco" (and in the gloaming, afterwards, upstairs on deck, we had a glimpse of her nestling her fringed head upon "coco's" little shoulder, while they both stared over the side of the ship in the direction of what once was Carthage, thinking of their humble beginnings). These frequent unbendings on the part of this splendid matron brought home to everybody on board the truth of that saying of the Universal Poet's—"a little touch of nature makes the world kin," or some similar saying, of universal application.

The French Military are the nicest people in Morocco, and the young officer was a pleasant fellow enough. But a colony is a colony the world over. He and the bureaucrat knew the same places and people, it was evident: and they exchanged anecdotes which never failed to secure a good hearty colonial laugh, about various *indigènes*—the natives they administered; and the droll sayings and doings of Ali and of Mohammed—of Si M'hamed and M'hamed *tout court*—were greatly relished.

Si Seddig was a queer fish, and Si Abdesselan was very odd and childish in all his reactions to the highly-civilized European world, and they all had many a good laugh over these worthies and many others too. It was a good solid colonial evening.

Before lunch I had been attempting to get hold of the Fräulein's tongue, to demonstrate how we pronounced our famous TH. I once did seize it in my thumb and forefinger and as I did so she said Oh *Thont Thease!*—the experiment succeeded. The slight compression of the air behind the front teeth is always difficult to bring about in a mouth unaccustomed to that operation. Later she had bitten her tongue in attempting to say "thoroughly thoughtful." Having then burnt it with the soup, she left the table, of course cursing English, and I had plenty of opportunity of listening to the talk at the High Table, and lunch was as good as dinner for that purpose. Its statuesque Queen was at her best however in the evening, dinner was essentially her meal: lunch was an *hors-d'œuvre*, or an undress rehearsal for the evening.

CHAPTER IV

A CHILD OF DON QUIXOTE

At five o'clock, upon the second day, we got into Alicante, and the Fräulein went ashore. I waggled my necktie in farewell, she waved her pudgy fist. The poor old girl will never be able to say "thoroughly thoughtful": she will always have to refer to the present premier of Spain as *Samora* instead of *Thamora,* for I doubt if she will find a Spaniard who will go into her mouth after her tongue as I did and run the risk of being bitten—she was no beauty was old Hedwig, but I have a liking for all of German blood.

A large *Valenciano* with his arm in a sling came over the side, that is to say up the plank. We both looked down at the Republic. There were Civil Guards by the gangway, to stop *emigrés* smuggling out gold, and communists bringing in Red Tracts—looking both ways at once—to Left and Right (between the horns of a dilemma really). I asked the big fellow with the white sling how Spain was and he looked at it and said *tranquil all over.* He fixed his eye on the holster of a Civil Guard and said it was *a good revolution* and that it was led by very intelligent persons. He said that if the king came back they would kill him. I said what I thought of that Plus-four Gossip-star and generally of all Suck-up-to-the-Subject Royalties, and he agreed: for he could see I was speaking ill of Royalty and that was enough: the mere word—*Rey*, I could see, awakened all his superstitious wrath. He was a Lerroux republican. He described the priests sitting in the cafés with long pagan cigars, and abusing the Republic, while they had their shoes blacked. "Priest," like "king," was a word that caused him to see pink. I left him and went to examine the other Spanish passengers.

There was one only who was interesting. From behind he would be mistaken for a very tall backward sixth-form lout fresh from school— still rapidly growing out of his clothes—his jacket creeping up over his bottom, his sleeves stealing up his arms and leaving the boney wrists bare or merely shirted and boyishly becuffed. He had his hands in his trouser pockets. As aimless as the wind, he stood about and stared fixedly into space: but when he wheeled about he unexpectedly re-vealed a long El Greco mask. He turned out to be a blue-grey person-age of sixty or so, with the large brown eyes of an innocent doe, with brows most beautifully arched like an early heavily stylised portrait of

Bishop Gore. Although ill-anchored and aimless, and prone to drift hither and thither, he had the air of being completely at ease with no care in the world more than such as might visit a wild ruminant in the midst of its kind.

As always happens, the publication of such a masterpiece as *Don Quixote* gave birth to quantities of chivalrous grotesques all over Spain. They linger to this day. In the same way (minus the masterpiece) Edgar Wallace and his school are responsible for the great popularity of crimes of violence in England and cause our society to breed up an army of criminals and an ever-swelling police force. But this man was one of the finest Don Quixotes I had ever seen—painted by El Greco. I suppose that he was a small land-owner from La Mancha: I guessed that he left Alicante every few days with a few thousand pesetas in the heels of his shoes, deposited them in a bank in Oran, went back to La Mancha, got another note or two, and smuggled that batch out by the next Packet, and had been doing this for weeks—for he seemed well satisfied, and was not at all unlike a squirrel, whose depository was already packed with nuts, out of reach and well-concealed. Or if you cared to allow some lean and dreamy stag the habits of a squirrel, then you would have more accurately the effect produced—though he may have been a Spanish solicitor's clerk sent to Alicante upon a mission, returning to report for duty next morning.

The quixotic physique will set the most prosaic dreaming, after the manner of Cervantes. There may have been no smuggled notes in the heel of this person's shoe. He may not have been a Grandee of Spain. He may never have noticed that there had been a Revolution. All I can say is that his appearance lent itself to the more sensational interpretations.

Apart from whether my discovery was one of the escaping *ricos*, or not, he was of great interest. At dinner he sat among a herd of French bagmen. The dining-saloon was now far busier. These jolly drummers were spinning yarns. These yarns were followed by this Spanish gentleman with the keenest relish. He neglected his food entirely in order to miss nothing of the story; when the bagmen lowered their voices he craned his long neck forward, he approached his head so near to the narrator as almost to brush him with the bristles of his beard. Once he actually got his head in between two of them. He drank in every syllable. When the joke came he lay back and laughed without restraint: and if the steward asked him whether he had finished (though he had not even begun) he quickly waved his hand and dismissed the dish and the steward too. These troublesome interruptions on the part of the personnel occurred at every course: always with the same half-impatient surprise this last of the Hidalgos waved his hand without looking round, to indicate that the plate could be removed.

He never spoke to any of these café wits whose yarns he so greatly appreciated. They, on their side, accepted him as a deaf-mute, evidently a little "soft"—except once or twice they gave him a sharp look when he laughed too loud and long.

But all good things have an end: these Good Companions rose from the table to go out, and the Spaniard seemed extremely taken aback. Hurriedly he arose as well. He thrust his hands half in his pockets (his trousers were too small for them to go in altogether): he followed the jolly bagmen to the door, stood for a moment scratching his grey beard, the thin fingers of his fringe sticking forward from the top of his lofty forehead. But they evidently disappeared. So he drifted off in the opposite direction. He had lost sight of this laughable troupe of resourceful clowns, he had resigned himself to their departure!— Later I noticed the group of bagmen in the smoking-room playing poker. My Quixote I came upon with his hands in his pockets looking down into the Engine Room. With the same childish curiosity in his noble, beautifully proportioned face, he gazed down at the inexplicable operations of the lethargic engineers.

Next morning the sun rose over the mountains of Africa. I watched it through the porthole: and as in one of those foreshortened panoramas, modelled in plaster and roughly painted, used by the *Syndicat d'Initiative* to show you the position of the main touristic plums and show-places, I could imagine behind the folds of the Kabyle cliffs, only a stone's throw beyond, the swamps of the Congo, the hinterland of Lake Tchad. Sunrise over the tropics was the sunrise I saw, reflected up and embuing with a peach-red glare the mists of Oranie, and the terrestrial plane of the sunrise seen between the crevices of the rocks.

At six we entered the port of Oran. And the delicate saffron and rose of this important, but purely commercial, city, is much to be preferred, I think, to the uniform smart whiteness of Tangier.

CHAPTER V

ORAN

Oran is a stereotyped French city. The Place d'Armes is its centre. Facing this, in the Boulevard Séguin, is the Continental Hotel, and its enormous roofed semi-circle of café-terrace. In all such coastal cities in Africa you get two or three big boulevards with palms. Here it is the Boulevard Galliéni and the Boulevard Séguin. There is the Lafayette or similar store, and of course the Posts, Town Hall, Churches and Police Stations—the little model of French Civilization is complete. More or less entangled with it, is the "native town"—*la ville indigène*, or the "Medina" as alternatively it is called. At Tangier these *barrios* are pleasantly fused: but in Oran not so. You must walk up the hill to reach the "native" districts. There at last you come upon a vast parade-ground, fringed with cafés and *fondouks*—I scarcely know what to call it, it is an open space with two lines of sun-blanched trees, as long as Whitehall and twice as wide. There at once is the Berber world.

This *place*—square, truncated Boulevard, promenade, or whatever it is—is to my mind more interesting than all the European Mediterranean put together. The people who fill it are as they have always been. Is not that enough? Their archaic nobility sticks out in stark elevation, like a grand black forest above the depressed levellings of our Western life. Our Machine Age civilization has pushed its obscene way into the heart of their country: but for the Berbers nothing is changed, except that, by God's will, we are there, and they wish we would leave. Anything that is, is. The Nazarene is accepted for God's sake, since God has willed it—that certainly is the secret of their docility. Meanwhile they proceed about their business, wrapped in their togas and cloaks, hooded or veiled, just as if we had never existed. That is at least the impression you receive when you first pass over into this archaic zone, this "Barbary," when you reach that part of the French coast-city where there are nothing but "natives" (that is to say the people to whom the country belongs, as much as anything belongs to anybody).

A century hence, naturally, when all these cloaks have fallen from their shoulders, veils dropped from their faces, *babouches* left their feet, *haiks* been unwound from them, and the last turban has left the

41

last shaven poll, when in place of which all sport the inverted scarlet flower-pot, the *chequia*—when all are bobbed, water-waved, shingled and helmeted—then will Berbers be just like us. There is no inalienable, inherent, "mysterious" dignity about Berbers. Need I say that? It is the *time* or "period" they represent. That is better than ours—*better* if you mean by that adjective possessed of more dignity, possessing all the grand attitudes and habits impossible to that "hurried man" of transatlantic pattern.

So it can be said quite soberly—with none of the emotional romancing of a Lawrence—that Oran is more interesting than anything upon the European side of the Latin Sea (without setting up Carthage against Rome, because the former is so deliciously "oriental" or any such exotic shallowness of the marvel-loving savage of the West). With us it is *the time* that is out of joint, not the place.

Passing out of the boulevards of the French Occupation you step into the first ten pages of the universal history book—you are behind, or beyond, *la cité antique*. Or it is, in other places (in the urban centres of this backward life, for instance Fez), as if you could embark at St. Mark's, and discover yourself in the midst of the Venice of the grandparents of Canaletto (who was already getting a little Lawrence-like about his own canals) or go to Athens and find the Attic world of Pericles intact.

Oran is of course not the best example to take—Morocco carries all this out far more fully. The farther south you go, again, to the Atlas and the Sous, the more complete is the illusion of a radical temporal displacement. But the temporal break is quite marked enough even in this enormous "native" meeting-place at Oran to justify my claim. For this immediate effect, even in Oran, the scale and shape of the great meeting-place in question is responsible, I think.—The two main features of the city of Oran are the out-size Café Continental, and this out-size Berber Square at the top of the hill. Both are too big for Oran. It is like a man whom you remember distinctly because for some reason his extremities, his head and feet, were furnished with head-gear and foot-gear unnecessarily roomy.

CHAPTER VI

BY WHOM IS FRENCH NORTH AFRICA INHABITED?

Oran is, in this story of a particular journey, important. In visiting a country for the first time, your head is stuffed with preconceived anticipatory pictures, is that not so? Travel to Warsaw to-morrow, if it is your first trip, and you will enter it with a fancy-town (a sketch only perhaps, but quite solidly built) installed in the foreground of your consciousness. Then will come the confrontation! The two towns, that of fancy and that of fact, will without your noticing it slowly begin fighting. At once there are certain fundamental things, which, usually unexpectedly, you discover, one after another. This is of course very much the case in North Africa. It was at Oran that for me those fundamental adjustments occurred. Hence, as far as this book is concerned, the moment has come (since I have reached Oran) to acquaint you with them, too.

There was first the place, and then there were the people in the place. I will take the latter first.

To start with, then, when you first begin looking about you after landing in French Africa you gradually come to discover by whom Algeria and Morocco are at present peopled. Beforehand I should have said, if asked, *By the Arabs and the French*, and have left it at that. That is, in fact, not the case at all—unless you extend to the word "French" a significance far more inclusive than is generally meant by that term—and unless you realize that "Arab" is in no way identical with the autochthonous Berber population of Maghreb, but that it can only properly be used of the ruling and administrative class, or the tribes of certain well-defined areas. (The "Gich" tribes of the plain, about Marrakech, and the Ma'qil of the Sahara, or what is left of them, are the best examples: though many Arabic-speaking tribes are no more Arab it seems than you or me, however much they may claim Arab descent.)

Now in the cafés, shops and hotels you will find quantities of Europeans, as opposed to *indigènes* (as the Englishman would say, "natives"). They all speak French. But you will notice at once that their French is most peculiar, sometimes more and sometimes less. Often they speak Arabic with a suspicious ease. And then at last you realize that the number of French-born Frenchmen even in Oran, is surprisingly small, or even French subjects who are of French blood.

If, for convenience, you divide the inhabitants into "White" and "Coloured," you will find that eighty per cent of the "Whites" are Algerians, Maltese, Italians, Spaniards, Jews, Levantines. Several generations ago some may have been French, but now few of them can properly be called that. The true Frenchman is a rare bird in French Africa, it might almost be said. And some of the French spoken by the Algerian and Levantine *métis* is even difficult to follow. They cannot even be called French in speech.

In Tunis, up till this year, I believe I am right in saying, the census showed that the French were considerably outnumbered by the Italians. There seem to me to be more civilian Italians than Frenchmen in Morocco even. Outside the personnel of the administrative offices a real Frenchman is not often seen.

The most authentic Frenchmen in Morocco are the Soldiers, and they are by far the nicest Europeans there. But those are the officers: the rank and file of the Foreign Legion are three-quarters German. The average *légionnaire* speaks an even more peculiar French than the Levantine or Algerian man-in-the-street.

So on the whole I do not think it is at all an exaggeration to say that the true Frenchman (outside the Officers' Corps) is a rare bird in Morocco. It is the exception, not the rule, to find him, or her, among the Arabic-speaking "White" personnel of the Post Offices or Banks. With the waiters in the cafés and restaurants this is even more the case. With the cabs and transport staffs it is the same thing. [. . . .]

CHAPTER VII

ARAB, TURK, BERBER, BLACK, AND JEW

In asking yourself by whom Maghreb is peopled, if you turn to the "native," or *indigène, he* is, in Oran or Tlemcen (my next stopping place) either Arab, Turk, Black, or Jew. In the towns he is mostly Arab, Turk, or Jew. In the country, the *bled*, he is mostly Berber. The latter are the agricultural *indigènes*. The Jews are the whitest of this town-dwelling trio. Indeed the Jews are usually, especially the women, noticeably whiter than those technically "Whites" (if you are using the Colour Bar for statistical purposes). The Berbers are the darkest, because they are more often out in the sun than the others. The Turks I was never able to distinguish: I was not in that part of the country long enough to tell a Turk when I saw one—they dress just the same as the Arabs. [. . . .]

The Jew dresses in *Black*, the Arab in *White*, and the Berber in intermediate colours (*Brown* perhaps predominates in the North, *Blue* of course in the South). The Negro dresses like the Berber peasant. In Tlemcen I saw masses of Riff tribesmen: they mostly were dressed in striped sack-cloth *jellabas* of tawny chocolate and enormous coloured palmetto hats, tufted with silk, steeple-crowned, and with the brim strung up to the high crown with cord, not unlike the huge parasol palmetto-headgear of the Mexican. (Morocco is very Mexican.) Generally the Berbers are half-turbaned, bareheaded, or if in the *bled* they may have these vast straw-hats. The crimson "fez" or *chequia* is worn by everybody (except Jews) of the merchant-class in the cities: red "tarbooshes" are the cap of the city populace. Often the turban is worn round a low tarboosh. Also in the *bled* you get the circular skull-cap of wool, horizontally striped, and top-knotted, which is said to be a Punic headgear.

As to the stature and so on of these various component races: the Arab, since he lives in the town, is sedentary, and better off—he as a rule is fatter than the Berber, who is particularly lean and often very tall. The Jew is any size: but generally he is lean and as a matter of fact famished-looking and wolfish, *et pour cause!* since he undoubtedly in the past has had to work himself to the bone to keep body and soul together, with the Arab always interfering with him, and apt to take any money away as soon as he had made it; so he had to make twice as

45

much as anywhere else, and work twice as hard, unless he was a usurer—when again he had to be a really hard-working usurer. To-day lots of poor artisan Jews don't seem to know what to do with themselves, life is all of a sudden so easy. One is inclined to pity them. They ride about slowly on bicycles to while away the time.

CHAPTER VIII

ISLAMIC SENSATIONS

It was at Oran that I experienced my first "Islamic Sensations," as the author of a guide book to those parts calls them—gracefully dedicating its pages to "tous les aimables visiteurs qui viennent si nombreux chercher ici du ciel bleu, de l'air pur et embaumé . . . ainsi que des sensations d'Islam!" Certainly I breathed a "pure and balmy air" for the first time for many long months. And I also had the "Islamic Sensations." The Islamic Sensations grew more intense as I moved inland. But at Oran already they were present.

When I went with a German chief engineer, met at the Continental, to a Berber brothel, for instance, there at once Islamic Sensations were present (not because it was a brothel, but because it catered for Islam). But as I have already, in another and quite recent book, made a liberal use of the brothel atmosphere, and been rebuked for my coarseness, I will refrain from describing, the moment I reach my destination, another of these places. I shall have to refer in the sequel to the *boîte* at Agadir: so all the other *boîtes*, all along the line of itinerary, I shall suppress, though to neglect them for such motives may be a mistake. I know that my more facetious critics would say that my book should be called *Maisons Closes*, not *Filibusters in Barbary*, if I did not, and so injure it in the eyes of my Irish provincial clientèle. (I may follow this by another study, however, entitled *The Quartiers Réservés of Northern Africa.*)

So leaving the harkos-painted, tattooed harlots in their tinselled *boîtes* (and also leaving out the delightful conversation of the German engineer—I might as well suppress the whole book at once as print that, though he knows a great deal about Morocco from Casa to St.-Louis-du-Sénégal) I will confine myself to the Islamic Sensations—those I got at no great distance from the Place d'Armes.

There is a small *café-chantant*, with a dais at the end of it, and there five Turko-Berber instrumentalists sit, fezzed and trousered, and dispense "native" music. While I was there a large soft-tanned man, in a light tweed suit, and handsome fez, evidently a Colonial Briton gone badly native (I am afraid very far gone), rolled placidly in, with a couple of Jewish *copains* (man and wife). He was exceedingly noisy, giving a lot of money to the musicians and inciting them to sing songs

Design for "Islamic Sensations."

about him which the cross-legged Turkish guitarist who was the principal did over and over again. Plucking away stolidly with his plectrum of whale-bone at the *ginbri*, or perhaps small Spanish guitar, he fixed his large blue eyes upon a far-off spot, and as though reaching for a good hoik, spat his aspirated recitative out of the corner of his mouth. As his voice droned on the praises no doubt of the big soft-brown moustached Colonial Briton who had gone Turk or Berber (I could not tell which) our fellow-countryman got so excited shouting out answers to the pentatonic balladist, springing to his feet, and sending more money up to make him go on, that I thought the big white boney guitarist (whom I took to be a Turk) would get tired or be at a loss for something to say. But no, he went on and on, and the big Anglo-Saxon fellow was flushed with Paloma after Paloma (that is Spanish absinthe) and his Jewish friends—a middle-aged spectacled couple—put away a good few too.

At last, after shouting back, unctuous and noisy (the great rollicking optimist) in an Arabic more royalist than royalty, with all its raucous complement of harsh gutturals and more, quite beside himself—Tarboosh-and-chibouk-man, so to speak, literally intoxicated with Islamic Sensations—he sat down in his chair at the table, with his heavy, tanned and moustached face dropping forward upon his manly chest, perfectly exhausted. After that the musicians had a rest, and a Paloma or two apiece.

The musicians differed widely in appearance and behaviour. One at the end was noticeably nervous. He kept pinching his nose and pitching his heavy-lidded, bitter-mouthed head back, reckless of fractures, upon his contorted shoulders. He was about twenty with a big tarboosh, too big for the sunken bones of his head. He would beat a skin-stopped cylinder that he hugged under his left arm, and pluck his nostrils alternately. When they sang together in chorus, suddenly he would out-howl the rest—tossing his head about and plucking at his nose, beating feverishly upon his *agwal*. He made no pretence of handling a snuff-nut—he had a vesper-packet: he did not *go aside* to take cocain, but sniffed it up without stopping his performance. Tossing and twitching without remission, he did one solo recitative, which was one breathless howl of suffering. Stamping and twanging came in the others. With the same sad nasal howl they joined him, in one long wolfish outburst. And it seemed quite natural that the doped drummer should stagger at their heels, within an inch of collapse (certainly they took no notice of him). Never once did any of the others look his way or hardly at one another for that matter. He writhed upon the flank of the indifferent sextet. He would sweep the audience bitterly with the tail of his eye, sick and detached, but occasionally leering.

The contortions of the doper-drummer, nursing his *agwal* like a restive brat, beating its bottom—now drooping over his instrument and twitching, now rolling his head from side to side upon his double-shouldered back—this studied epilepsy suggested the birth then and there of a new dance-form, invented for the harsh pentatonic howling. He was side-on to the café-audience, cross-legged and round-shouldered: especially when he was drumming and howling out the words of an incantation, his dance gave the effect of an endless dromedary odyssey. It was a nightmare desert-ride, with camels pushed to the gallop to avoid capture. It was the shattering jolts of a wounded rider, returning at top speed from a distant razzia. Would he reach safety in time? Hardly it seemed! It appeared almost certain that death was near. Such was the only solution, death must bring this dark course to a close. A distinctly "Islamic Sensation," I think, and Islamically interpreted. I remembered the story I had read of a wounded Chaamba runner, who, when forty out of fifty of his comrades had been killed in a surprise attack upon their camp by "Berabers,"[1] had got away in the night, and ran a hundred kilometres in the heart of the Sahara to the nearest French Post. He was so exhausted that he fell at the feet of the officer-in-command, and no one could get anything coherent out of him for a long time. All that could be gathered were the words (weighted, in their form, with the authentic, "Islamic" fatalism)—"Those who are dead are dead, and those who are living are living!" This meant that most were dead of course.

The sick drummer, when it came to his turn to sing, did so in howling spasms, pumping the dismal hollow sounds out of his vitals. He might very appropriately have been recounting the last *étapes* of that desert Marathon of the wounded Chaamba—and, with a frenzied mimicry, a dying voice, have been representing what, for the sitting posture, was all that could be done to convey to the audience the horrors of the last few kilometres. Anyway a quite good "Islamic Sensation" was to be got out of him for a first night, and I went twitching to bed, racked with spasms of the coke-djinn, or was it haschisch too? He certainly drank more than one Paloma.

---

[1] Saharan bandits.

CHAPTER IX

TLEMCEN

Tlemcen is a very important town in the history of Maghreb; it is geographically important: thirdly it is of first-class interest to the sight-seer or student.

It is placed at one end of what the French call *la trouée de Taza*. It faces Fez, at the opposite end of the long hole in the landscape in question. It is the first town, going west from Algeria and Tunis, where you get the Andalusian Civilization (the Hispano-Mauresque) and so it is the first Moroccan town.

But it is even the first *city*, that is old-settled city—autochthonous and not one run by the European overnight—between Tunis and Fez. "In Maghreb," says E. F. Gautier, "urbanism has only, in fact, developed at the two extremities of the country, around monster cities—Tunis at one end, Fez at the other. Algeria has no *citizens*, properly speaking, except at Tlemcen. The Algiers of 1830 was nothing more than a garrison and Turkish port, in spite of the presence of a few Andalusian immigrants, called by the French of 1830 *les Maures*. One can only understand native Algeria (as distinguished from the Algiers of the French Occupation) by recalling that it is essentially rural."

So Tlemcen is in Algeria the only surviving city of the Middle-Ages of Maghreb. The Bedouins, the Spaniards, Turks, Armenians, etc., etc., destroyed all the rest. It is the only city of old-standing at all. Of great cities like Tiaret, there is to-day not a trace—no one even knows where it was. So the well-informed traveller (and I was a very well-informed one, indeed, as I have said) approaches Tlemcen with respect. Tlemcen, as a city, is not *la première venue*. Archir, La Kalaa, Tiaret, Archgoul, El-Batha, all swallowed up in the destructive rage of the Arab, with the others to help him—from Kurdish archers to Norman chiefs. Only Tlemcen is left. *And* it is the first Andalusian city, the beginning of Morocco: and a place of great character and attractiveness. As I moved towards it in the train from Oran across the Rio Salado (I suppose), through the headquarters of the Foreign Legion, and at last up into the mountain-chain north-west of the Tell (definitely continental, rather than coastal tracts, at last), I knew, as

51

well as if I had been there, that in the Mellah[1] a foreskin was probably being tied up in flannel and hung over the mother's bed as an amulet, whereas the Mauresques—why *they* would be on their way to their Marabout to burn incense, or *haoufi:* while elsewhere a punctilious old Reb[2] was bastinadoing a Jewish corpse, preparatory to burying it, to spare it trouble in the next world: all the cycle of birth and death, in short, of Arab, Turk, Berber or Jew, all that the visitor ought to know, to take an intelligent interest in—just as I knew that it was the Zenata of "the second race"[3] that had founded the Abdenwadite dynasty: and the name of the first king, Yar-morasen, I knew as well as I knew my own.

The dolomitic cliffs of this mighty *massif* are more impressive than the Tarn I discovered (though the wild country immediately north of the Tarn is the only part of France that is able to give you an idea of these African desert-mountains, invaded by sand and salt, as is everything else in Maghreb, everywhere spotted with the flat nomad tent). The enormous, rufous battlements of nature thrown up about this entrance gallery to the Cherifian Empire are of course vaster than the works of man, but, because they have a regularity reclaiming chaos, these cliffs should be classed with the tremendous Kasbahs that the chieftains of the High Atlas have built. For a traveller entering Morocco by this route the Massif of Tlemcen is indeed a worthy gate to Barbary.

The city of Tlemcen is lost in an olive forest. The train, after leaving the great red bastions of rock, where you have been passing from Oranie into the dominions of the Maghzen, goes to hunt for it in its cloud of olives: and when it finds it, it is not the best approach, as it turns out afterwards; you do not at once recognize why the position of this town is so much vaunted.—However Tlemcen is on a rock itself—it was called *Agadir* to start with, which means "precipitous rock" (whereas Tlemcen means "source"). You may distinguish the distant sea-line from it upon a clear day. In winter, we are told, the almond blossoms are covered with snow. "The Winter of Tlemcen occurs in the Spring" is an Arab saying. How delightful when "winter" means snow, and "spring" the sun, with the most absurdly vivid, violent blossoming! With us these marriages of the seasons are deadly. They but result in worse mud only. Winter wins. But that is not all: there is *no autumn* in Tlemcen, either—only three seasons. A sudden frost—and the summer is all over: except that the sun goes on shin-

[1] Jewish district.
[2] Short title for Rabbi.
[3] The Zenata tribe in its great Thirteenth Century revival.

ing, though not so hot. *To liquidate Autumn*—what a good arrangement! Then to plant a spectacular winter in the midst of the flowers of spring! What happy climatic transformations!

"Well, if Tlemcen is all that you say, Mr. Guide," mutters the traveller, "it must be a premier city." But everything points to its being something of the sort. When its patron saint, an Andalusian mystic, Sidi Bou Mediene, first caught sight of it, he exclaimed, "What a jolly space to sleep one's last sleep in!" and died the same day. There are so many chances and accidents (I suppose he thought) that take us away for ever from these beautiful places! So he settled down once and for all, and put a stop to the destructive vagaries of Fate, as far at all events as he was concerned.

Tlemcen is in fact all that they say and more: but you must have a good smattering of the history of Morocco, or more properly of Maghreb, to be able to breathe its balmy citron-scented air intelligently—in addition to staring at its storks' nests at the top of all its minarets, and remaining open-mouthed in front of its Fondouks and Synagogues.

Often in the past I have stared stupidly at vast systems of machinery—in factories and power-houses—for many minutes, until it got too hot or I was moved on, without having the least idea what these monstrous concatinations of steel might be for. A city and its history are the same as that. Wherever you get people you get this: it is all meaningless and really rather silly unless you know what it's all about.

There is an opposite difficulty of course: namely that when people know what a thing signifies *historically* (just as they might be informed of the uses of a complicated machine) often they see too much, and much that is not there at all. Thus nothing will persuade me that the Koutoubia (the celebrated mosque-tower at Marrakech) is anything but a pleasantly arranged square tower. The lyrical flights of fancy regarding it are aberrations merely of the historically-minded—a triumph of history over the eyes in the head.

For one popular authority upon Morocco, for instance, the Koutoubia possesses "the stern harmony of the noblest architecture": and this writer adds: "the Koutoubia would be magnificent anywhere: in this flat desert it is grand enough to face the Atlas." That, to my mind, is a pure exaggeration: the Koutoubia, the Giralda at Seville, and the Tower of Hasan at Rabat, are the three star-pieces of Hispano-Mauresque. The ruined tower of Mansoura, outside Tlemcen, must have made a fourth, had it been left intact. But because, come to Marrakech, the traveller knows, or ought to, that "the Victorious," "the Golden," El Mansour, himself, built that tower, with the assistance of a million Christian slaves, to be a monument not easily demolished to the splendour of Arab arts and arms, that is not to say that the traveller should see it larger than it is—in its "severity" a match for great mountains for instance: nor that, just by itself, it constitutes more than a good tower, of a certain style. Also there is a better one near it, namely that of the Mosque of the Kasbah, beside the Saadian Tombs.—The ruined tower at Mansoura (two kilometres from Tlemcen) is I think more impressive, in its ruined state: all these works would be better as ruins. It is useless to claim for the Hispano-Mauresque more than a relative interest. Hispano-Mauresque is Arab. The Berber Idea is much grander than the Arab idea. It is best expressed in that rougher *genre*—in the giant Atlas Kasbahs. And those you do not see till you reach the High Atlas. Nowhere north of that is there anything approaching them in interest.

It was at Tlemcen that I saw my first *Souk:* and Souk is "market," or, in this case, "bazaar." In a city like Tlemcen "souk" means Bazaar, also the daily and weekly food and live-stock markets. The Souks, or the Bazaars, a chaplet of fly-blown shops, are, as elsewhere in the Orient, the main feature of Berber or Arab life.

"Souk" is an Arab word: the sound in Arabic is not "sook"—there is a complicated guttural tail to it. But the French have made this sound into "souk," as the nearest they could get to the original.

In English I have seen this monosyllable variously spelt. On the analogy of "Sus" for the French *Sous*, it is often spelled "Suk." Also I have seen it "Sok." The first looks much more like the sound of "suck" than the sound "sook," the second "sock." You miss the "oo" sound. Similarly if I spelled the French *Sous* as "Sus" (they sometimes spell it that way too, only with an accent on the u—"Sûs") it would merely confuse the general reader, and make him think it was something to do with *Jew Süss*.—It is such considerations as these that have caused me throughout to stick to the French spelling, for these sounds often have no equivalent in a European tongue, and a conventionalized spelling is necessary.

The combination of lethargy and incessant movement is the first thing that strikes the traveller in these Moroccan Bazaars, should he be as I was a novice in the Oriental picturesque. They are narrow cobbled lanes, often steep as well as winding, meandering in all directions, ending in covered markets; or they are open-air workshops doubling upon themselves, disappearing into tunnels or losing themselves within the lofty walls of private gardens. People swarm in them, and winged insects, especially where there are food stalls: mules, camels and asses, with sacks of salt or flour, pass up and down them, or sometimes a merchant on horseback, with the great peaked saddle of the Berber, so different to the Arab one (though the horse must be Syrian, and not a "Barbe," if the rider is to be pleased with himself).

The shops generally are cupboards in a mud wall. They start two or three feet from the ground. In these the merchant squats or crouches, often asleep or dropping to sleep, or if awake majestically resigned as regards the customer-question. The customer-question has been solved by Islam. That is left in the hands of Providence. The shop-keeper appears to have climbed up into his shop and sat down there, rather because it had been the Will of God that he should play his brief part upon life's scene as a merchant in a Bazaar, than animated by any feverish desire to sell something. Even the Jews in the Mellah seem tarred with the same brush, and have the airs of whiling listlessly away their time—though I dare say underneath they are aching to effect a sale, and live up to their reputation. But they do not show it, they act the same as the Arabs and as though Fate were their God as well.

On the other hand, the Producers (carpet-makers, cobblers, potters and so forth) work very hard. Someone after all has to *make* the beastly article—Fate decides who it shall be. Only, once the thing is made, it passes into the hands of an indifferent guardian, rather than an eager salesman. It is expected to sell itself. It sells or it does not sell, at all events: if it sells, it sells: no one is in the least surprised when it sells, nor disturbed when it doesn't.

This great rule of massive mercantile indifference does not apply to the large establishments of the big rug and curio merchants. They, or their scouts, dart screaming out upon the visitor. Their emissaries lie all day long outside the European cafés, and when a new person drops in to drink they go in after him, and get him. Rug after rug is unrolled—some so large that they stretch right across the road to the opposite pavement. But these are people who have learnt restlessness from the European, who is their main customer for such goods. Also their shops, at the heart of every Medina, are doubtless the cells, the small *succursales*, of some well-organized Levantine Concern, having its headquarters in Tangier, or perhaps in Alexandria. They probably stock anything from a miniature Pharaonic *cartouche* to a wax-inlaid *kiff* pipe.

Fanning the flies with a palm-fan then, a bearded personage sits impassibly, legs under stomach, behind a pair of scales, prepared to sell some *couscous*, healing herbs, goat's meat, or what not, if asked—

that is the rule of the Bazaar. When no one arrives he may crawl out and put down his shutter, or else he may go to sleep upon the spot. When it gets cooler he wakes up, palm-fan in hand. Meanwhile incessant swarms of silent and athletic tribesmen pass, occasionally saluting a friend, with the *Hush*-gesture of the finger to the lip, without looking otherwise to left or right. Up and down this tortuous and stinking lane, the rocky bed of a mountain torrent as Burton described it, the phenomenally silent inhabitants of the *bled* pass from morning till night.

That is, of course, "the Eastern Bazaar," which has been so often described before. To see it is a first-class "Islamic Sensation." As a sensation it is to be warmly recommended. I am told that the sensation is more truly Islamic in Morocco than even in Damascus, I dare say even than in Mecca.

It is naturally delightful to be in a place where industrialism has not put its squalid foot. Here it has not. You can see the ornate saddles and harness used by the rich merchants and notables cut out and sewn in a workshop open to the street. In the same way the shoe-factory does not supply the *babouches* as yet. All Berber footwear is made where you can stand and watch the phases of the workmanship, until there it is ready (if you are a Moroccan, or have gone native) for your foot.

Luxurious slippers, for great notables, their wives or well-paid prostitutes, have the traditional patterns being sewn into the flat sheet of Moroccan leather before it is attached to the silken welt. These consist of patterns as invariable as the tattoo spirals and constellations upon the skins of the Mauresques.

There are of course factories. I was taken through a daedalean labyrinth of passages and courts, and so into a large carpet-factory. Upon three sides of a courtyard were ranked looms. The large wooden looms are like the up-ended frames of big English spring-beds. At these upwards of a hundred girls, of thirteen or fourteen, in a profound hot hush, a stagnant studied gloom, manufacture rugs. They sat or stood before the looms as they worked. This was a very large workshop or factory, certainly: but none of the oppressive hustle and slickness was to be noticed of "the Works," when it is the Machine that is paramount. These fat brown children, the Fatmahs of to-morrow, occasionally whispering, made far less noise than a single gramophone, playing a waltz with a soft needle. One of the outstanding "Islamic Sensations" of Maghreb is the absence of what the coster calls "loud-mouthed"-ness.

No argument is possible, I think, when these two modes of life are contrasted. At a period when man has not been powerful enough to transform the accidental dispositions of nature—with no dynamite to blast, or rock-drills to disintegrate—and is compelled to build the streets of his cities in and out and up and down, inventing, as he goes along, untried architectural devices, delightful deformities and structural freaks, then, it is too plain, the result is more agreeable and stimulating to the eye. By following the vast, non-human, lines of nature, our human arts score their best successes. Projecting his tortuous, not yet oppressive, geometry, out upon the chaotic superstructures—being methodic where he can, in the teeth of natural disorder—man is seen at his best. He then produces something of intellectual as well as emotional value, which the unadulterated stark geometry of the Machine-Age precludes. Without arguing pro or contra—whether some day the Machine will be put in its place—it is sufficient here to affirm that the labyrinths of these ancient Souks are far more imaginatively pleasant places to be in than is, say, Hoboken, across the ferry from Manhattan, or (on a small scale) the Casa boulevards.

Passing from the subject of Souks to that of Kasbahs, I think that something else can be safely asserted. The appeal of the great Kasbah—of the crowding, many-towered silhouette of Animiter, for instance, facing the Sahara—that is the same as the appeal of the swarming Skyscraper. "Down-town" New York is from that point of view really the blood-brother of Tagontaft or of Animiter. But the Kasbah makes the greater impression.—I have however gone on ahead of my itinerary—there are no Kasbahs at Tlemcen, only Souks. I will take up this theme later, when rising out of the Souks of the plain (the vast walled Souk, which is all that Marrakech is in fact) we ascend into the sun-baked Atlas valleys and first come face to face with the incredible many-towered castles of the great Berber Lords. But that is such a special subject, and might, I have felt, be of so little interest to the general reader, that it will form the subject of a separate volume, which I shall call *Kasbahs and Souks*. I recognize that my great interest in the Berber Kasbah is in part a technical one. I noticed in *Mogreb-el-Acksa* that even such a sensitive observer as Mr. Cunninghame Graham dismisses the Berber Kasbah (that of his host of Tagontaft) in a few words. And I could scarcely expect the average reader to be more easy to interest at second-hand, than was the distinguished Scottish nationalist when face to face with these tribal structures. This will fully explain the hiatus where the Kasbahs of the Atlas are concerned. I shall often mention them of course. But for a detailed consideration of their significance I refer you to *Kasbahs and Souks*.

CHAPTER X

IMPORTANT INTERIORS

Any guide in Tlemcen has his path made smooth—he does not have to be much of a guide, all he need do is to go out and wave his hand and some "sight" for the sightseer is sure to be there as though he had conjured it up. Yet a guide you must employ, otherwise you cannot get inside the baths and brothels and other important interiors so easily. Also you must have the things explained to you. You discover say a small female child in the middle of the road, stockstill, grasping the ends of two pieces of stout thread. These disappear into a dark shop beyond. It is perfectly useless to follow the thread: ultimately you would find, fifteen feet away, in the obscurity, a man at the other end of the threads, working with them upon some garment. But you have to be told, or so I found it, how he requires the child to hold the two threads in order that he may be able to sew the cross-pattern of the elaborate hem of the men and women's silk jackets, ceremonious vests and the rest.

But now for some *important interiors*—for in the Mohammedan East you must contrive to enter behind the rebarbative walls or battlements. The *fondouks*, they are most important interiors. You must get into these interiors. A *fondouk* is an inn (the Spanish *fonda* must be the same word). There is a large gate and massive arched entrance, in the shadows of which, in the poorer *fondouks*, men sleep wrapt up in their hooded cloaks. An Arab coffee-shop is installed there too. Within it is a courtyard that is in fact a stable: generally full of animals, mostly asses and mules. A stairway leads to a balcony: that is above the court—it runs all round. As there is no roof, and no walls above the well of the courtyard, this balcony is what would be the passage: the bedchambers of the guests open upon it. There are of course rows of unlit boxes, crowded with visitors from the *bled*. For the Berber never ceases to move up and down, and a *fondouk* is a profitable concern I should say. Eight and nine people sleep in a room, bringing their own rugs for bedclothes. This, at twopence a head, is good business. In Tlemcen there is a *fondouk* for the Gipsies. There you observe numbers of this "reactionary" tribe of picturesque Hindu pedlars, encamped in an inn. A paradox—for why the Gipsy should wish to have an inn at all I was not able to find out. (Why not the *bled*?) Beneath the

58

enormous shadow-filled arch of the Fondouk of the Gitanos coffee was being made, the berries grilled over the brazier in a ladle, and people, with the same stony milky stare that these very especial nomads have wherever they are met, were drinking it out of minia-ture cups. My second night in Tlemcen I went into a *fondouk* that was full of Riff tribesmen: they were singing upstairs in a largish room. But there was a great commotion when I entered, sleepers swathed in white rose out of the shadows like the medieval dead in their shrouds, and approached me in surprise. There was a great deal of unneces-sary hurrying about. The song stopped, and so I left. I felt a few words of Berber were necessary and I knew none. That was a failure. There are *fondouks* of all grades, but the average costs a few sous a night. You must get into a *fondouk:* the morning is the best time, when it is comparatively empty.

The Moorish Bath—that is an extremely important interior, you must at all costs find out where it is and enter it. People spend the night there as they do in the *fondouks*—it is both a Bath and a *fondouk*. The atrium, a square block of bluish gloom, of this bathing and sleeping-house, decidedly affords one of the short-cuts to the secrets of Barbary.—It is of critical importance to get into the Bath. Only Moslems are supposed to enter, in the stricter Morocco.

For this book, I have placed a ban upon the Berber Brothel. You do not have to have travelled far, out of Folkestone or Harwich, to know that "brothel" does not spell licence, more than does any noisy café. It is merely a café, or pub, where the visitor may sleep with the waitress or barmaid, probably, if he likes (but he does not necessarily desire to).

In that respect it differs little surely, from most cafés and pubs. So of course it is only for an Anglo-Saxon audience that a writer is com-pelled to ban these institutions, as being not fair sociological game. I still may venture to say, to any serious student of the place—though the recommendation would be quiet unnecessary, that it is under-stood, with such an investigator—you must get inside all and espe-cially the cheaper ones! They are all *important interiors*. They cannot be looked at from the outside—there is nothing to see. They are packed with "Islamic Sensations." If you only have say forty-eight hours at your disposal, then it would be best perhaps to stay at the Bath. Go straight from the Station to the Bath. Having chosen your mat, go straight to the humblest brothel. Apart from a sortie to the Synagogue, and a crawl round the worst Souks in the morning, that will be all that is strictly necessary. (Always avoid the Medersas.[1] They

---

[1] The colleges.

are Hispano-Mauresque bores of buildings: or if you visit one you have seen all—go once, it is enough.)

He who has not seen the handkerchief-dance for instance, now—the shuddering feminine body covered with bangles and charms, gradually working its way down the room, upon its pounding naked feet, that retard it as much as they advance it—the handkerchief held taut, before the breast-plated busts, alive with vibrations: but more important, the motionless male peasant audience, gravely expressionless, and then the regulation sticking of a small banknote upon the sweaty temples or on top of the tattooed eyebrows—the lowered eyes heavy with black Kohl—while the dancer abases herself in a traditional curtsy (to receive what was formerly a coin upon the glutinous skin, dampened with her gymnastics)—not to have seen this is to have missed the spectacle of an essential ritual, peculiar to this people. But I need not insist.

Wot else? (as Ezra[1] says, before finishing a hasty note). I do not say that the Synagogue is an *important interior*, but I should go there, it is best to get into it: you certainly should understand the Jews better then. What a disconcertingly sensible race! You can enter their prosaic little temple with your hat on the back of your head and a cigarette in your mouth—*they* don't mind! It is so much part of their everyday, almost domestic, life, they are so familiar with the godly, that they would as soon show you the place where they pray as the place where they cook, or kill their chickens—for them it is all the same. They are such *professionals*, such born religionists, that they leave their tabernacle open upon the street, as if its four walls enclosed nothing more than a few chairs—or as if, rather, no mere human walls *could* enclose much more than that. *Privacy* is the enemy, perhaps (no man shall be closeted with God?). In scorn of the solemn Moslem prigs round the corner they prove themselves the most offhand worshippers on earth. I have not seen them on Saturday, but their nonchalant devotions have often been described: there they all sit or lounge about apparently, some of them nasally humming a little, while others gossip about business—the fall in the peseta, or the price of wool. It sounds like a very very mellow Quaker conventicle. *Sans façon!* says the Jew. For such past-masters in religion it is almost like an outrageous swank.—Yes, it might be worth while to give the local synagogue the once-over. I regretted I was not able to drop in on Saturday, leaving Tlemcen as I did in the centre of the week.

The Mosque, although you have to take your shoes off, and the

---

[1] Ezra Pound.

place is dark, is of a most puritanical bareness, and thoroughly uninteresting, without the agreeable *sans-façon* of the Hebrew temple. Not an important interior—though it has to be walked round for the say-so. All the powerful "Islamic Sensations" are elsewhere. The *Koubahs* the same—*Koubah* is a saint's tomb—a white-domed cube: they swarm everywhere—they are all the sanctuaries of Andalusian Saints, expelled from Spain, and all date from the time of the Arab expulsion. *Never* fret because you cannot get inside them (it is forbidden). There is absolutely nothing inside!

CHAPTER XI

THE RIFF

From Tlemcen, the passenger train goes no farther than Oujda. After that you must proceed by motorbus to Fez. The road lies through stony tufa-steppes—salt, sand and rock—system after system of barren mountains. The *Minerva* set out at 2 o'clock, and reached Fez about 8. All the afternoon and evening we went on at top speed (to keep the lead of other buses) always through desert plains, flanked by the mountains of the Moulouya and those closing the Riff in the South.

The river Moulouya crosses this route halfway between Fez and Tlemcen. This, it seems, has been generally recognized, at all times, as the conventional frontier of, on the one hand, *Maghreb-el-Aksa* (that is Morocco) and, on the other, *Maghreb-el-Ouesti* that is Algeria).

It was across these deserts that the Spanish regiment, during the war with the Riffs, escaped in a headlong scuttle to safety, arriving without arms and practically naked at Oujda. The Berber thereabouts still has a good laugh over that. The French have never afforded them such mirth-provoking exhibitions!

Many reports were current in the Moroccan papers in May and June of the recrudescence of the traffic in arms. In Oran I read a Spanish account of the alarming extension of this particular contraband. *The Riff is arming again!* That was the cry. Gordon Canning, the famous English filibuster, had been signalled at Gibraltar. That spoke volumes—for the Spanish of Tetouan, and, for that matter, for the French. Wherever Gordon Canning is, there you get a brisk *va-et-vient* of cases of cartridges, carbines and Mills Bombs! For them, this Englishman was directing, as before, the flow of contraband. Every night a flotilla of small craft, under the cover of darkness, left the Spanish shore, and landed cases full of arms and ammunition upon the coast of the Riff.

It was then (May 1931) and is still, I suppose, punishable with death for a Riff to be found with a rifle. But the Republican Government, especially with Prieto there, would hardly allow their generals to give effect to such reactionary decrees. The General who was a recognized model Man-of-iron—a "strong man," a stonewall of the Old School, with a touch of Asiatic, "dago" barbarism—was still in the Riff. He was credited with exhibiting the heads of decapitated Riffian rebels in the market-place of some big centre, I forget which one. But it was unlikely that the new régime would encourage him to keep order with such thoroughness. (In June a civilian colleague was sent out—to keep an eye upon him, no doubt.) If order could not be maintained without barbarity, it is certain that Republican Spain (that of the "Workers' Republic") would prefer to abandon Africa.

In Morocco I have listened to many conversations upon this subject, of what would happen were the Spaniard to leave the Riff. The British Foreign Office, I am told, have tabulated, among the dozen likeliest causes of great wars in Europe, the withdrawal of Spain from Morocco. The French, it is believed, would then march in. But that might quite well precipitate a war between France and Italy. It is one of the danger spots, the Riff. And although the quantity of arms entering the Riff every evening—the Spanish authorities at Tetouan said they had positive information that enabled them to estimate this at roughly 500 rifles per night—was, all agreed, exaggerated, nevertheless, since the day when Alfonso cried *Viva España!* as with an elastic step he boarded the Spanish cruiser at Valencia after his flight from Madrid, there had been a warlike bustle throughout the mountains south of Ajdir.

These mountains to the north were beginning again to bristle secretly with rifles; and I followed upon a map, as we rushed along, the black outlines of this ominous geography. Afghanistan and the Riff must produce much the same sort of human wolf: nothing I should imagine has a less reassuring air than a busful of Riffs, such as you see rushed into Tlemcen for a day's shopping. The Riff is swarthy and hollow-cheeked, tall and phenomenally lean, inclined to be toothy and with that fixed mesmerized look of children often. He is evidently a machine—truly "a fighting machine" in the literal sense—a murderous, child-like, clean-shaven or bearded mahogany automaton.

Now, as I am writing this, it is reported that Abd el-Krim has escaped from his island prison and has been signalled off the Riff coast. He will soon, once more, be sending his envoys to Rabat, Fez and Tetouan, and also to Geneva! But I expect this "escape" is apocryphal.

The red tufa-steppes between Oujda and Taza, illustrate the irreclaimable salt barrenness of this country. The name of the main river between Oran and Tlemcen is Rio Salado; and that is not the only *salt river*. Salt indeed is everywhere here, both in the earth and water. The whole of Maghreb is saline and desertic at bottom. It is only in the neighbourhood of the big cities that you meet with methodic cultivation. At Tlemcen the irrigation works, responsible for the olives and vines, is the work of the Romans, in the first place. Sagniat-er-Roumi they call the canal system that brings the waters of the cascade at El Ourit over to Tlemcen. The attempts to reclaim this desert country are not likely to succeed. More and more the French are of the opinion that the only profitable form of cultivation in Morocco is that of *trees,* certainly not crops or vines. Gardening, not agriculture, is the cry—then wholesale *tinning.* Fresh fruit is too difficult to ship they say.

Fez, where I stopped some days, is a mass of Souks. Tlemcen or Fez, in the matter of Souks, is much the same, though Fez is larger and less altered by the European than Tlemcen, and so better from the point of view of the Souks. There is much Merinide art, if you like that; but what interested me most while I was there was a huge Film Company, preparing a film that was to be called *The Three Unlucky Travellers.* The waiters pointed out the three unlucky film sheiks. One was French, one German, and one American. But I will return to this a little later where I supply a brief account of their important industry—for side by side with real sheiks in Maghreb you are constantly running up against artificial film ones.

CHAPTER XII

CASA

Casablanca is a huge marine outpost of Europe. It is the last city of the coast to have a railway this side of Senegal—beyond it, travelling south, you must go by car. It is the Queen of the Atlantic for the *Vieux Marocain,* it is *Casa-la-Blanche*—or so its corps of journalists invariably refer to it. It is a hell of a *stink-fein* city in fact, and deserves more than a passing mention. Casablanca was the first town of the French Protectorate: the Moroccan conquest started there. As it appears to-day, it is pointed to as the city Lyautey built—it is the last place he saw when he left Morocco for good in the *Anfa*—it is "the pearl of the French Renaissance," emblematic of the precarious post-war power of France. It is perhaps the place that holds the secret of the destiny of this astonishing latter-day colonial conquest.

The history of Casablanca, or Dar el Beida, is not important. It is an ancient settlement, for some reason—the Anfa of the Phœnicians; though why it is difficult to see, since it is the world's worst natural harbour, with nothing to distinguish it from any other point of unindented coastline south of Rabat. It is cursed with an abnormal surf: it has an abordage calculated to prejudice any mariner against it.

Here is a description (by Dr. Arthur Leared, *Marocco and the Moors*) of how you got into it about sixty years ago. The morning of Dr. Leared's arrival, in the Tangier Packet, a strong sou'wester was blowing. "The roadstead is quite unprotected," he says: "a heavy sea was rolling into it from the Atlantic." Vessels with passengers and cargoes for the different coast-towns often had to pass Casa, after perhaps laying off for several days in the hope of getting in, owing to the hopeless weather conditions prevailing at this most unlikely of spots for a port, and go on to Mazagan or Safi.—On this occasion, as the doctor says, "it was long before any boats put off to us, and when they did arrive there was another long delay; for we had to summon resolution to get into them, and to parley as to the exorbitant demands of the Moorish boatmen. No wonder that these fellows ask to be well paid for their perilous work. It is no uncommon thing on this coast for boats to be upset and lives lost in the tremendous surf. What makes the idea of being upset particularly unpleasant is the presence of great numbers of hammer-headed sharks, as these voracious creatures abound all along the coast. Only a few months previously, four masters of vessels that lay in the roads, three sailors and a Moor, were drowned by the upsetting of a ship's boat. . . . At last we left for the shore, and my first impressions of an African surf are not to be forgotten. Once within its clutches, it was a neck-or-nothing game, and if ever delay was dangerous it was here. Watching the opportunity while outside the seething water, the men impelled the boat with their utmost strength on the crest of the ingoing wave. The tremendous velocity gained by this impetus caused, for an instant, the boat to rise high in the air on the swelling surface, and as suddenly dip down the sheer descent of the subsiding water. This was the critical moment; for were not the crest of the next wave as rapidly gained, that which followed inshore would swamp the boat. The wild excitement of the scene beggars description. With wild shouts and frantic gestures, the *reis*, or captain, at the helm, urged the crew to renewed exertions; and they, straining every nerve, yelled like madmen in response. Some Jews in the boat cowered down and looked like lifeless bundles; but though the foam dashed over passengers and crew alike, we were all, thanks to Moorish strong arms, soon safely landed, and with no greater inconvenience than a thorough wetting."

A *Vieux Marocain*—which means a "colon" of a dozen years standing—told me that when being a small boy he landed at Casablanca for the first time (in 1914 I think) he and his parents, sisters and brothers, were carried ashore through the breakers on the backs of boatmen. And to-day at Safi ships are loaded in the same manner: chains of men, standing up to their waists in the surf, pass from hand to hand the cargoes coming in or going out, which are then rowed in open boats to the anchored ship.

The Casablanca, or Dar el Beida, of 1870 is described by Dr. Leared as "the dirtiest, most tumble-down place ever seen." A still more emphatic observer, writing in 1889, describes it as follows: "Casablanca occupies a flat low-lying piece of ground close to the sea; the houses have not a single feature worth remarking; the principal street is a running sewer of filth . . . the people are more ugly and dirty, the donkeys worse treated and more mangy, the dogs more numerous and repulsive, and the beggars in greater numbers and decidedly more importunate and loathsome, than in any of the other places we had yet seen." (*Joseph Thomson*).

At that time it was a township of 4,000 inhabitants, surrounded by walls of *tabia,* or mud concrete, twenty feet high, well supplied with water, but often visited with cholera and plague—the former killing as many as a dozen Jews a day. Owing to the uncomfortable harbour-bar at the mouth of the river upon which Rabat stands, a good deal of the export trade of Rabat—wool, carpets and wax—was shipped from Casablanca.

There is one respect in which the Dar el Beida of 1870 is reminiscent of the *Casa-la-Blanche* of to-day, and that is in the prevalence of the dwellings of an auxiliary population of nomads. Thus Dr. Leared writes: "There are also many waste spaces. Of these not a few are covered with reed huts, in bad repair, in which, when we saw them, many Arabs, wretchedly poor, were encamped." These *encampements* of reed huts, or their equivalent, are still everywhere to be met with, wherever there is an open space.

But whereas the physician who visited it in 1870 said of it that "the worst climate on the African coast could hardly show a higher rate of mortality," it must to-day possess one of the lowest death-rates in the world, for its climate is in fact excellent, and of course Europe has brought its drains and lavatories with it, all stinks are banished and middens frowned upon.

Dr. Leared describes "an Arab village" outside Mazagan, "made up of conical huts, which resembled the barley-stacks of an English homestead." These are the *nouala:* but they are black cones of a coarse thatch of sticks or of reeds, and remind the traveller at the first blush much more of equatorial Africa than of Sussex or Kent.

Drawing into the station of Fedhalla, which is a small port between Rabat and Casa, upon the Rabat side, the traveller finds himself in the midst of an enormous *nouala*-village of this sort; and, with its cactus hedges and the naked squalor of its dusky infants, he would not have to be very fanciful to suppose himself in Guinea or the Congo, rather than in a North African nomad-town. Nothing indicates that this is not Fedhalla itself: coming from Fez or Tangier the traveller will have seen nothing of the sort, except here and there (associated with tents) one or two of these thatch cabins: and he certainly could be excused for jumping to the conclusion that either the activities of the Colonial Exhibition had shuffled the African colonies in some manner (was not this perhaps an equatorial village bodily on its way to Paris, which got left behind, or settled down en route, finding itself too late?) or else that a different race dwelt here—perhaps a stray community of the Hargatin, that is the negritic stocks of the desert or Anti-Atlas?

The black beehive-villages, built in orderly rows, are met everywhere in the south of Maghreb el Aksa: unquestionably they have something to do with the prevalence of Negro blood. That a thatch cabin of the order found in the Upper Volta should occur in Central Morocco is as natural as that a Zenetic tent should turn up

NOUALA

South of Tchad among the Massas.

The Negro shades into the Moor everywhere south of this. The famous White Touaregs even, of the Hoggar, have a delicate measure of Negro blood—just enough to put a shadow in the White. The greatest of the Lords of the Atlas (the Glaoui, the M'Tougi) have it more plainly still. Many villages in the Anti-Atlas are already definitely negritic, and all the Saharan oases are populated by the Haratin, a negroid race (descendants perhaps of the most ancient people in the Sahara, the peculiar Blacks whose last retreat is Tibesti).

No bones are made about this inky blood. The Sultans, and the great Cherifian families (their descent from the Prophet notwithstanding) all sport it without a thought. They have been visibly blackened with the blood of slaves—for this there is no help, in a society run upon the basis of the use of the Black *Untermensch* to do the hard manual work: and it has never occurred to anyone to call his neighbour "nigger" (in the way that one *rasta* will say of another "Es Indio!") for the excellent reason that in their vocabularies there is no such word. In the Berber and Arab tongues of Morocco there is no word expressing in any way what we mean by Negro. Apparently the shading-off has been so effectively *nuancé* that no such idea as that of a White and a Black, starkly contrasted, has ever presented itself to a Moor or Berber. They must surely have noticed the enormous ethnical difference between a "buck nigger" and a typical Berber. But if so they have been so little preoccupied with it as to find it unnecessary to make a new word for the phenomenon.—Indeed, in the plain of Marrakech ("the Plain of Morocco" for the men of the last century) and the Valley of the Sous, the Soudan is already there—already you have entered the Saharan World of the great steppes and deserts between the Noun or Tafilalet and the Niger.

In contradistinction to all this, however, the Soudanese are conscious of *Whiteness*, as a thing differing from the Soudanese norm. They have their words to indicate a person upon the other side of the Colour Line—not necessarily a European. A Berber for them would come under that head (unless, it is to be assumed, particularly negritic).

The *nouala* (or *kabbousah*—"caboose") is technically a cylindrical mud hut, with a conical thatch roof. Often the roof extends to the ground: then it is a ten-feet-high or more, dark conical dwelling, made of branches and sticks, secured at intervals with hoops of the same material.

This *nouala*-town which you see from the train is however not Fedhalla, which lies out of sight of the station. It is merely an important nomad or semi-nomad settlement composed of many hundreds of families, come there to work. They come from anywhere, they are always moving around: it is the works going on in the port, or the fish factories, that attract them. First they pitch their tents. It is the low-slung black roof of coarse home-spun cloth, made of camel and goat hair, palmetto and other vegetable fibre—high enough for squatting but not standing—that you see all over Maghreb. Next they prowl round and smell out the work and the money. If it is all right, they build a *nouala*. Others build *noualas*. If hundreds of hands are wanted, soon there is a Caboose-city. If these sources of employment fail or slack off, or if they get tired of the place, they abandon the *nouala* (of course without the slightest hesitation—no one would regret a dark insanitary *caboose*): they load their ass and move on to any point of the compass they fancy. Then the same thing happens again.

These people come under the head of semi-nomad I expect. They are of the same nomadic category as the *transhumant*—those who alternate between pastoral tent-dwelling, and highland village life.

The Berber is a foot-nomad. The Berber is a matchless walker. Mr. Cunninghame Graham scoffs at this born foot-slogger, comparing him unfavourably with the Arab (whom he pictures as always mounted upon a priceless and high-spirited steed). But I think it is a great pleasure to watch these romantic athletes, in Indian file, undoubtedly setting up, daily, desert records.

They should be trained for Marathons. They cover prodigious distances, it is said. It is nothing for a family, starting in the Sous, to go and do some harvesting in Tunis. Their brains are like those of animals, they photograph the desert landmarks; doubtless they know, too, the smells, and the characteristic geology of the soil—that must be their embossed map, which they feel with their feet—since they all go barefoot. Flint and broken glass mean no more to a Berber (especially "transhumant") than to a good solid shoe. (The feet of dead Berbers should be utilized for shoe-leather.)

Everywhere, throughout the thousand miles from Oran to Casa, groups of *nouala*, or most often the low, dark-brown, nomadic tent, are met with incessantly. It is a chain of encampments—or strings of wandering families, pressing forward, in Indian file, with loaded asses.

Wherever there are mines, or farms, there are groups of tents, and occasionally rough cabooses. And, in this country where the day-labourer is a nomad, who pitches his tent against the field or mine he is to work in, the question that presents itself to the statistician is no doubt whether these people are "transhumant," "nomads," or, on the other hand, uprooted "sedentaries," in search of work. No one I suppose can quite say, in such a fluid life. The "sedentary" is always apt, upon the slightest provocation, to become a "transhumant." And the "transhumant" is more than likely to develop into a nomad. So what is the ratio of nomadism, what of settlement, must remain uncertain.

In Casablanca, for instance, there is a vast settlement that the French have named "Bidonville." It is a city within the city, in fact. It consists of small huts mainly composed of petrol-tins. "Petrol-tin Town" (a blemish in *Casa-la-Blanche*) is again a mushroom settlement of nomads, attracted by the dollars to be picked up in this Babylon of the Nazarene half-finished. Thousands of these petrol-tin dwellings already exist, day by day they are added to: they have streets and squares.

Bidonville is quite "sedentary." It lies in a hollow. Above it tower the dazzling white palaces of the *Quartier Réservé*—which could be called "Brothel-Town" or, to make a joke to show you the idea, "Strumpet-ville." Let us call it "Strumpetville" to match "Bidonville."

By the Petrol-tin Town, or Bidonville, of Casablanca, one is irresistibly reminded of another excrescence of the same sort, recently described in the English newspapers, namely the sub-city, or shack-town, growing up outside Chicago. *Capitalism and Barbary breed the same forms*—but how odd! The world-slump that hit America with the velocity of a tornado, spewed out on to the streets millions of decent people, not necessarily passionately nomad. So many have gone to live in the "Bidonville" of Chicago, we are told: they are sardonic, they name the principal boulevards of their Hobo-city "Prosperity Avenue" or "War-debt Drive." Their hovels are numbered, like the dwellings of any other town; they have their letters addressed to, say,

Mr. So-and-So,
No. 486 Hoover Road.

So the enthusiastic Frenchmen, who point to Casablanca as the "pearl of the French Renaissance," and emphasize that it is a great city upon the latest transatlantic model, could even, if they wished, adduce the existence of Bidonville, to make the flattering comparison even more apposite! It is a parallelism which is, however, in no way dishonourable for the French, for *their* Hobo-town is the creation of born nomads, who are, by choice, the inhabitants of a tent or a caboose. No capitalist laws could drive them out of these hovels. It is different in the case of War-debt Drive, in the Hobo-town upon the shores of Lake Michigan. *There* our White stock is being forced down into a

semi-savage sub-world of the down-and-out, or Untermensch. It is being thrown back into Barbary—not invited to issue out of Barbary into the advantageous plane of the civilized European life.

Strumpetville is of course another matter. Both Bidonville and Strumpetville are typical of Casablanca, itself a mushroom city. When I described the houses of its *Quartier Réservé* as palaces, I was not dealing in hyperbole. I do not suppose that any *Quartier Réservé* on earth is so sumptuous. With its own shops, gardens and so forth, it is situated, by some irony, cheek by jowl with Bidonville. Yet considering the two together—the cloud-capped towers and gorgeous palaces of the one, and the kennels constructed of petrol-tins (looking like a savage congeries of small barbaric shields) of the other, it is difficult to decide which in fact looks the more impermanent.

Casablanca itself is an enormous whitewashed fungus-town. Fifteen or twenty years ago it did not exist. One of its old-established hotels— its premier-hotel, a place about the size of the Strand Palace—the Excelsior, a decade or so ago was not there. The Excelsior was built upon the bed of a river. This may have been the river that turned the wheel of the little flour-mill in the days of Dr. Leared. The river was in a ravine, and all "ravines" in Moroccan cities are shoots for refuse. So it was built, also, no doubt, upon a refuse-heap. There is a pump in the basement of the hotel: every day they have to do down and pump it out. Not many London hotels provide as good a dinner as the Excelsior table-d'hôte: there is a first-rate American Bar, lounges, great and small. Upstairs, in the passages, as full of incense as a Caïd's palace (as a result of the cigarettes of guests thrown into the cuspidors or trash-trays filled with sawdust, igniting the aromatic cedar wood) storey above storey, are luxurious bedrooms with bath, douche, etc. As a hotel it is in every way more "modern" than most London or Berlin hotels, beneath the Ritz class. But in the basement the water of the *oued* is flowing, and it has to be pumped out daily, else, presumably, this Grand Babylon would tumble down, or the subterranean waters would rise and submerge the guests and their Porto Flips in the American Bar.

Casablanca is a city upon the American model then. It is semi-skyscraping, "Block"-built, as modern as modern. An impression of kaleidoscopic unreality of the same order as that that disengages from the "canyons" of Manhattan, assails you as you enter it for the first time, a passenger from Europe (all allowance made for the inferior importance of this French colonial fungus, as against the staggering impressiveness of the externals of New York, seen from a Cunarder's decks in the early night by a London visitor). From both emanate the

73

same unmistakable sensations of violent impermanence. But in Casa it is in some ways more striking, since the civilization it apes, namely the Mediterranean, is traditional, whereas the American is frankly upstart—it is the uprush of a New World. The "forcing" operation whereby Casa has suddenly come to be, is, upon all hands, starkly apparent. Its shell, the dazzling balanced plaster walls, what are they, the suspicious traveller asks, but a gigantic architectural confectionery? Tap them, they must be hollow, or filled with *marsh mallow*— certainly of a mushroom flimsiness, porous rag-pulp or paper-mulberry-hearted. In fact no one has been there long enough to saturate any cubic foot of it with his presence. There is no personality in its hasty palaces: this densely-peopled city might still be empty, for all the human aura with which it is charged. Organically it is a hoax: here is not an organism, but a preposterous assemblage of discrete and self-sufficing cells, which would collapse at a touch, administered with force enough, almost anywhere.

All its inhabitants, too, are a huge scratch-population, blown together by a big newspaper puff from the four ends of the earth, gold-diggers in posh city-quarters, ten-a-penny filibusters in plaster palaces: the "big noises" in this mushroom metropolis are adventurers of a decade's standing at the longest—not like the old and crusted harpies of Tangier and Tunis: the biggest "men of substance" here, you feel, would, anywhere else, be straw-magnates, with big question-marks against their names. So this half-caste, ex-legionary, citizenry, is, again, racially unreal. Its cohesion, such as it is, is its tongue, which is kitchen-French, little more (and even that will shortly grow to be a mere *sabir*, full of German and Berber). What is it doing there all of a sudden then, *Casa-la-Blanche* in the midst of an ancient piratic empire—pretending to be a European "conqueror"—with all the white, impressive power it has brought together, or that has been brought together for it (that is nearer the mark I think!). Will it not all as suddenly disrupt, escape perhaps with the hiss of a puncture, one fine night—one of the Thousand and One Nights of Arabian phantasy! Meanwhile the pseudo-Paleface is far outnumbered by the dark faces come out of the *bled:* Casa is swarming with nomads, just as half its *soi-disant* permanent population are nomads of some kind as well: it was built by nomads: perhaps one day it will be destroyed by nomads!

Such is *Casa-la-Blanche.*—But this fair city is the creation of Marshal Lyautey—that is a paradox, however. It is the bastard child, I fear, of that great governor, of that old Roman. [. . . .]

For "European civilization" is no longer Roman, the Machine has no nationality nor is it a matter of hemispheres: and Maghreb is a desert, where nothing will ever grow except desert things. The military genius of the European is part and parcel of the past, I think that is self-evident, the War was the proof of it. It is a retrograde force. It still dreams its military and administrative dream, it is awfully useful for police-work, and all right in its place. But it is divorced to-day from the world around it in an absolute sense—a soldier, a great military administrator like Lyautey, is a throw-back: true to the military mind he had inherited, he built his castle in Spain (or Empire in Morocco, the same thing) in the grand Roman style of his ancestors. An anachronism. Then the political riff-raff and job-snatchers (pals of Oustric and patrons of the Bonnet Rouge) who had been watching his altruistic proceedings from the distance, biding their time, more powerful than he, spat in his eye and kicked him out of his castle and turned it into a bank. Such are the fortunes of war, in a world that has out-grown war, in which the soldier will never be honoured again—however much he may yet be made use of and sometimes paid lip-service to—which of course would be magnificent, if a worse man were not likely to be honoured in his place. But let us hope that will not be the case.

A few observations are called for, as a consequence of the foregoing account of Casa.—The gamut of human advance is to the stable from the unstable—its poles—I take it. The most potent insult you can offer to a Riffian is to say "Your dad died in his bed!" The Touareg has a proverb, "With the plough enters in dishonour!" These two races are evidently at the unstable end—the Riff is shown, by the specific nature of his touchiness, to scorn *peace*—the Touareg, *agriculture*. And the German tribesmen of antiquity is said to have regarded with great distaste all towns, or any enclosed settlement. (Hence, they say, *Wandervogelismus.*)

But our civilization, with the impetus given it by machines, is turning from the settled to the restless ideal—from "civilization" to "savagery." The gist of my remarks regarding Casa was this: if you pitch a tent or project a skyscraper—if you camp in a "Caboose-city" or in a "White-City" run-up overnight, or from one year to the next, that is all one, if you are of the nomad sort. The roving, versatile, American workman works a while in one place and then is apt to move on—he "guesses he'll beat it": and if you observed him "beating it" in his two-seater Ford, looking for work, you would be observing a "transhumant" of sorts, as truly as if you had beneath your eyes a family roaming the *bled*, though quite willing to get some mud and sticks and build a caboose, if it was made worth their while.

75

The French Protectorate in Morocco, then, is a great European enterprise—the last of that order, I should think, that we shall see. An administrative genius, Lyautey, did it with his eyes shut, I should say—because it was his nature to behave in that manner, and the nature of those who worked with him: he was allowed to do it because you must have soldiers to make wars with (according to politicians) and when you have soldiers they behave automatically in that way when you're not looking, unless violently stopped—they, it is their second nature, indulge in martial alarms and excursions, bully niggers, encircle accommodating sultans, and before you can say Jack Robinson (if they happen to be great guys like Lyautey) come running back with an "empire" between their teeth! And then, of course, the old imperialist framework—the old sentiment of the *épopée*—was still there: such institutions die hard.

French Morocco is the last great European enterprise of that order, magnificently carried through by a great soldier—one of the last of the great European military figures. It shows the French at their best—as the humane, civilizing, most genially-acquisitive, of all powers, able and good-humoured—something like what the Normans must have been, when mellowed a little by the benefits of conquest. But their protectorate is built upon sand, in every conceivable sense. The type of "European" who is running it is as unfixed, restless and incalculable in everything as is the nomad, semi-nomad, "transhumant" or only technically "sedentary" population he is invited to boss. All that is essentially stable is the military. They however are never left for long in the same place, lest they should become attached to this or that *popote*, city-quarters or out-lying post—that is the great military principle of *change*.—And the civilization behind the military power, and upon which it depends, has made a virtue of disequilibrium. Must not we consider, then, this admirable outburst of the old French genius as in the nature of a *sand-castle*, built upon the sands of a desert, without the promise of much permanence: we should admire it all the more, because it must be transitory, and the last thing of that sort our society will witness. Can anyone imagine the post-war English building such a pretty empire, for instance, twice the size of Spain? What a pity that the whole world cannot be governed by such people as Lyautey! Instead, the *Barbarians* have taken to building! And we are returning to the hair-tent once again—"picturesque and poetical," as Budgett Meakin said, but the death of science and of art: "not an ideal life."

PART TWO

RIO DE ORO

CHAPTER I

MARRAKECH

[We are at Marrakech. And Marrakech may be regarded as the
Chleuh capital. But it is also more than that. It is a big vortex of
life where the Northern Berber, the Chleuh, and the Saharan
come together—stagnating, with a considerable blackening of
skin owing to the Soudanese influx, about its busy Souks.
                                                   —*Kasbahs and Souks*]

There is no particularity of the City of Casa to which I need draw
anyone's attention. I stopped there on two or three occasions, spend-
ing I suppose ten days within its whitewashed circumference. Most of
that time was spent in attempting to undermine the colossal indifference of the French Postal personnel to the welfare of the Public—I
was the Public, for the occasion: and I could inform you of course that
the large German café in the Avenue du Général d'Amade—upon
which I invariably fell back when heavily repulsed at the Post Office—
is much the best in Casa. So let us turn, with some relief, from *Casa-
la-Blanche* to the "City of Morocco."

Up to a point, *l'un vaut l'autre*. All that can be said, upon the lines
laid down in the last chapter, of Casa, can be said—indeed very often
has been said—of the Capital of the South, Marrakech. It stands in a
fifty-mile-wide stony tufa steppe, and is in fact nothing but a huge
walled oasis, supporting a multitude of palms with the waters that
come to it from the wall of the Atlas, at its back. The most populous
city in Morocco, larger than Fez or Rabat, Marrakech is yet a vast
rendezvous rather than a capital. It is a walled-in converging-point of
nomads or of extremely restless peasants. The Brothers Tharaud
refer to it as "this city of the South, which, in spite of a few fine
remains, is still nothing more than a great camp of nomads"; or again
they refer to it as "Marrakech . . . this immense *fondouk* of asses, mules
and camels."

First of all, from the standard "Oriental City" of the north of Maghreb el Aksa, you penetrate, once you pass the thirty-second degree of
latitude, into a more definitely African World. Dr. Leared says:
"There was little to record of my first impressions of Morocco (mean-

ing Marrakech) except its likeness to the Oriental cities I had visited. Most things, however, wore a more African tinge. The black race was more numerous here. . . ."

Everything, indeed, as this writer says, "wears" a far "more African tinge." As you pass from Casa into the South, or the *Sous*, you find yourself in that part of Morocco that is least affected by the European, in the first place, also (and that is more important) it has come less beneath the influence of the Arab, outside the direct administrative sphere of the cities, and of course the areas occupied by the Chich tribes. There in the South are to be found the densest Souks, the greatest Kasbahs, and a climate, too, which, approaching more to the tropical, brings in the banana and the date-palm as a natural part of the décor—thereby heightening the "Islamic Sensations," with great novelties for the northern eye.

Here in Marrakech the Saadian Tombs (ramshackle and ruined as that precinct is) are alone suggestive of a more settled society, according to the two Tharauds. They are a little piece of civilization in the midst of this indifferent Barbary, or its huge camping-centre of dried mud—Marakeh or "Morocco." But, say these two quite readable brothers, "should you wish to find a sepulchre made after the image of this already Saharan city," you must turn your back upon this little island of orderly beauty, "go a few hundred yards farther on, following a mud enclosure, and have a look through the planks carelessly knocked together of a miserable patched-up gateway. There, in the shadow of a fine apricot tree—beneath a few bricks assembled without art, and then slapped over with whitewash, which is scaling off in patches—lies Yousseff ben Tachefin, who founded Marrakech, and led his hordes of veiled Warriors to the conquest of Granada and Cordova." This is indeed a tomb in keeping with the city. "Often pious hands have attempted to raise the walls of a *koubah* above his head: but every time that this happened the illustrious defunct, accustomed to the open spaces of the desert, of life beneath the tent, has kicked away the roof that it was proposed to provide him with, for his last sleep, for he wished for nothing above him, in death as it had been in life, except the roof of the moving leaves!"

So the great Almoravid, the first and greatest of the Saharan princes who galvanized the Berber world with their desert energy, and held it together for a spell, lies buried under an apricot tree, beneath a few bricks in the wild oasis-city he founded almost a millennium ago: and the city is the image of the man and of Berber life as well, in short of *Barbary*. That is what the Tharauds have to say.

But Marrakech is far more real than is the tall white city of Casa, fully organized upon the most ample industrial lines, all the resources of Western Civilization contributing to its quick uprush. Then, again, Marrakech is a city after the image of Tachefin: but Casablanca, on the same principle, is *not* a city after the image of Lyautey, or even of France.

What the Tharaud Brothers say of the *revers de la médaille*—or the hot mud-city of the first nomad-dynasty—may be accepted as fact as far as it goes; the other side of the picture, especially regarding the impressiveness of the Saadian Tombs, is another matter. There are a lot of long plain gravestones—they *are* like small stone boats, if you like, keel-up: and these tombstones are to be found in a couple of lofty ill-lighted chambers, *à l'Alhambra.* The Tharauds are thinking how all these Sultans died a violent death, one after the other—one at the hands of his Renegade Christian Bodyguard when he was drunk, another through the agency of the same fine body of men when he was sober: another slaughtered by his treacherous uncles, another poisoned by a Barbary fig, at the instigation of a Palace Eunuch, and so on. They are perfectly right, as I have already pointed out, to think like that: a man is a brute merely, who does not. I thought of all that too as I looked at the stone boxes. Only when I hoped to see in them "a simplicity, a divine proportion," that should remind me of the greatest masterpieces, then I had to confess that where the Tharauds saw so much I saw nothing at all—little more than I see when I pass the monumental stonemasons in the Euston Road, before you get to Great Portland Street Station.

But there is another point upon which I think the Tharaud Brothers, and many others, are gravely mistaken. I refer to the assumptions behind their terms "civilized" and "uncivilized," as applied to what we find in Barbary. For me the polished and empty Hispano-Mauresque, the Andalusian Art, is simply dull: it is, as someone has said of it, little more than a dazzling *luxury-garment* thrown over anything that can pay the price asked for the tiles, fretwork, and mosaic—mosque, palace, or Tolba School all getting the same mechanical adornment, the same one stock-outfit. The sheer architecture at the bottom of it is nothing, or next to nothing.

This certainly is "civilized," in a Parisian way, but it is too narrow a definition. The finest architecture in Morocco is to be found in the High Atlas, according to my view. There the great Kasbahs are splendid works of art, or at least very impressive works of art, however rough sometimes, in a very great tradition. And all the best of these Kasbahs are built by a desert, or semi-desert, tribe, the Ouled Yahya. These people come from just north of Tiznit. (Tiznit is a *ksar* upon the

81

Saharan slopes of the Western Atlas.)

But there is something else which makes the sort of statement I have quoted from the Tharauds particularly superficial. It is generally believed, according to the latest researches, that the best contemporary architecture in Maghreb is as a matter of fact the Saharan. Very little is known about the oases in the neighbourhood of Tatta, since only two or three Europeans have ever seen them. But they are said to be particularly finely built. And Gautier (*Les Siècles Obscurs du Maghreb*) insists upon the great superiority of the type of building in the Saharan cities (Figuig and its neighbourhood for instance) to the Kabyle or other "sedentary" architecture farther north.

If we compare, then, the monuments of the Hispano-Mauresque with the adobe hovels around them in Marrakech, this very chic Turkish Bath Architecture would no doubt discover itself in the role of the polished gentleman over against an African hobo. But that in fact is not quite the contrast, all things taken into account, that a wider inspection would suggest. The Soudanese home-land of the Berber chief, Tachefin (the first Almoravid), was not necessarily quite the savage spot that the Tharauds and the rest assume it to be. On the contrary. There is every indication that the civilization of the Sahara was of a higher order than that of the Tangitanian Mauretania. The monasteries and famous centres of mystical scholasticism of Senegal and Mauretania were not, evidently, mere deserts full of wild animals and untutored nomads. Mauretania, or what we call loosely the Rio de Oro, has been termed "the intellectual centre" of Islam in the Berber World. There have at all times been cities and monasteries in those deserts as well as nomadic brigands. So Tachefin should not be regarded exactly as the chief of hordes of veiled brigands.—But I will take up this question again in a moment.

Even if you like the Hispano-Mauresque, however, there is not much to see in Marrakech. There is the famous Koutoubia, whose silhouette dominates everything; there is the Palace of Ba Ahmed—it is a vulgar descendant of the Alhambra, there is nothing in it that is not coarse and summary in workmanship. But this huge peach-coloured adobe town must not be judged by its few Andalusian remains. It must be judged, on its own merits, as something like an immense human personality.

Marrakech is indeed "the mouth of the Sahara," as it is described by Graham. It is a huge, red, windy metropolis of mud and sand. In the centre of it is "The Place of Destruction" (*Djemaa el Fna*) which is a small desert in the midst of a city (as "a square" it is vast) full of the vigorous African crowds—acrobats, potters, Chleuh boy-dancers (like bands of depraved but still strictly-disciplined surpliced acolytes)—many sorcerers and palmists (before whom squats some silent mountaineer, drinking in the words of fate, while the prophetic quack holds fast the tell-tale hand, mesmerizing his victim as he whispers to him the secrets of the future) with, at the busy hours, a city of fantastic tents. The tent-making capacities of the natural nomad are here seen to full advantage, in the structures of mats and poles, which take the shapes of a pachydermatous beast, or hollow-carnival giant, sheltering the salesman and artisan—cobblers, locksmiths, *couscous*-vendors, herbalists, butchers, letter-writers.

The Djemaa el Fna has often been described: half a century ago it must have been in most respects the same as to-day, except that the unlovely Post Offices (of a Moorish Operette type) and the slick Paris-Arab pastiche that it is considered necessary to indulge in when building a Bank, does not improve the view. The large café in one corner of this Djemaa el Fna affords a select, arcaded meeting-place for officers and Berber notables: the great Caïds, it is said, go up to the roof if they wish to indulge in an extra drink or two, so as not to be observed by their tribesmen: but the "Islamic Sensation" is necessarily lessened by the presence of this commanding European building. Also much of the dancing that used to occur in "The Place of Destruction" has been, since the French Occupation, driven underground, or persuaded to remove itself into houses set aside for such strange African licences, which is a pity.

Still the desolation of cracked mud and sand, endless fine upstanding palms, loaded with dates, miles of these plumed plants—everywhere, wall within wall, peach-pink mud-concrete battlements, of which earlier travellers speak, is still perfectly intact. "This heap of ruins, sand-heap, desert-town"—this "city of the Mahdis, halt of the Sultans of the South, on their way to capture Fez"—has not capitulated to Europe, it is still the "Morocco City" of Dr. Leared, or, last and worst of all Black Vizirs, of Ba Ahmed. "Morocco City is purely African," says Mr. Graham; and that is it after all. Those "handsome Arab types" so beloved of the travelled Briton (of Mr. Graham of course) are conspicuous by their absence. There are no magnificoes, in this huge adobe Souk, who hold as heirlooms the monster keys of the houses in Granada unwillingly vacated by their ancestors five hundred years ago. Marrakech belongs more to the Soudan than to Spain.

CHAPTER II

FILM-FILIBUSTERS

Before going south of the Atlas into "the mysterious" Sous—a land so pregnant with plots and so overrun with lawless outsiders as to make a mere tourist's hair stand on end—before rushing for four hundred miles up and down the sides of mountains in a mighty bus, and at last dropping with a dull roar into the ocean valley of Santa-Cruz-du-Cap-de-Gué,[1] the very home-soil and breeding ground of the essential Filibuster (whose filibustering is the principal industry of the place), I will give some account of an important Filibuster met with farther north—not in the Sous—namely the Film-Filibuster. I fell in with a huge caravan of them at Fez. And then (in more aristocratic surroundings and in a much grander form—juvenile-lead and magnate rolled into one) at Marrakech.

But if I take it upon myself to refer to the Film-pro or Screen-king as a "Filibuster," it must be understood that I am casting no reflection upon his rectitude. At least, the ramp is elsewhere. The gulls are in the distant theatres, in such centres of civilization as Chicago or Glasgow, much more than among the natives of Barbary—among whom the Ufa and Pathé magnates send their troupes (not troops) merely to afford their sham-sheiks a Hispano-Mauresque photographic setting. The whispering masses in the Film-palaces—it is for them that this description of filibuster filibusts—throwing up shoddy mirages, with his photographic sausage-machine, of the desert-life—so falsely-selected as to astonish into suspicion sometimes even the tamest Robot. As to the filmable populations—true, this mechanical Vandal degrades them as he does everything he touches, but for the rest he puts many a lightly-earned peseta in their pockets, and is a pure benefactor as far as that goes. And as to the Italian hotels of Barbary, it is difficult to see what they would do at all if it were not for those truck-loads of queer fish brought from Paris and quartered on them by the gross. The touring film-rabble make up for the absent tourist—the latter a rarer bird every minute, with every fresh oscillation of the world's Exchanges and every fresh currency ramp or tariff wall.

---

[1] A former name for Agadir.

At Fez, the Hotel Transatlantic was closed—it is open only for a few months in the cool season. Similarly all over Morocco these huge hotels were shut down—they are the "follies," as in other days they would have been called, of a Steamship Company, I believe. The Grand Hotel, when I arrived, was open, but it was very large and it languished—it had been conceived to meet the booming requirements of a "Renaissance Marocaine" which has not materialized, and for a volume of sightseers and filibusters far in excess of what can now ever again be expected. The enormous dining-hall adjoining the café, with its numerous staff of white-jacketed Algerian waiters, its Italian managers, was perhaps a quarter full upon the first evening. Then upon the second day the train from Casa came in with all its compartments packed with a super sheik-film company. Its fifty-odd personnel poured in for lunch, and immediately the winter of our discontent was turned, at one blow, into glorious summer. These fifty dumb characters in search of an author dumb enough to concoct a plot and text for them (accompanied by the sharp-shooters of the mechanical staff) swarmed forward, vociferous and replete with a strident reality that was so thin as to stamp them anywhere as screen-folk—creatures that is of an art at one remove from the shadow-picture. With all the prestige of this idiotic industry (as practised in our Western savagery) they gave the hotel-staff something to live for, and a scene of great animation was the result.

They swung (if of the Mix-class)—danced, shuffled, dashed, sidled, stalked or tottered in, each according to his kind: noticeably *two-by-two* (as if picked out into sex-pairs by an official Cupid) like the animals entering the Ark—for of course each of these Stars, however impotent a one-candle-power washout (even according to Box-office canons) must, off the Screen, move in a triangle of bloodshot adultery—to satisfy the business-end of the racket—in order to suggest the bombardment of an anguished fan-mail (if to no one else, to their fellow-actors). Only one or two dared to be solitary, for however brief a time.

This company had come to Fez to enact a rather elaborate arabesque of kiss-stuff, crime and contraband of arms, to be called *The Three Unlucky Travellers*. My informant was a half-caste waiter—pock-marked and with the scars of several other epidemics as well to underline his attractions. But he felt himself nearer to the great dynamic heart of the universe than ever before with these people—he told me that he had been remarked at once by the Film-boss. At sight he had been engaged for a minor part. What part? Oh, that of a blind mendicant, not an important part! They had *wanted* him to take a more important part, but he hadn't time. He wished in a way he had! They had asked him to go away with them. Yes, they desired him to become one of them. But he did not see his way to do that. He could not be spared just then, so must remain at Fez. At that moment one of the Three Unlucky Travellers (the Polish one, the least lucky of the lot) clapped his hands impatiently in our direction, and shouted for a straw for his ice-water. When the waiter returned to me (after watching for some minutes the Star make use of the straw) he informed me that the one he had just obliged—who had just asked him to help him about a straw—was the first of the three to fall a victim to the spells of the magician's daughter (who was the leading lady) and to fall over a cliff. The cliff as it happened (by this time everything was ship-shape—Fez had been ransacked scenically) was the other side of the Medina. It was a very big rocky lump, which the *Fési* has accounted for by attaching it to a local legend—it is supposed to be the colossal detritus of an indignant divinity, who was disgusted with the people of Fez, and took this rather objectionable way of showing it.

The Unlucky Traveller Number One was French, as was right and proper in a Parisian film. His were the almost matchlessly empty histrionic blend of attractions of the French Music Hall—those throaty troubadours of the Third Republic who mouth with a mealy sweetness the songs that are hawked in broadsheets afterwards by tenoro-guitarists in the provinces. Only I had been accustomed always to see that figure in a *tuxedo*. Therefore at first I was somewhat puzzled, for he considered an Aertex vest and canvas slacks sufficient clothing even for dinner in these sporting tropics, and in that form he was at once terribly familiar and yet absolutely strange. Of course in that way his athletic proportions stood revealed, but they were pallid (as one would suppose the city songster's to be in spite of his cave-manly cawing and basso-profundo cooing). He looked in fact not unlike those half-naked bakers who occasionally emerge in pastrycooks' at the time the hot cottage-loaves are brought up from the subterraneous ovens.

When this clumsy Hearty, the first juvenile-lead, entered the restaurant, he *swung* himself over to his place at table, as if in the atmosphere a system of massive ropes had been secreted—his torso, which was flat but very wide, swung in one direction, his arms (which were a clerk's and not a blacksmith's—but large-boned at least, if innocent of muscle) swung in the other direction. And he remained at all times a Man-of-the-hour, although he would not be "released" for a twelve-month. If he went over to the kiosk, which stood in front of the hotel, to buy a newspaper or packet of cigarettes, he inflated his chest beneath the proud fabric of the Aertex beforehand—*then* he started: he swung across the road, again as if ropes upon either side of him, suspended in a fluid medium, led direct from café to kiosk. "Unfortunate Traveller" for six weeks (the troupe was to remain there for at least as long as that they said) he was a most melancholy gymnast, his existence a footlight one, overshadowed by an epic struggle on the other side of the Medina—on the Tarpeian Rock, then out in the pitiless *bled* with a bloodthirsty Sheik—never off-duty, compelled to remain stripped (to his Aertex) for the fray, by the etiquette of his profession. Did the poor chap ever relax? Did he in his bedroom relax, and become the clumsy, slouching clerk of his early youth once more—or did he sleep bolt upright, even in his sleep an "Unlucky Traveller," with his chest stuck out three inches beyond the norm of its recumbent silhouette?

These simple universal problems (for the onlooker) are provided in common by all those who live by impersonating "unlucky" characters, cast for abnormal episodes, of great physical violence. But it occurred to me as I watched these film-cattle that the stage-actor, the backgrounds for whose work are the scenes of everyday, though they have much in common, must differ very widely in important particulars. The stage-actor for instance could at all times be spotted out of the theatre, in his non-public life. Likewise the film-actor, but less so. For on the whole with the latter the actorishness must be of a more insidious sort. His artificiality has to be more intense, since the demands of the *real* everyday background are more exacting. In his professional displays the Screenworker in the nature of things is the last word in *naturalism,* at the opposite pole to a formal art. His actorishness therefore (the stigmata of the trade of Makebelieve stamped into his features and attitudes) must be rather a distortion of a very common-or-garden norm, rather than the reflections of a transcendent, an abnormal, existence. The Film-man will tend to be a very intense, very slightly heightened Everyman: whereas the Garricks and Irvings would carry about with them in private the impress of successions of great Individuals of the Imagination—separated by all the arts of the formal stage-play from that everyday nature of Everyman, which is the particular province of Film-photography.

The huge company that came to the Cherifian capital to reproduce the great dime-drama of *The Three Unlucky Travellers,* was polyglot. One of the luckless heroes was a German, but there was every nationality represented, even English. The spectacle of this cosmopolitan social organism taking shape beneath one's eyes was a mild diversion.

They arrived as a mere chaos of personalities, upon the scene of the Grand Hotel. But at the end of three or four days they had separated out into well-defined classes. The Leading Parts (irrespective of nationality, age, salary, or looks) sat at a smaller table. This became a sort of High Table. There was a second table for those not quite so eminent. But from this second table people were occasionally promoted to the first. This was usually as a consequence of successful love-passages with a male or female of the first rank. This necessarily brought them into the charmed circle of Stars (if the love-passages lasted above twenty-four hours that is). But upon the first day of one of these adventures the couple involved in the new intrigue would separate upon arrival in the restaurant, and would go to their respective tables, according to class. Sometimes after a day or two at the High Table, a Second-Classer would have to return to Table Number Two, upon being superseded in the affections of the Star in question. There was therefore a constant going and coming. It was an evolutionary pattern, supervised by Cupid, the *motif* divorce, of course.

After four or five days a new phenomenon was to be remarked. A pair of important Stars would roughly break away from the central tables, and go off into a corner by themselves—to a *table pour deux*. At the end of the sixth or seventh day most were back again where they had started, in their original groupment. Others had, meanwhile, broken away, and were to be seen with their heads together alone at a table, even perhaps going so far as to order a half-bottle of rather better wine (say two francs worth of Sauterne) than was supplied gratis with each meal.

As two would come in—and, instead of going to their usual seats, according to class, at a common board, were observed to pass down the room and establish themselves in a distant spot—all the other tables would be in a fulsome momentary ferment—people would turn round and point, chatter and signal from one table to the other. In short, the attitude of all these people to their own actions—of "passionate" couplement and further violent separation—was exactly the same as though they had been a crowd of *fans*, instead of a crowd of pros. They acted the *fan* for each other! Their shop was as much, or a great deal more, *publicity*, than it was the art of acting, that goes without saying. The goodlooker, not the good actor, would become the Star. It may be regarded as certain that each morning a *fan-mail* would come up with the principal's breakfast. It would be composed and dispatched overnight by lesser members of the flattersome company. And from the camera staff such attentions would come particularly well no doubt. All day long the individuals of this herd were showing off to each other, attempting to convince the rest that they were "coming" Stars, or if already by way of being Stars, that *this* show would give them a place in the centre of the world-spotlight, with semi-Garbo-like laurels—or recall the days of Valentino, when Stars were Stars indeed.

The quality of the female élite of the company, I regret to say, was exceedingly low according to any standards. They were all under-sized, almost like another species, and their intense artificiality took the form of an odd degenerescence. In *forcing* the normal everyday reality as it were—in compelling it to conform to what was certainly a vulgar average, but a particularly odd variety of the vulgarest commonplace—they suggested the exact opposite of the *heightening* said to characterize the finest art. Theirs was a *lowering:* but it was a descent so much *below* the *average* level as to be eccentric and extra-ordinary. Here were indeed the authentic *depressed* levels of the universe of the *Untermensch,* in all their blatant pretentiousness. Seeing that their departure from the norm was in the direction of a dwarfishness, an eccentricity, an air of impaired health—with the demented self-assertiveness of the *Asphalt*-folk that they of course are, and the demented concentration upon *effect*—an impression (even necessarily) of a *degeneration*—from power, law, dignity, and sense—was conveyed by their presence. It was as if some patently *inferior*—some less healthy, less excellently balanced, less beautiful—some half-mad midget people, were, father to son, Film-pros. In Maghreb all the acrobats come from a particular tribe in the Sous—all the builders and masons come from a particular tribe in the Great Atlas—in the same way all the personnel of this Film-world might come from a certain district—say in Galicia or in Czechoslovakia. One could imagine them as a diminutive, pthisic, gutter-people, who had started in gutter-theatricals, prospered, spread over the world (as the Berber tumblers of the Noun have done) caricaturing any eccentric-ity, or imitating any particularly brutal behaviour on the part of the full-grown, "normal," master-people by whom they were surrounded—falling in and out of love, to show that they were *real* and not just puppets, and even taking their desperate pretence of reality so far at times as to blow their papier-mâché brains out—a small vampire, or vampish, kohl-lidded, heterosexed clan, an impor-tant subdivision of the *Untermensch,* selecting for their imitations for preference Crime—some specializing in gangster parts, some in coke-addict parts, some in lesbian roles—some partial to blackmail, some to arson, some sticking to "straight" Murder-Club stuff, some having patent side-lines of fancy homicide—but *all* violent—*all* guaranteed to be intelligible to the least talented, to the most adenoid-stifled gutter-infant, or to the lowest average level of City-serfdom—always the crudest Box-office "appealed" to—everything imitated by them to be vulgar and violent *de rigueur*. So, restless and keyed-up to jazz-concert-pitch, this swarm moved about the hotel: to overhear a dialogue in the elevator was to be let into a secret of the heart of a Star. At the mere presence beside them of a stranger (a potential *fan*) they began talking feverishly, so that you should feel that when they passed out of sight a pistol would be fired—a pipe of opium resorted to—an illegal operation consummated—or (at the mildest and meekest) a fruity adultery be instantly forthcoming. This *atmosphere of climax* in this great hotel became somewhat oppressive at last. It blotted out the Arabs finally, and made the Berber a little dim—I was of course grateful for the eclipse of the Hispano-Mauresque Babs and Minarets, Medersas and Mosques! They certainly cast a spell over the "capital of the Islamic World" as the Sultan's good town of Fez is often called. They swarmed everywhere—they whispered in the passages, danced in the café, wrote masses of letters and cards (to languishing *fans*) in the writing-rooms, monopolized the Bars.

The three he-men and their three he-friends were the principal American Bar guests—one in puggaree and pipe, two walking ads. for underwear—and then the three understudies of course to match, though exaggerating the absurdities of their principals—dressed in an inferior quality of men's vests, and with even an inferior quality of skin—though the latter was in fact somewhat of a feat, in the way of subordination!

The younger officers of the Fez garrison mingled on terms of equality and patronage with the Film-folk—not of course sitting at their tables, but occasionally inviting one or two to theirs—or often a Film-man would come up and sit down with them unasked, and they suffered this with a good grace.

I take it that this big Film-troupe was a second-rate French one, dispatched to Fez on the cheap, on a Lunn Tour basis—probably "done" by the Hotel at ten francs per day per head, for six weeks—everything found, the least choice Algerian wine thrown in and glad to get rid of it. Trade was at an abnormal ebb—the Economic Blizzard must have emptied every hotel from the Bermudas to Bombay—and this ill-favoured herd certainly filled up the hotel and gave it a spurious air of prosperity.

But it was at Marrakech that I was privileged to catch a glimpse of quite a different type of Film-folk. There in the local Ritz-Carlton I found myself the fellow-guest of a Film magnifico. (I was of course travelling in the strictest incognito, and I am sure that he was perfectly unaware of my presence. I had the better opportunity in consequence of observing him.)

CHAPTER III

FAKING A SHEIK

To name the personality in question here is entirely unnecessary. He *had* a name—it is a name that is "world-famous," which has been bellowed in the ear of the Robot-rabble for over a decade. Producer, Director, Author, Continuity-man, Supervisor, Star—all rolled into one—he was rather unique. But it is a uniqueness in futility. To be *versatile* in a hundred such ways as those were, is very much what it would be to have a "world-wide" reputation for being able to play *God Save the King* on the piccolo, accordion, violin, Jew's harp, oboe, piano and saxophone. To be so constituted as to be able, *first* to scribble out six pages of a *Peg's Paper* or *Gem Library* romance, *second* to be able to undertake the duties of the "Continuity" hack (and expand the six-page story, puff it out, and then cut it into suitable breathless slices—a mosaic of nonsense), then *thirdly* to possess the talent necessary to conceive (in the capacity of Director) how a crowd of puppets could be made to carry out, scene after scene, the foolish injunctions of the "Continuity" hack (as handed over to the Script-Clerk)—further, to be sufficiently accomplished a *moron* to be able *in person* (having written the silly words oneself) to interpret them in the flesh—in short to become a Star—if to possess all this galaxy of undesirable gifts does not deserve *a name*, well, I don't know what does; but all the same it is a detail that can be dispensed with I think. After all, this kind of thing is widely advertised as a *folk-art*, and a folk-art is nothing if not *anonymous*. We do not know the names of the hundred million box-office gulls who are this fellow's masters (however much they may be gulled), so why then perhaps should we know this fellow's name either? It is immaterial.

Still, this was no ordinary figure in the vast imitative Underworld of the Screen, and this was for me an exceptional opportunity of studying a "Sheik" on the spot, as it were—of observing the sham-article in process of manufacture, out of the raw material of the Real—the Film Sheik taking shape in contact with hundreds of authentic Sheiks. And there is nothing more curious than to observe a person modelling a lie *from the life*—upon the living original—in an odd process of deliberate misrepresentation. It is the sort of work upon which the Propaganda Departments were engaged during the War—of always pondering how they could make a stupid lie out of some insignificant fact that came to their notice. And *ponder*—that is what this Sheik-faker was always doing in public—whenever I saw him he appeared to be *deeply pondering*—he *pondered* on his way downstairs, he *pondered* in the hotel lounge, he *pondered* at his meals, he *pondered* all over Marrakech.

But this was not the last of his oddities. Perhaps the oddest thing about him from my point of view was that in spite of everything he was, or had the appearance of, a gentleman, or to put it in another way, notwithstanding his profession, he did not exude vulgarity, as did the Film-Folk at Fez.

His record was a very bad one. It seemed that this was by no means the first time he had come to the *bled*, to fake a Sheik. He had formed the habit, *de vieille date*, of Sheik-faking. He was one of the first men to fake a Sheik—an old confederate of Valentino, and he had been in at the birth of this tradition. Every summer saw him prowling thereabouts—pondering—upon the extremities and fringes of the desert, plotting new "sets" of blood and thunder lollypops. But this was the first time, it seemed, that he had proposed to impersonate one of the principal characters himself. This was perhaps a turning-point.

He was thoroughgoing. They said he had become a Mohammedan—at least his publicity-staff interpreted his fascination for Islam and for Islamic Sensations in that way. For the public of Sheik-fans at all events he was a follower of the Prophet. He had built himself a Berber *timgremt* or Kasbah, upon the Riviera (where no doubt, dressed as a Lord of the Atlas, he gave people three thimblefuls of sweet mint-tea). Yes, not content with living amongst shamsheiks, false Black Palace-guards, Mokhaznis, and Vizirs, for a few months every year, he actually wanted to *be* a Sheik for ever—at last hoisted with his own petard and caught in his own trap! What an odd thing that was!

From the point of view of the French Colonial Authorities—the *Bureau des Affaires Indigènes*—this Sheik-complex must have been fairly handy, and this "Sheik" of the Riviera certainly was afforded every facility to proceed with his vulgarization of the Berber Steppes. When he built himself a Kasbah in the Provençal *bled* (where of course there are a good few Berbers in one way and another) they must have been rather pleased than otherwise. It would be like an annexe of the Colonial Exhibition. (If some idiot could be found to put up a Cochin-Chinese feudal residence in the same neighbourhood—and another to install himself in a Sonhrais temple-fort, with a Gambian touch or two—then the colonial-publicity departments would no doubt regard the interests of France as well-served by these ingenious visitors.)

This was the first American Film-magnifico I had ever encountered. Fifteen years ago I had seen his first great hundred-reel wow. But he differed from most of the Film-kings in being, as I have already indicated, instead of a Jewish businessman, an Irish-American of agreeable exterior and pleasant manners. Undoubtedly there was field-work for the psychologist here, if I had been such a person. I could see what a juicy little problem this would be for the professional analyst—namely what obscure motives lay behind this strange decision of his—suddenly to come forward at what I judged to be somewhere round the age of forty (though a very prepossessing, tanned, blue-eyed, healthy forty, as I have said) and concentrate the glare of all the Kleig lights, green mercury lamps—the "scoops" and "wampus"—the "babies," "suns" and "broads"—in his studios upon his own person, so far immune, as far as I know, from the life of the Star. It was not that he regarded himself as an irreplaceable "caster" for the role of Sheik—for as a matter of fact he had decided to play the part of a French subaltern. It must be something else. I idly wondered, as I watched this constantly pondering, a little ponderous, figure, going about its strange business: but I suppose the impulse that had led to this was a matter for an expert film-fan rather more than for a psychologist—why this veteran, measured by the time-standards obtaining in the Film World (one who had witnessed and participated in all the most demented excesses of the vogue of Valentino, with Wisconsin and Idaho flappers blowing their brains out right and left upon the news of the Star's decease, in front of a signed photo of that rather oily waiteresque gentleman)—why at this distant date from such epical events this wirepulling dictator should wish to take a hand himself in the sets, at the dead-end of the wire, where the automaton capers—and smile out in debonair close-ups, or prance in wistful middle-distance-shots, for the benefit of a gum-chewing World-pit—that was difficult to see.

Meanwhile here he was in the full splendour of official favour. The Rabat and Casa newspapers were full of his projected exploits. How he was to take his absurd pack up into the gorges of the Saharan Atlas, and *hunt the Sheik*—the national sport of America, as fox-hunting is that of England. A special Arab interpreter—in the most spotless costume and brand-new, blood-red *cheqhia*—had been detailed by the Residency to accompany him wherever he might choose to go, attached exclusively to his person. And a few nondescript individuals who had come with him from France, to reconnoitre, and mark down fresh Kasbahs to be *shot*, composed a select (unostentatious) retinue. In six months he was to return with a large company, like the one that had overrun the city of Fez, following upon what at present might be arranged between him and his technical consultants.

For his own part, he was quite reasonably dressed (as a cowboy—with khaki shirt, belt, riding boots, etc.). But his lieutenants were in Aertex vests (or some similar make of sport-suggestive gentleman's hose) like the people I had encountered at Fez. His manners were gentle and pleasant, and one felt that had not this Industry attracted him and conferred upon him an emperor's salary in early life, he would have been an agreeable fellow enough—handsome, healthy, and unassuming, if of no particular note. And for how many of those filling the higher ranks of the Film Industry can as much be said!

However, for many years this individual had been a deafening Noise, way up in the Film-firmament. He possessed many of the tricks of his elevated and noisy station. This was my second visit to Marrakech: it was the hottest period of the year, so the hotel was almost empty and the restaurant in the palm-court had been closed down, the waiters going north to do a bit of café-work. The handful of guests were directed to a restaurant upon a neighbouring boulevard. There night after night, upon a *terrasse* consisting of no more than six tables, in a cloud of flies, in a subtropical temperature (123 degrees in the shade) I sat almost in the company of this engaging magnifico, I was much more than within mere earshot of his conversation—I was bombarded by his dreamy bombast.

The first words I heard him utter were these, whether you believe me or not:

"I can understand," he announced dreamily, "killing *a man*—I can understand *that!*—I can't understand killing *a child!*"

I looked up, I gazed over, and I saw that, "bull-throated—bare of arm," this fourth-form hero was dreamily thrown back in his chair toying with a crumb—*pondering*. He was this time pondering *a kill*. He *could* not see himself as the Ripper of a defenceless bambino! Someone had evidently canvassed the murder of a child—and his mind had drifted away to two-gallon hats, at the news of this cowardly crime. As he expressed himself upon this delicate distinction in homicide, his staff and two French visitors hung upon his words.

Resigning myself to this study (some are born among the famous, and some have the famous thrust upon them) I next heard my man laying down the law of Islam. He was quoting the Koran. And he was laying it down to his rather jumpy young Berber interpreter, who was, no doubt, a fairish interpreter, but perhaps not much of a Tolba student. When corrected in this way upon some matter of Islamic doctrine by his Sheikish boss (who even at times, when feeling particularly fine, taught him a little Arabic, as well as a little Koranic law, and the young Berber's eyes danced up and down with annoyance) he often showed signs of great strain. The Berber voice would rise a little hysterically, to get above the slow deliberate accents of his Irish-American master, battling in his clipped French. But his French was never corrected, only his Arabic.

But in this connexion the Berber was able to retaliate, though it was I believe in spite of himself he did so. I have in mind an awkward moment in the hotel lounge. It was when the film-magnate and his retinue had just returned from a day in the high mountains. A little-frequented Atlas lake, ten thousand feet up, had afforded his lieutenant and himself the delights of a headlong he-man-dip and as he came in past the clerks' office—a little dreamily as usual, he told the lady in the office what a refreshing dip it had been and she said that it must have been. Then with a ponderous grace, frowning and casual, and stretching himself a little, in answer to her inquiries, he began to tell her about the route they had taken. But forgetting some detail, the name of a village had gone out of his head, he turned towards the Berber interpreter. He asked him in Arabic suddenly (or he thought it was Arabic) what was the name of the village—what was the name of the village—what was the *name* of the village! But the Berber interpreter—not expecting at the moment to be addressed in any tongue but French—could not for the life of him make out what he was being asked. (At least so it seemed, though it may have been put on.) So he inquired *in French* what it was that his master wished to know, and his master again insisted *in Arabic*—attempting sternly to mesmerize the slow-witted Berber into understanding. But the latter merely looked very confused and stuttered in French, turned this way and that and showed every sign of nervous strain—for he made his living after all as an interpreter, and if this big drawling transatlantic *enfant gâté* went back to the Residency and said he did not think much of the interpreter they had given him, that wouldn't help his career. It was a very painful scene.

The great man turned away from him with considerable languor (*pondering*—about Berbers it was clear) as one turns one's back upon an instrument that has been found wanting. But as an involuntary assistant at this characteristic scene I could not help thinking that if the interpreter did not recognize the single Arab sentence "What is the name of," it could not have been very correctly uttered.

Then this great Producer was an inveterate sketcher. The entire table at the restaurant was reduced to silence and an embarrassed inactivity upon one occasion for upwards of three quarters of an hour, while the great man was in travail with the sketch of a filmable "Fatmah" they had encountered in a hill-village—sketching away upon the back of the Menu he bent bare-armed over his work, in a sullen anguish of cross craftsmanship. When completed, it was handed round, amid exclamations of obsequious approval. Flung back in his chair, he smiled upon his handiwork.

On another occasion after dinner he whistled a great deal. And also he would buzz and jazz through a comb, used as a mouth-organ (the comb had to be sent for). These were, he said, airs he had composed during his early days in New York. This performance was very painful to everybody. The sickliest of grins transfixed the faces of all the assistants. The inveterate publicity habit *ne chôme pas*—it never rests. It was certainly *plus fort que lui*. It would have been impossible for him to understand that these people, not being "fans" in the ordinary sense, took no interest whatever in the early history of his personality, nor gave a hoot on a lousy comb for its early struggles upon the sidewalks of New York! Nevertheless I make a point of believing the troublesome *permanent childhood* of this over-public man was an accident, in the sense that left to himself he would have been a perfectly inoffensive, nice, commonplace chap.

This order of film-filibuster comes into these lands to take poisonous nonsense out of them, not to bring his poisons into it, hence (as I have said) he may be regarded as a benefactor. Those he exploits to their detriment are quietly seated far away, in the European filmtheatres and those of the U.S.A.—it is they who absorb all the childish *Sheikery,* the sweet-toothed and soft-brained city-mobs—their minds parched in the vulgar emptiness of the false-desert. But there is another order of film-filibuster *who brings the stuff in,* from outside—reels upon reels of kiss-stuff and crime. In an excellent account of the American Film industry called *Star-dust in Hollywood*, by Jan and Cora Gordon, we are given a glimpse of that sort of immigrant ruffian. I will quote a passage—especially since it demonstrates how the characteristic *arsenic-habit* of the North and West African natives is taken over (if not improved on) by the interlopers, the *filibusters.*

The Gordons are speaking of the experiences of a friend, who was a film-filibuster.

> A friend, intent on gain, once took a travelling-cinema plant to West Africa. He wanted to set up a cinema near the desert's edge at a town from which the caravans started toward Timbuctoo. He hoped to reap a small fortune by the enterprise, for here was a real example of the mountain coming to Mahomet. The ordinary cinema theatre, as the

Albanian promoters had found to their loss, must continually change its films or audiences will fade away. This entails no small expense. But at this town a full half of the population changed every month, collecting gradually to join caravans and emptying as soon as the caravans set out. So, instead of the owner having to bring new films to the audiences, Nature contrived to bring new audiences to the films.

That he never reached his destination is part of a longer story, but on the road he naturally tried to minimize expenses by showing as he moved. Thus, landing at Lagos he hired a huge courtyard with a balcony, open to the skies of heaven. This was by no means the first movie enterprise to delight the black population of Lagos, for he had two rivals. One was a Portuguese half-breed who tried to poison the new competitor, but dosed the wrong man; the other was a Negro woman, she who insisted on running the life of Christ upside down rather than cut her film.

The lucky film-filibuster, you will note—he who remained in possession, the top-dog of his class—was handy with the arsenic. Also he was Portuguese. But most of the masters of the contraband trade in the Sous are Portuguese. And of course all filibusters are either themselves poisoners, or are affiliated, more or less closely, with poisoners. The amiable and romantic author of *A High Wind in Jamaica* was as a matter of course introduced to the most eminent poisoner in the Sous when he went there—every British tourist (who isn't a filibuster) is introduced to the local Star-poisoner.—But already we are in the atmosphere of the Sous. And so we will leave at once for those regions I think, having given a glimpse or two of the Film racket, which should serve to show one of the uses to which "the romantic policy" of Lyautey has been put.—I did not go directly into the Sous however. First of all, from Marrakech I went up into the *Haut-Atlas*—the "Great Atlas," the English say. The Atlas Mountains rise to a height of fourteen thousand feet, are without glaciers, extremely hot in the summer, and of the most impressive magnificence. They are like the sierras of central Spain, but higher, hotter and even more denuded. The people who live in them are called *Chleuhs*—which is the name given to the Berber dialect spoken all over the south of Morocco.

Mountains, like the ocean (height and climate being equal), are much the same everywhere in the world. In Mexico, Abyssinia, Afghanistan, or Morocco if you describe one you would have described the other probably. Their inhabitants and the places they build, differ—not the clouds, rocks, torrents, snows.

To describe, in rhetorical or literary language, an Atlas Kasbah, or *timgremt*, would serve no object in a book of this sort. But I might have given certain details regarding them, had I not been preparing a separate volume, with plates and diagrams, which provides both a picturesque and historical account of these remarkable strongholds. For the more general reader it would appear as a matter of specialist interest rather, once the thrill had been administered. So at this point I pass over all that mountain-world, and pass immediately beyond the barrier of the Atlas. In so doing, we arrive at length at the ultimate object of this book—namely the extreme western and southern limit of Maghreb, and the queer filibustering confraternity that makes up its pioneer population, and the "Blue" deserts into which it melts.

CHAPTER IV

AGADIR

Agadir has its name in our European history books. For us *Agadir* is a word that consorts, in a rather cheap and sinister fashion, with *Kaiser*. If the "Exile of Doorn" should read this chapter, he will see a Haupt-Quartier map bristling with beflagged pins—he will remark a black spot, all by itself, with, for nearest neighbour northward, Mogador: and beneath it a little yellow-coloured patch (yellow for Spain) marked "Rio de Oro." A gunboat of the name of *Panther* will then steam into his ken, coming from the north, an insignificant unit of his old High Sea Fleet. Its guns (considerably out-of-date) will be trained upon the black spot—the spot by itself, above the no-man's-land called *Rio de Oro*—where there are no black spots, because there are no habitations to speak of, except the tents of the Mauretanian nomads. *Agadir* will stand for a dream-town in the old *Welt-politik* world, whose horizons were swept with clattering imperial eagles, a vanished breed. At Agadir—for Doorn's bearded ex-war-lord—an ominous hush will come over Europe once more—a hush of *his* making! For all the millions who violently died in the ghastly Epic of which he was the central figure, might they not all have died a few years sooner, had Agadir, not Sarajevo, been the starting-point? The name Agadir would then have been even more famous.

For me, who stayed for some time upon that black spot, which is all the map gives of it, Agadir has a quite different significance. At *Agadir* I see a crowd of images that compete with the imperial pre-war fustian, of course. As nearest to me, I perceive (above the bright teeth of the waves under the Trade Wind) a Souk of tents and booths, and beside it, between the edge of the low cliff and the high road, a concourse of asses and camels: there is a wild and gesticulating maraboutic figure (a segment of the magic circle drawn by him is in the dust of the high road) pretending to charm a cobra, while his assistants beat tambourines and blow into oboes. The cobra's dark flat-fish of a head and neck are erected, they rock with a gentle motion, indeed not at all unlike a solid black plaice on-end, moved hither and thither by an ocean current.

A Berber crowd surrounds the frantic quack. Meanwhile a European doctor hurries from spectator to spectator. Seizing them deftly by the left arm with a well-satisfied "caught-you-my-lad" look in his hunter's eye, he lifts up the sleeve, and with a knife scrapes the skin over the biceps. Following upon his heels is a Berber acolyte holding up a saucer. From this the doctor takes the serum—the operation lasts at most a few seconds. The whole crowd is vaccinated inside ten minutes or a quarter of an hour.

With one doctor they told me of, this fascinating game got the whip-hand. He was known to the Berber for twenty miles round. Driving his car along a road through the *bled* (even were he at the time on his way to perform a major operation) if he caught sight of a Berber in a field, he would bring the car to an abrupt halt, leap out, and rush across at his prey, needle in hand. But the Berber would take to his heels as soon as he saw the doctor stop. So this fanatical physician would chase the flying Berber up hill and down dale till he caught him: both blowing like porpoises, clutching the Berber tightly by the bicep, he would vaccinate him.—At the word "Agadir" I see (metaphorically) the wild-eyed maraboutic figure, gesticulating above the serpent, and the no-less-wild-eyed physician, rushing down the field after the barefooted Berber. Both come to life, the doctor at second-hand—for obliquely I am aware of the placid military grocer telling me about the doctor, fifty kilometres beyond Agadir, in the *dir* of the Anti-Atlas, in the country where it occurred (the local Berbers still with the doctor's mark upon their brown biceps doubtless—*better-than-to-have-a-face-pitted-with-Small-Pox!* you can fancy the doctor's retort) while *bled*-tramping peasants lift their right hands in that "Hail and Farewell!" gesture, as myself and the official pass them in our Citroën—"dissident" mountains upon our right, the steppes between Agadir and Tiznit upon our left.

"Lyautey built Casablanca. I will build Agadir!" that is reputed to be the destiny reserved for this spot by Mr. Lucien Saint, the present "Resident."—But there are difficulties. I will attempt to explain these difficulties.

In the year 1551 Captain Wyndham sailed into the beautiful bay of Agadir, in "a tall ship called *The Lion*, of London." Captain Wyndham was the first European trader to get his foot upon these shores, although my informant says that a certain Aldaie "professeth himself to have been the first inventor of this trade." But how shall we name the "trade" Captain Wyndham (or was it Aldaie?—I prefer to think it was Wyndham) "invented"? I fear his "trade" was that of a *filibuster*. My informant calls him "flibustier plutôt que marin véritable," and says that before that Wyndham had been a pirate.

101

The following year, in 1552, Captain Wyndham came with three tall ships instead of one. That is *The second voyage to Barbary*, that may be found in Hakluyt. And with him he had the right worshipful Sir John Yorke, Sir William Gerard, Sir Thomas Wroth, and Master Francis Lambert, a lot of brother pirates I suppose, and fellow filibusters.

A certain Mr. Scott O'Connor gives it as his opinion, in a travel book, that this coast "has always attracted filibusters and adventurers." But its filibusters have formerly come in "tall ships called *The Lion*" and done the thing in style. To-day there is absolutely no question that there are more filibusters to the square-inch at Agadir than in any other part of the Globe. A census would immediately demonstrate that. But the ships they come in are not "tall"—they are usually dirty little schooners packed with contraband carbines and pistols; they are bound for Ifni, flying for preference the Portuguese flag for some reason—those are the birds of passage, with others passing through by land in tempestuous Tin Lizzies, or big green bulbous Peugeots: but many are domiciled at Agadir. They are perhaps "stout fellows" (I can recall one with a large red egg of a head and a first-class colonial belly—*stout* maybe, but not in the picturesque Tudor sense)—stout filibusters all for sure, but shorn alas of all romance (just as the one above-mentioned is shorn of hair). When one is first confronted with the squalor of our actual filibusters (and one is at once up against the filibusters the moment one sets foot in Agadir) one looks round to find some other term for this "trade," invented by Captain Wyndham of "the tall ship, *The Lion*," as it is practised in the Petrol Age.

A middle-class British filibuster with the manners of a polite grocer, engaged who can doubt in most revolutionary plots, but going about them as if he were an indignant burgess on a Watch-committee, out to catch the dirty dog who scribbled offensive remarks on the walls of the local chapel—perpetually flushed in a sort of righteous watchfulness—that is what we find, alas, *en fait de flibustier*. But that is like a bad joke—a damp squib that *will* not filibust—for all the explosive glamour of Africa, in spite too of that splendid Wyndham of Hakluyt who spoke a Tudor tongue, with the same *label* certainly as that still current in Tooting or Mill Hill, but ah, who did not hide his piratic light under a bushel of legal technicalities, nor present the appearance, I am sure, of a smug City Worthy, paunchy and self-righteous.

The position in Agadir is this. The "Situation is Such"! Agadir is situated in a perfect bay. It would make a first-class port. Its climate is a blessed perfection of moderation, never too hot, never too cold. Its sea-road is another Corniche. It will make a Nice or Cannes—except that its mountains are rather too African—sandy, tufa-ish, crusty, cactus-spotted, with palmetto-rashes, not high enough (that is, just here) and would not pass muster without a fall of snow. All the same, one says *Corniche*. Corniche has often been said. But the port is the thing. Here will end, when they get it through, the railway by way of Bou d'Nib, which, by the Sahara route, will join Tunis and the Sous, and so link up (with luck—for Spain soon might cede Rio de Oro) the French Empire in Africa. There is no other possible port anywhere this side of the desert. From it you are in St.-Louis-du-Sénégal by the Aero-post in a few hours—how many? not much over a dozen. *So it must be Agadir.* Agadir must become as great as Casa. Its destiny is implicit in the map.

If the French develop the Sous—Agadir is at the mouth more or less of the Oued Sous—if they scrape some copper, zinc, coal or iron, out of the Anti-Atlas (those best placed to know are not so sanguine as others regarding these mineral riches) that will help the port. But it must be a big port anyway if the French stop in Morocco.

Marshal Lyautey however had a portentous saying. This they repeat in Agadir. And Marshal Lyautey was a very great guy who knew Morocco like his pocket. What he said was from the horse's mouth; and he always said, with an ominous emphasis:

"We must never open Agadir!"

The French respected the advice of this great administrator, until two or three years ago. No one could go to Agadir, without a military permit, up till then. Needless to say all the people who had no business there got there all right. Years before the place was "opened" every person against whom the *Not-open* order was directed was comfortably installed, and making as much of a nuisance of himself as he could, without risking his precious skin (and the French are a humane people, and a man has to do a great deal before he begins to run the shadow of a personal risk in a French Protectorate).

Then, Lyautey out of the way, his policies under a cloud, the Paris politicians in full power (where formerly it had only been the admirable soldier)—bang! the door was thrown wide open. *Agadir was open!* Santa-Cruz-du-Cap-de-Gué was open to the outer world. In Agadir everyone held their breath! Every European and every "native" in Agadir was spell-bound with expectancy. When would the wave they felt suspended over their heads break? When would the first batch of the great horde of pioneers come storming in? The "Old Moroccans" from their usual seats upon the terrace of Barrutel's, the principal café of the town, shaded their eyes, gazing down towards Founti and beyond, for the first immigrant bus-loads.

103

But nothing happened. No more strangers than usual rolled up, day by day, and month by month, in the Mogador buses—respectably seated (inside only) about thirty, no more, of which two-thirds are Berbers or Jews, who go back or go on, their business done.

This however almost anybody might have foreseen. Anyone who *wanted* to get into Agadir had got in long ago; it was full to saturation-point of equivocal "pioneers," who lived on air and seemed to have nothing better to do than go to Barrutel's and have a Paloma or two, or a double Scotch, and cheat some other pith-helmeted pascha or smooth-tongued little gold-digger, as *oiseux* and seigneurial as themselves. All the licensed filibusters, and sedentary "pioneers," who had any interest in Agadir, had been there living snugly under the wing of the military for years, plotting their squalid plots—about little strips of land for which false claims in faked Hassani deeds had been forged and reforged (by lettered Arabs in Taroudant or in Tiznit), sealed and delivered, lost and found again, about cargoes of rifles in Portuguese bottoms—they were already "Old Moroccans" as it is called, "des Vieux Marocains." Squatting and plotting in the midst of the pleasant bustle on the café terrace, airing their kitchen-Chleuh upon a pack of armleted shoeblacks—old habitués, watched by the police and each other, as large as life.

Everyone was surprised all the same, except this filibuster ring perhaps (namely half the White population).—Although Agadir was *opened*, the embargo off, all that occurred inside the town itself was that the civil authorities took over from the military authorities, did not do the job so well, and the town got disgustingly dirty. Everyone cursed the day when the military had ceased to administer it. Meanwhile no more houses were built—a few were pulled down perhaps. That is all that happened. The White Town was still hastily-stuck-together shacks, and large shelters upon the edge of the sea—temporary premises of the Bus-offices, Barrutel's, and in short all that ragged one-sided, one-storeyed street that makes Agadir still resemble a Wild-West mining camp.

CHAPTER V

THE FILIBUSTER OF TOOTING BEC

What was the cause, you may well ask, of all this stagnation upon the one hand, and this filibusterish activity upon the other? Just apparently what Lyautey had foreseen—the motive for his formula: "We should never open Agadir!"—namely an embarrassing impasse, which could no longer be accounted for on the score of aggravated "dissidence," and prolonged Insecurity. That was the cause for this paralysis. It appears that the French were not upon quite such sure ground here as elsewhere. The Berber Resistance, that was a bagatelle. It was the undergrowth of treaties, "capitulations," leases, and counter-leases that made Agadir a kind of jungle, in which only the slowest and most painful progress could be made. It was only too true: nothing whatever was to be gained by "opening Agadir"— though for that matter not very much to be lost: except that, from the French standpoint, they would to some extent be forced into political action, to precipitate changes which on the whole it would have been better to allow time to effect.

The Germans (Mannesmann Brothers and a lot more) had acquired extensive, exclusive rights in South Morocco. Agadir, they had hoped, would become a German port. The Sous would be theirs. Many of these rights were bought up by British subjects, when the Germans left. But "British Subject" in Morocco means anybody. The most powerful of the local Caïds was a "British Subject," the French found, as well as a star-poisoner (even for Morocco, a past-master with arsenic), an old ruffian in fact of the first order. Being "British"— being established right upon the limits of the Protectorate, upon the edge of irreconcilable "dissidence"—it may be imagined how awkward the French found it to deal with this old dog, this swarthy British Bulldog—as indeed with all the other Britons—the Bulldogs of Mogador, the Mastiffs of Safi, the Bullpups of Casa, Tangier, and Fez—not to mention those jolly old John Bulls of Gibraltar and of Malta, of Berlin and Timbuctoo! And then behind these genuine passported Britons came all the "British-protected persons." It was indeed a nasty, ticklish mess for the poor old Frogs!

But why should a victorious French Army, rounding off its unchallenged protectorate over the Cherifian Empire, hesitate to send an aprocryphal Bulldog of Old England about his bloody business? Alas (from the French point of view, which in this case is certainly my own—and the longer I remained in Agadir the more pronouncedly pro-French I became—I felt like sporting a little Tricolour, so ashamed was I of the poor appearance of the local British filibusters)—England and the United States still possess what are called "capitulations" in Morocco. That means that those countries have never given up their technical rights to behave just as they choose there: there is a *British Post Office* in every Moroccan city, as an emblem of British independence of French Control.

In Morocco an Englishman (or an American) cannot be arrested by the French police. No one is allowed to touch him. An Englishman is far safer in Morocco than he is in England. Unless he murders somebody he is above the law, and even then it is questionable if they could get him inside a French police-station.

A year ago a violent dispute occurred just south of Casa between a Frenchman and an Englishman. It was about the usual thing in South Morocco—namely the question as to which of two or more worthies a certain piece of land belonged. Both claimed it. But the Frenchman at the moment of the argument was actually on it. There the matter rested, till one day he went to Mazagan for the afternoon. The Englishman at the head of a band of pals—armed with rifles, tin hats and the rest, got into the house. When the Frenchman returned, there they all were spluttering in bandy-legged Bulldog fashion, "J'y suis, j'y reste!" It took half the police-force of Casa to evict them—in this case bloodlessly.

You can see from this how very inconvenient those "capitulations" can be for the French; and the farther south you get, the more the "capitulations" are to the fore. The more warily the French have to tread. The international booby-traps of an absurd, out-of-date, imperialist diplomacy lie thick and menacing on every hand.

It is not of course the British Consular authorities who are responsible for this state of affairs. They are not only most amiable people—as willing to help stray Bulldogs as are the French—but actually they have a great deal of trouble with other sorts of Bulldogs, who take advantages of "capitulations" to defy the French police—engaging in every lawless activity under their noses on the ground that they are Britons.

But the land question is beyond all others most intricate and troublesome. That fine old British Bulldog, the Caïd of Inezgane, whom I have already mentioned, thought nothing of selling a piece of land in Agadir—which did not belong to him anyway—to half a dozen people at the same time. Sometimes he would sell the same piece of land twenty times over. To whom does this piece of much-sold land to-day belong! It is almost impossible to say! The French rack their brains to discover some issue, perspiring in this tangled undergrowth of claim and counterclaim.

What immobilized the march of progress upon the sea-front was however mainly a wholesale claim upon whole blocks of land, on behalf of a whole kennel of Bulldogs of one sort and another—all of whose interests are in the hands of a queer middle-aged middle-class Bulldog Drummond of an ex-Temporary-Major. This odd, smug, highly respectable-looking filibuster lives outside Agadir in a smug white "Arab" house he has built for himself. What is this gentleman exactly? It is hard to say. He is a house-agent of a peculiarly Moroccan order. No doubt he was selected for the job on account of his typically British appearance: *he* is the real thing all right—the good, solid, pink, fetch-and-carry order of faithful dog-Toby of a man—his honest baldness inflamed with exposure to the African sun, with an invaluable air too of righting wrongs, about him, and assisting the poor down-trodden Arab against the wicked French, and really I dare say charged with a good bit of beefy romanticism of the station-bookstall shilling-a-volume order (the Briton in foreign parts what what!—a bit of "secret service," a dash of free-lance, but always sure to be anywhere where there's a "scrap," what what) though doubtless aware which side his bread is buttered.—This strange plump Cockney-Scot was organizer and commander-in-chief of an assortment of pith-helmeted, Mill-Hill-Schoolish, Tooting-Bec-bred hangers-on—he ran the principal estate-office of Agadir, had a "dinky" dairy farm and his milk-cart affected to take milk to the town, but the town complained it was none too easy to get milk out of the Temporary-Major. But the milk may after all have been a blind. Also he owned rustic auto-buses, which took natives out to their villages in the *bled* (but this may have been to have the *fellaheen* under his thumb—a bus-driver is a very influential person in Morocco). Me he regarded immediately with hostility and suspicion to my very great surprise. If it rested with him he would keep Agadir closed against all visiting bulldogs, I came to the conclusion, over the Lunn's Tour standard of intelligence.

To the natives, hotel-proprietors, and so on he represented himself as the unofficial British Consul (Agadir has no official English representative at all—though I venture to think it is about time it had and that he is badly needed): and the hotels send you to this local Briton-in-chief for information. When I said I wished to visit some *magasins collectifs,* especially of the Ikounka tribe, this excellent man was puz-

107

zled. Doubtless he had always been far too busy bull-dogging about, and defying the French, to find out anything about the ancient social organization of the people of the Sous, or any such boring subjects as that, that was quite understood, though he regarded himself as a great authority. He seemed able to talk kitchen-Arabic, and probably to patter a little in Chleuh and claimed to know more than anyone— except perhaps his "Serbian" adjutant—regarding the Sous. He had never heard, at all events, of a *Collective* (the communal fortress in which people of an allied group of villages store their grain and valuables). Also he had never heard of the Ikounka. His face was as blank at *Ikounka* as at *magasin collectif*. He fetched his adjutant. His adjutant had never heard of a *magasin collectif*. He had never heard of the Ikounka. His adjutant retired after a little argument, in which he had questioned the existence of such a tribe at all, to consult with some especially louche-looking Arabs. After a time he returned, sat down and said, "Ça y est!" The "Serbian" adjutant now knew who the Ikounka were. Also he knew what a *magasin collectif* was. I was quite right. There were such things. But there was one very grave obstacle regarding the Ikounka. It was this: *it was quite out of the question* that the *Bureau des Affaires Indigènes* would allow me to go so far outside the limits, or rather within the limits, of the *Zone d'Insécurité*, as the territory of the Ikounka. Did I know what was the *Zone d'Insécurité*? Well, the *Zone of Insecurity* began at ten kilometres outside the town.

The more I talked to these two birds, the farther off, the more inaccessible, the territory of the Ikounka came to appear. The more irrealizable it seemed, my purpose of visiting a *magasin collectif*. The red-pated bulldog middle-class filibuster, he set his jaws and narrowed his eyes, and exclaimed that if *he* wanted to go to the Ikounka, he would go to the Ikounka! The French wouldn't stop him!

"In this country you have to have, well—to use a coarse expression—you have to have *guts*, you understand, yes, if you have the *guts*——!" I cast my eyes down, and stopped them upon his waist-line, and saw that he had *guts;* but he looked very fierce and chewed his pipe in true bulldog fashion, and I wondered what order of *risks* these were, that this prosperous unofficial British Beadle and perfect picture of a Special Constable who had taken the wrong turning, might conceivably run: instinctively I knew that it must be one of those bogus-risks and cheaply earned thrills, so dear to the romantic soul of that particular fresh-coloured off-shoot of some well-policed Tooting Bec; and looking up modestly, depreciating the indecorous word, I said:

"But I am not brave. I do not wish to defy any of these charming and good-natured Frenchmen here. I like the French—it is peculiar!"

He scowled. But he said nothing (*Like the Frogs!* By the Roast Beef of Old England, what traitor is this!). It was difficult to know what to do! He would have liked to take me—*without permission* (I flinched and whitened—I threw up my hands) but his car was so big, it would be spotted at once! They would say—What is that bloody Englishman up to now! Besides the car was being repaired. And his "Serbian" adjutant said he was the only man in Agadir who knew the road—he knew it backwards—he had been on it at all hours of the day and night— also of course he could speak like a native the patois of all those parts—(how absurd of him not to have known when I said *Ikounka*— why he had been there only last week) it was a pity he could not take me, but his pal's car was engaged—he *knew*, yes, he was positive—for the next few days.—But we should have had to have gone *without permission. That* I would never get! He could tell me—*that* they would never give me!

I visited the *Bureau des Affaires Indigènes* next day. The Colonel-in-Command of all this part of the Sous saw me himself, without any difficulty. I found him a most charming French officer, thoroughly acquainted with the social organization of these small Berber Republics; he was a personal friend of Montagne. The latter is the author of the standard works upon these subjects. (My equivocal compatriot had sneered at Montagne—the trouble about Montagne, said he, was that he thought he spoke Chleuh, but no Chleuh could understand him.) The Colonel made no difficulty at all about giving me permission to visit the Ikounka. He wrote a personal note to the Commandant of the Military Post at Aït Baha, within whose jurisdiction were the Ikounka villages. Let me place on record that I have found (with one exception) the French Military authorities the pattern of politeness, ready in every respect to place at a foreigner's disposal every facility for studying the places and peoples they administer.

On the other hand, the strange figure giving himself out as "Representing British Interests" in the Sous put every obstacle in my way. Lyautey himself could not have wished to occult Agadir more than did he. From the start he breathed discouragement, and exuded obstructiveness with every drop of bulldog sweat that the warmth of the climate and the strenuousness of his peculiar house-agenting brought to the surface of his pink and polished cuticle.—Why? What was there, I asked myself, that I must not see? And I began of course looking round with idle curiosity. A puzzling situation! For some reason this strange semi-political house-agent—who threatened, if the French authorities laid so much as a finger upon *his* land, or the land

109

over which he mounted his bulldog British guard, that he would put machine-guns on it—did not desire my presence in this rather ticklish part of the world. I had told the man who I was. When I said who I was he blushed. The fellow was familiar with my books. He asked me twice if I was really myself, and I said I was certainly that identical filibuster of letters, and we had a good laugh as one filibuster to another: but he kept looking at me and blushing all over the crown of his pink billiard-ball of an occiput. He was both better and worse after this. He said he was a writer too—before the War he had been a reporter in Pittsburgh I think it was, and also Johannesburg. A rolling-stone, I said to myself—he has gathered no moss! But I suppose he must have read something in my books or in one of them that made him think that I was—what I imagine he would call "always looking for trouble." Or he may have thought I had the Evil Eye. It would cast a spell over his cows—it may have been that: they gave strangely little milk as it was. The magic of my presence might have finished it.

I describe all these incidents because they show you the temper of this little frontier township. It is at once a fierce and a bourgeois little hole. The suspicious sniffing at one's heels of rather questionable bulldogs was natural enough—they have the sullen fixed idea of *trespass*, and scent in the most detached of indifferent analysts a "Nosy Parker," that is understood—I did not even attempt to send their consciences to sleep. But the French, especially the military, were everywhere frank, well-behaved and sensible.

At last it has been decided, however, rather suddenly, to build this city that has hung fire so long. It is to be some kilometres out of the town, to the south. All the boulevards and so forth are mapped out, land is changing hands with lightning rapidity, gangs with chains and tapes are busy in the *bled*. In a year it should be there—not quite where they had intended it, not quite where it should be, but still built—at least that. Certainly when I left in late July, 1931, there was an increasing bustle. There will be enormous waste spaces, in between the different bits of the city, no doubt (which will necessarily be fragmentary)—blank spaces over which shady and vociferous house-agents of Casa, Bulldogs of Mogador, deposed Sheiks and others are wrangling with the French Commissaires and will wrangle till the Crack of Doom. But a city of some sort will no doubt rise up, and can scarcely fail to flourish. It is a very interesting spectacle indeed to be in at the building of an important mushroom-city—which will represent, when it is up, enormous capitals, and observe closely if not sympathetically all the spiders (who will be for ever underneath it) spinning their preliminary webs.

110

Meanwhile the French officials and civilians seem a little dubious about it all. They are uneasy at the quagmire of intrigue, bluff, brigandage, threats, obstructions, that they feel incessantly beneath their feet, and who can wonder? Ever since the days of the *Panther* this has been volcanic soil. The "Capitulations," since they are of no use to the People of England, should of course be given up. But that I suppose would be like hoping for a repeal of the 18th Amendment.

Agadir is cut off from the world by mountain, ocean, and desert. A hundred kilometres south of Agadir is the desert city of Tiznit. In appearance Tiznit is much like Marrakech, though of course a tenth the size: the same massive gates, gardens of date-palms, and outside a more complete tufa-strewn sandy wilderness than the "Plain of Morocco." The Anti-Atlas is upon its eastern flank. They are very wild and barren mountains indeed. Tiznit is the extreme southern limit of the French power in Morocco. At its gates almost begins the great desert of the Rio de Oro. There are a thousand miles of desert between it and the Soudan.

To the north Agadir is blocked with mountains, the road to Mogador, the nearest town, being much of it a coast-road. Inland, the Valley of the Sous is enclosed by giant mountains. Agadir is therefore particularly isolated from the civilized world. It is natural that the German Imperialist should have selected the Sous, and its natural port, Agadir, for his activities. And of course in the future it might again be found that the isolation from the rest of Morocco of the Sous Valley would tempt the enemies of French rule to use this backwater, with the enormous deserts to the south, in the same manner as they did the Riff. For the Politician, one feels, this must be a highly interesting spot. For the Artist, is is even more so.

CHAPTER VI

THE BROTHEL OF AGADIR

(Virgins 25 francs apiece)

To demonstrate, in the physical field, how the battle of land-rights must result in trisecting, throwing off its axis, mutilating and scattering to the four winds, the future city of Agadir, I had intended to describe how the hills, ravines and flats lay, of which the potential city is composed. But when an attempt is made to tell one how the rooms and passages of a house occur (in the murder story this is often done) most readers, it is quite certain, cannot follow, most only skip. Language is not suited for that abstract map-making. What is the use of saying—There's a big hill upon the left, then there's a lower one, to the right, flatter on the top, and so forth? None whatever—Agadir is a hilly spot. There are big sands, covered with seagulls at low water, where they are wet—enamelled and glittering. Like a white cock's comb, with heavily milled edges, there is a Kasbah upon a mountain—"véritable nid d'aigle" the French writers always call it. There are a lot of uncouth and often filthy ravines: the "front" is overgrown with cactus and the spiked candelabrum of the *Euphorbium*, and what I suspected to be juniper, and all sorts of thorny bushes—it is a wilderness of sandy gashes, steep mule and camel tracks leading to the sea; garages and impromptu one-storey hotels present their untidy back-yards to the shore. But there are many wide level gaps too in the road-line and big sandy playgrounds for tethering animals or ones squatting for want of something to do—these are accounted for by the stout bulldog claims of our passionate compatriot, on behalf of other Bulldogs in the background—bigger and wickeder Bulldogs than he.

At the foot of the mountain, in a wild disordered gully, is the brothel, the *bousbir*, the *quartier réservé* (the whore-shop, the lupanar, the mud-nests of official love). Sitting on a stone, upon the opposite hill, looking down into the brothel, I could see all its alfresco mud cubby-holes. A weather-rotted curtain was fixed over the openings to the miserable dens of the females of this sad menagerie. "Deep-throated" German chanting came from a mud-cell stuck onto the nearer wall. So I could not see this choir of the Legion. The queen of

112

the colony—a girl of about fifteen—was holding a reception at the opposite end.

One brothel inland which I met with was more peculiar even than this: it was like a large mud-built pig-sty; or like the empty many-celled Souks you come upon in the *bled*, only made of adobe instead of stone. It was quite open, or seemed so. Each cell contained a woman—I saw it about noon, I walked down this repulsive tropical lane, full of fierce houseflies: a stout snore came from each sty. This was in the mountains. The stable for loose women in Agadir was scarcely fit for mules, but it was better than the Tenderloin of the *bled*.

To the *bousbir*, the love-Souk of Agadir, I went one night, in the company of three Italians—it was the day after that I drew it. There was a tent at the gate, with an armed policeman in it. He let us in, and we found ourselves in a large empty court of mud. This was un-lighted, but there were lamps behind the curtains of the women's cells, occupying three sides of it. There must have been thirty women in it. Each cell was about seven foot every way, except from roof to floor, which was under six foot. Against the inner wall was the bed. We all crept in at the hole or door on all fours. We sat on the floor of beaten mud, with our backs against the mud-wall.

We were visiting the queen of the brothel. She was a bright Berber girl, with good features, with eyes like a squirrel's, good teeth and a little chin. Her face was painted and tattooed. (There was a row of vertical spots where in a man the chin-cleft would be.) As she was so young probably her eyelids had less kohl than those of her older mates, whose eyes oozed ink; they kept crawling in and out (she usu-ally drove them away with a harsh indignant shout). Two Foreign Legion non-coms crept in and sat down. They were German. Al-though drunk they were very quiet. The Roman Legionaries at Volu-bilis must have had much the same square countenances.

Our hostess was extremely grave and the small cell was oppressive with her matter-of-factness: with an attentive frown she made the green tea and mint, and handed everybody present a small glass—not small enough, for it is extremely sickly.

The senior of the three Italians, an ex-Foreign Legion sergeant (or commissariat non-com), was talkative, he wanted the girl to undress at once. She ignored this pointless suggestion. We all drank our tea and talked of one thing and another—no one except the Italian who had brought us paid much attention to the girl. When several cups of tea had been drunk, the chief Italian again commanded her to undress *tutti nue*. She frowned and then gave a few Berber giggles. "Oui met-toi tutti nue, Doho!" At length she went to the two beds (like ships'

113

bunks against the wall) and took off her clothes and stood looking at us like a squirrel—showing after much coaxing its winter *cachette* of nuts. Everybody looked: when I remarked upon the stoutness of the belly, at fifteen, an Air-force non-com who had crawled in said:

"Evidemment! *C'est le ventre colonial!*"

"Elles ont toutes des bedons? Quel dommage!" I said.

"Evidemment!" he said. "Que voulez-vous! C'est bien le ventre colonial!"

She soon covered up her "colonial stomach" again, and when all harnessed up in leaden and silver bric-à-brac, sat down. She poured out more green tea with much mint.

"Eh bien, je m'en vais me coucher!" said the Air-force corporal. He crawled out.

"Moi aussi!" exclaimed one of the Foreign Legion visitors.

They crawled out—one rolled out, the other crouched and charged out through the hole head first.

We all crawled out into the pitch-black yard. There were a few white figures moving down the sides of the cells. Several Foreign Legion privates moved listlessly up and down, smoking. The other women we had seen were savage blousy bundles of grey rags— battered old flowers of the *bled*, a fat Jewess, with beady eyes in a mask of pallid dough.

"She is the best!" one of the Italians said, meaning the one we had been with. "She is the only one here."

The senior Italian remained inside; the curtain fell violently over the hole by which we had issued on all fours. We went out of the gate, *bon-soired* off the premises by the police-guard in the tent outside.

This brothel is not unknown; a book by Joseph Kessel (in its fiftieth thousand) has an account of it: he writes that in going to have a look at it he knew "that there could be nothing comparable to Casablanca," but that he was not prepared for this, that he "was stupefied by its miserable aspect. . . . At the bottom end of a squalid, dirty, and stinking lane, a wall of *pisé* enclosing a court more cramped than a farmyard, hid the sensual joys of Agadir. Even at Dar-es-Zor, on the Euphrates, even at Palmira, in the Syrian desert, I had found more room to move about at least, more gaiety, than in this place set aside for prostitution."

It is the large, muddy farmyard without even a street lamp in the middle—the high walls and the rows of squalid niches the size of a small lavatory, built into the wall itself, that calls forth these exclamations of disgust especially from the Parisian traveller. Even if a rough pavement existed (it would cost nothing—the women could beat into

114

the mud the flat stones required—most of these women have worked on the new highways with a hammer, stone-breaking—it is not as though they had had no practice)—if there were a hut or two in which you could stand up, or even if, covered with bugs and reeking of stale rose-water, one of the women were a credit to her down-trodden people—with a couple of bold black eyes, or an uncolonial stomach! It is such things that make people write about the *bousbir* of Agadir, especially if Parisians.

I write about it mainly because its brothel does demonstrate the extent to which Agadir is still the wild frontier township—"*Here* we are in the *bled!* In the *bled!*" as someone shouted at me when he asked me if I liked his langoustes and I did not answer quickly enough to please him—though I knew the Breton fishing-boats came all this way—and as far as St.-Louis-du-Sénégal—for such langoustes: and of course therefore the *bled* in that respect was the *bled* and not the *bled*—since we were where the luxury fish of the cities come from.

It is the *bled* (you cannot translate *bled* champaign or countryside, nor yet quite wilderness. It is what is not *city* in Maghreb—it is the steppe with its cactus, and its mud-concrete fortresses, its donkeys and well-wheels, argans, walnuts and palms—but nine-tenths wilderness, sand or tufa steppe).

Many talks with the men who look after the "reserved quarter" tended to crystallize my notion of prices. A virgin costs round about fifty or sixty francs three years out of the four. The fourth is invariably a bad year, then she is cheaper. She goes for as low as twenty-five francs. (These are all girls of about thirteen or fourteen—there are no virgins much after that of course.) There are years when—oh, anything will do it: a franc, a Hassani peseta. The father gets the money. (This is in the *douar*—in the *bled*.) There is a great deal of extreme misery, which I am sure is no fault of the French, though they naturally are blamed—even the *bled* is not worse than the Middle West (U.S.A.) in that respect (*cf.* reports *re* the starvation in the cotton-belt). Numbers of Mauresques work on the road, breaking stones. After some months of breaking stones on the road it can be readily understood that a woman does not stand on her dignity or sniff at a two-franc piece, even if she would before, which in Morocco is scarcely likely.

Under such conditions it is not surprising that the *quartiers réservés* are besieged with women of all sorts (mostly no oil-paintings, you can be sure) imploring admittance.

The Foreign Legion are the chief patrons of the *bousbir* of course. But wherever they are quartered there are women who are only too willing for a few francs to do anything: a legionnaire takes a bottle of wine and a blanket and retires into the privacy of the *bled;* others follow suit, and so it is that, in spite of every regular prostitute *passant la visite* daily, there is much venereal disease.

CHAPTER VII

MARSHAL LYAUTEY AS THE CREATOR OF "THE GREAT LORDS OF THE ATLAS"

Before turning to the Rio de Oro, that enormous and unknown district immediately to the south of Agadir, I must state an opinion, then attempt to outline the French position up-to-date in this part of the world. After that we shall return to the subject of the filibuster. Then the romance, as also politically the menace, of these deserts will be easier to understand.

First I must divulge my bias. In so far as I can be said to have an opinion regarding French Politics, it would approximate to the *Action Française* outlook, rather than to that of say Mr. Briand.

I find once more in Budgett Meakin (the classical English authority on Morocco) an attitude that I should endorse. In *Life in Morocco* (1905) he wrote as follows:

> All England cares about is the mouth of the Mediterranean, and if this were secured to her . . . she could have no cause to object to the French extension. . . . It were better far to come to an agreement with France, and acknowledge what will prove itself one day—that *France is the normal heir to Morocco* whenever the present Empire breaks up.

This statement, he tells us, was published in 1901, and was naturally not at all popular.

> Unpopular as this opinion was among the British and other foreign subjects in the country . . . so that at first it had no other advocate, it has since been adopted in Downing Street, and what is of more moment, acted upon.

In 1905 that was the position, and to-day it is doubly so: England, with a scattered Empire everywhere shaken with revolt, is not the England of 1905. And as regards Morocco, English trading interests have almost entirely faded out: the continued presence of the English Banks there is only justified by the requirements of "British-protected" persons (of which there are a good number) and the native "Bulldog" of course; but otherwise the English have no more interest in Morocco than they have in the Moon. Even the most mischievous

117

soldier-of-fortune with a British passport could scarcely trip or entrap England into a dispute in those parts.

Under these circumstances it may seem otiose to say that the French Protectorate, as far as I can see, is the best of all possible protectorates for Morocco. It is nevertheless advisable to proclaim it, since there are great numbers of people in Morocco—Italians, Spanish, and a few English—who spend their time abusing the work of French penetration and pacification, and squandering much passionate and stupid eloquence in vilifying France.

There are however *two*, or three, Frances—as there are two or three of everything else. It is the France of Lyautey that I for my part admire. And the France of Lyautey has nothing to get out of Morocco, of course. "What France will gain by the change," Meakin writes in 1905, "beyond openings for Frenchmen and the glory of an extended colonial empire, it is hard to imagine." Hard indeed. "So far [in 1905] the only outward evidences of the new position are the over-running of the ports, especially of Tangier, by Frenchmen of an undesirable class." These Frenchmen belong to the Other France, not that of Lyautey—not even of France (geographically) at all. And to-day, as I have said, the most notable thing about French Morocco is the scarcity of actual Frenchmen of any sort to be found there.

But this scarcity of the French, even in Algiers, was noted by Meakin thirty years ago. He wrote in this connection: "The European colonists [in Algeria] are of all nationalities, and the proportion which is not French is astonishingly large"; or again, "Among the foreign colonists it is a noteworthy fact that the most successful are not French." Of course they are not. Who ever heard of the majority of a nation getting anything out of their country holding another country as a colony?

But no "native" population gets anything out of being a colony either: and the native population of North Africa are no exception to the rule. [. . . .]

To leave everything scrupulously *just as he found it*—such was the policy of Lyautey. He left the Sultan of Morocco with just as much, indeed rather more, power than he had upon the intrusion of the French—the Cherifian umbrella still over his head—just as much periodic "powder play," the prayers still said in his name in the mosques. If an *indigène* commits a burglary or stabs or cheats another, he "goes up before the Pascha," just as before. And a really incredible scrupulosity has been shown in leaving Souk, Kasbah and village intact—except perhaps for a surreptitious house-drain or two, and numbers painted upon the doors of the houses of the Medina, to guide the postman I suppose.

119

These are the *romantic politics,* as they have been called, of Lyautey. If Lyautey had been Governor of Paris, the boulevards, fairs, and markets would still be there intact, and the wholesale destruction of historic landmarks would not have been tolerated. But it is not difficult to see how this anxious consideration for the local-colour of the Berbers must have enraged the "socialo-communist" elements that had to stand by and watch it, also those who wished to see a clean sweep of the old life, in order to be able to secure lucrative contracts for the Europeanization of Morocco. No. *Nothing must be touched or changed:* there all the Europeans, come out there to get rich quick, had to remain at a respectful distance.—*Respect for what?* For the Berber filth, the useless bric-à-brac? The only way the military, under Lyautey's orders, would keep them all at a distance was to label as much as possible *Zone d'Insécurité (Zone Militaire—Zone Interdite)* and to explain how terribly *dangerous* the Berbers were—though there were plenty of non-Berbers in Morocco competent to know that there was nothing *dangerous* about the poor child-like Berber, and whose fingers were itching to get at the loot.

Probably in the administration of the High Atlas more than elsewhere this *romantic policy* inaugurated by Lyautey was violently criticized and bitterly resented. [. . . .] The actual root of the business, and reason for the great violence with which Lyautey was attacked, was LAND. The Great Caïds, the "Lords of the Atlas," refused to allow their subjects to sell land to the foreigner: and they employed every method and weapon at their disposal to prevent the transfer of a single acre. A hundred stories of violence done to some Berber peasant who was about to sign away his patrimony to the "Nazarene" are told by the opponents of the Lyautey Régime.

Here are the words of the advocate of that Opposition I have mainly used in the foregoing *exposé* of the anti-Lyautey case:

"A entretenir dans les tribus, l'idée dangereuse que les Caïds défendent la liberté de leurs territoires en s'opposant aux vente de terres par les indigènes, quel but poursuit-on? Veut-on fermer simplement le Sud Marocain au peuplement français?" etc.

When El Hadj Thami says to his people "If you want to sell your land, sell it to *me*—don't sell it to the foreigner!" he should decidedly be checked. That is very "dangerous"! It is also highly inconvenient for all the real-estate-agents and that swarm of adventurous folk like our jolly red-faced compatriot of Agadir (who operated at Marrakech before he went to the Sous).

Whether it is the M'Tougi, or one of the Khalifats or El Hadj Thami, or Goundafi, or Ayadi, or the Ouriki, the Caïd M'Soudi, the cry is always the same! *"Any sale of land to a foreigner is an offence in the eyes of Allah!"*

But what do we find that Lyautey—representative after all of the "foreigners" in question—does in all this? He supports the Caïds, and so *assists* in preventing the "foreigners" from getting the land out of the Berbers—protected (for selfish motives) by the Caïds. Why, he is scarcely behaving as a White Man even!

The literature of this subject is full of tales of poisonings, of people found murdered, the title-deeds of their land vanished out of the corpse's pocket, of shady lawyers, of Arab clerks who are deft forgers of old Hassani title-deeds, and *ainsi de suite.* It is a mist of speculation and peculation, and it is all about LAND.

In the Sous, at Agadir, it is just the same thing. Land, *Land—Land* is the cry! There you are told all the old stories as soon as you get there of Germans found murdered at Inezgane, bundles of title-deeds of land vanished into the blue out of the victims' pockets, of the interminable faking and forging of documents, of all-time-jobs for masses of crook notaries, of the incessant overtime of unscrupulous Arab scribes. One particular old ruffian is proudly pointed out to you as being the star-poisoner of the district (and romantic Anglo-Saxons when they visit those parts as I have said are taken to tea with him— the thrill of thrills—"oh observe how he lets you drink first, in *case* the pot has been tampered with!").

So Agadir is much what Marrakech was some years ago. There is of course no right or wrong in all this violent mess, all are in different degrees to blame. Everyone is a *filibuster* of some sort who is installed upon the territory of a race that is not his own. Lyautey—yes, Lyautey was a filibuster too. Extend the term far enough, Lord Irwin at Delhi was a filibuster.[1]

Then, of course, the romantics, of one order and another, are as much ugly customers as the plain unvarnished sharks, if not more so. It is impossible not to pity the Berber peasants. And of all the enemies of these distracted people, those who advertise themselves as the "friends of the oppressed" are apt to be the biggest ruffians of the lot, as is always the case, we know.

Such are the dark backgrounds against which the brilliant figure of Lyautey has been silhouetted. It is a picture full of irony. This great "Man-of-action," the disciple of Vogüé and de Mun—is (how can one tell? but one has that sensation) perfectly scrupulous—a passionate *ambitieux* no doubt, but one whose hands have not been dirtied with

---

[1] Irwin, later Lord Halifax, had been Viceroy of India.

money at least. So this chivalrous monument is destined in history to stick up paradoxically in this African and Levantine landscape, the gloved and booted statue of a typical Gentleman, in the military uniform of a radicalist Republic.—It is a very odd position to have chosen for this statue. Destiny has amused herself!

CHAPTER VIII

THE CLUBMAN FILIBUSTER OF THE 'NINETIES

(Portrait by R. B. Cunninghame Graham)

It would be a great pity, since you are getting such an insight into the filibuster up-to-date, for you not also to become acquainted with Major Spilsbury. That gentleman has been immortalized in Mr. R. B. Cunninghame Graham's book *Mogreb-el-Acksa* (which will be read again some day—it is one of the daintiest dishes of "the 'Nineties").

"Quiet but determined, a linguist, leader of men, and one of those willing to risk his life ten times a day for any syndicate, upon most reasonable terms, Spilsbury was a born filibuster." There you have Cunninghame Graham's strong, silent hero.

Evidently little has altered in those regions since 1896, except in the rather important matter of *personnel*. There has been a sad change in the quality of the personnel. There are still men possibly willing at a pinch to risk their little fingers, now and then, and at a price, for any well-backed passably open-handed syndicate. And their terms I am positive are "reasonable," as of old. But whereas we gather that Major Spilsbury was a gentleman, as well as "a born filibuster," to-day the filibusters are not gentlemen. That is an important difference, because, not being gentlemen, they probably make less good filibusters. It is I think freely admitted in all the best-informed circles and by all the best organized "syndicates," that the best filibusters are what we call gentlemen. The bounder (or worst of all, the demi-gent, the inclined-to-be- "refayned") he busts up a shade too soon, or a fraction too late! That is fatal.

No really important "syndicate" can at present be working that coast. Such is the conclusion to which I reluctantly came. Else there would be a lot of really top-drawer filibusters down there—instead of rather highly-strung ex-temporary army-toffs with their nerves not adequately under control. Spilsbury now was a lad of a different temper. "But for an accident," Cunninghame Graham assures us, "Spilsbury might have been Emperor of Agadir." To-day there are no people of that calibre in the Sous. There are no potential "Rajahs of Sarawak" upon the horizon of the Oued Sous or the Oued Noun. I am sorry to have to admit, for the credit of my own latter-day account of these parts, that this should be the case.

We are shown Spilsbury in a London Club of the 'Nineties, who "sat smoking quietly without a trace of 'Union Jackism'." It is very aggravating, but I am compelled to admit that "Union Jackism" is rampant to-day in those latitudes. "No word," with Spilsbury, "of moral purpose, not a suggestion of being . . . a sort of John of Leyden going to set a people free." How different to the vulgar emancipatory humbug so prevalent among the half-baked Bulldog Drummonds into whose hands this captivating "trade" of Captain Wyndham's has fallen. You see Spilsbury, the pure type of the *gentleman-filibuster*, as opposed to the coarse flag-wagger or vulgar humanitarian who affects to be the friend of the "poor *native*" (who inveigles the poor *fellah* into transactions undertaken oh! entirely on his behalf, and then proceeds to rob him of his land or whatever else he may possess).—*Spilsbury* was the genuine article. He was the real British *luxury-object*—for export in small quantities, but guaranteed to stick together and do the work of any "syndicate" through thick and thin, on a minimum of pay. "Simply an ordinary clubman, talking of what he was about to do, as he had talked of fishing in Loch Tay." Ah that Scottish touch—ah me! Loch Tay! "A well-dressed quiet-mannered filibuster, not bellowing that he would make the Arabic language popular in Hell, after the 'fighting Bob Tammany style. . . .' "

But it does one good to think of Spilsbury all the same—it is the bouquet of a filibusting vintage that is lost! [. . . .] The schooner of our "Clubman" filibuster of the 'Nineties would to-day have found schooners, brigantines, and yawls of all descriptions passing and repassing him—for according to all accounts, arms are pouring into Mauretania from Las Palmas all the time. This coast, "which is one of the most deserted in the world," is certainly not frequented by anything but smugglers, but by those to-day it is infested. Only, the power of France does not reach beyond Agadir, on the coast. So there is no danger of interruption from anyone in the world. It can scarcely be called *smuggling*, in fact.

I hope this portrait of the Clubman-filibuster of the 'Nineties lifted (with apologies) out of the brilliant and lively pages of Mr. Graham's book, will have served the purpose of showing the unalterable nature of this coast—how, from the days of Wyndham, in 1552, until this year (the year of the bursting of the capitalist War-debt Bubble), the Sous and its southern marches have been the haunt of that queer bird, peculiar to European climes, *the filibuster*. The latter change from age to age. In the elegant 'Nineties they were "Clubman-filibusters"—

Champagne Charlies on the piratic lay. To-day they are middle-class Stockbroker's clerks, ennobled by the Great War into "Majors" or "Lieutenant-Colonels." But the more the Sous changes (and however the quality—never the quantity—of its filibusters may deteriorate) the more it is the same thing, from age to age.

CHAPTER IX

THE *BLED* HOTEL

So, in the very teeth of one obstructive filibuster, the Union Jack one, with the sham-farm, in an atmosphere rank with "capitulations" and with veiled *Verbots,* I went to the country of the Ikounka. I went across the Ikounka country, I saw their communal fortresses. But I did not visit these embattled "shops" of the Ikounka, as things turned out, but went farther along the Atlas instead. How this came about I will briefly relate.

By five in the evening of the day in question, there I was with the permission. I had an army at my back that meant. It was the most powerful army of any—the army with THE FRANC behind it.

But if I was equipped with this exclusive permission, it was literally in the teeth, as I have said, of the world of Agadir, and moreover it was not thanks to the landlord of my glittering little *bled* Hotel, who vanished into thin air at the critical moment. It was a very odd affair indeed, that of the permit—*every* official upon one's side, most anxious to provide one with every facility, for innocent studies—but *every* non-official banded to circumvent this touristic trespass (by passive resistance and by strategic *vanishes*). I have never before this found myself with the status of a Commission sent to pry into an abuse— Dreiser in Kentucky could not have been met more sullenly, avowed Nosy-Parker that he there was, than was I in the Valley of the Sous, in contact with "British Interests." So little am I concerned with politics, however, that even now I am at a loss to imagine what particular Bluebeard's Chamber I was supposed to threaten to burst into or about which I could blab.

Borzo was the name of the *Patron* of this Splendide-Astoria of the *bled.* He was an Italian ex-legionary, who, like every Italian, in or out of uniform, thought in terms of *hotels.* His time being up in the Legion (which according to his own account he likewise did his best to turn into a sort of hotel—a Hotel-on-the-march as it were, in his capacity of commissariat noncom), he received his last month's pay, I suppose— he stepped out of the barracks (in a cracked pair of patent leather shoes I am sure) once more a civilian, lighted a cigarette (inhaling very deeply indeed with his eyes closed up tight), went at a rather precipitate shuffle round the corner, and founded a Hotel. He founded a

126

Hotel as naturally as a German would go round the corner and enlist again—in a second army, having served his time in the first.

It must, I imagine, have been not very far from Agadir that he took his farewell of his mercenary duties in the African battalions of France. He probably went straight to the nearest house-agent, rented the nearest available Arab house, converted the central court into a restaurant, put palms all over it, collected a half-dozen other Italians together, had *Hotel* painted in giant type upon the whitewashed wall of the house he had rented, and started being a hotel-keeper, without thinking twice about it.

He did not engage an Italian cook however, but a German one. The reason for that was that the thought of Germany excited him very much. He had come under the spell of Germany. He was *so* Germanophile that the chef was the principal personage in the hotel. He was Germanophile to an eccentric degree. Whenever the opportunity presented itself he spoke (or rather gave forth in a headlong staccato buzz) the bastard German of the Legion, German that is mixed with Berber, French, Arab, Neapolitan, and even English.

He was well pleased with me at first. But slowly, as the days wore on, his manner changed. He had been seduced by the filibusters, who were now in open revolt at my continued presence in the place. I am quite aware that this will sound as if I were romancing. But romancing it certainly was not for me, the protagonist on the spot. As protagonist on the spot I was compelled to bear the full brunt of the *agon*. And at certain moments the pressure was extremely severe.

On the morning of the day on which I got my permission it had been arranged between us that Borzo should take me to the military in the morning at ten. But he was absent all the morning and did not go with me to the military. Ten came and went. There was no sign of Borzo whatever. Eleven found me at my window, still sweeping the roads approaching and receding, in vain. Twelve, and still no Borzolino. At one, breathless and heavily button-holed, rushed up to his hotel this small, careworn, shabbily-elegant stuttering Italian, with profuse apologies to me. It had been quite *impossible* for him to get back—he had had to go to The Captain upon business of his own. Yes—to the Captain. Yes, to the *same* Captain! It was *the Captain*, what!—it was the *same* Captain! There was only *one* Captain! Why had he not fetched me? (For *that* was where I too had wanted to go?) Yes *he knew* I had wanted to go—he was exceedingly sorry but he had been detained at the market!—And so forth.—I bowed. That afternoon, when the luncheon siesta was over, I would go myself.

When Mr. Cunninghame Graham tells you, in the manner more or less that just now I have employed above, how mere Berbers, Caïds, "native" Agents, Jews or Turks tended to put obstacles in his way—why, you believe him at once! Why not! Was not he in a wild land? In dealing with "natives" one must expect both ferocious obstructiveness, and contemptible deceit!

Well, I tell you that Britons are just as bad as Berbers, and their personnel of mulatto Americans and "Serbians" hidden behind smoked glasses (quite according to Film canons)—why they are as bad as scheming Oriental Caïds and Congo "Chamberlains." After all, why not? Why should not the poor Briton have his schemings? Is not the European capable of plots?

But there is a law, an unwritten law, perhaps, and it is this. Nothing proper to *Chicago* can happen in London: all "Orientals'" (it is in their nature) are *mysteriously* obstructive and untruthful! Britons never! To tell about your *adventures among Europeans* in the same tone you would use for adventures among "Orientals"—that is absurd—I have offended. I apologize and pass on: in extenuation all I can suggest is that I am not an ordinary man and it may be I dislocate the pattern of the personalities in my neighbourhood.

By five or six I had the permission and letter, at all events. The hotel-car rushed round the hill with me. Borzo sat in the office of the hotel, his buttonhole awry, his face in his hands. But before his treachery I had agreed to go in his car. So I struck him on the back—I knew the cause of his torpor. It was *me*.

At seven in the morning the car must be there. We arranged. It was a long journey inland into the Anti-Atlas. Most of the route was by way of tracks or *pistes*, not roads. It was not only the *Zone of Insecurity*, it was on the edge everywhere of the line of "dissidence." None of the available chauffeurs in the town were acquainted with the tracks, they had never been at all to some of the places I was to visit. A sugar and tea merchant in a large way of business loaned Borzo, my *patron*, his Berber boy-mechanic for the day, with him a dignified young Mohammed who (if the military failed in their duty) would pass me through the Ikounka villages and if possible fortified shops, as he was friends with an Ikounka *Amghar* or small chief.—I went all over Agadir as well to buy pellicules for my camera. When at last the Russian, who called himself "Serb," of the *Bazar du Sous*, had disgorged two small 26 x 6 Kodak packs—the pellicules—the hotel rang me up at Barrutel's to say the packet of pellicules sent for the day before had arrived from Mogador. (The "Serb" had a monopoly of the pellicule-trade of the town: he created an artificial scarcity of Kodak pellicules, because he wished to sell a type of camera, at 900 francs, which did not take the Kodak pellicule. Of the pellicule required for that camera there was a surprising abundance. It was on sale everywhere.)

That night was a red-letter night in the Splendide-Astoria, in my little hotel. All the flying Aces in the Sous and several naval pilots were meeting there. The German chef had made a colossal piece of Fatherland pastry to flatter the ornamental Air Boys and the big Air Magnates expected—a Flight-colonel from Marrakech, and a fat, much-begallooned deep-sea Air Specialist of the French Fleet, and perhaps the Commandant himself.

I talked with Signor Borzo shamming sick in his office. The young Mohammed and the chauffeur were there. Holding his head in both hands because it ached worse than ever, Borzo swore he had marched, three years before, with a column, over the route we were to take (which he had helped to make, besides) and he kept stammering to the chauffeur, "Don't forget the *second* bend—it is not the first. Don't be deceived! I know—I built it!" And the Mohammed lent me by the big grocer nodded his head: there *was* that hairpin bend, yes! Evidently the *patron* had been there—he had built it, perhaps. Mohammed surveyed the Italian rat before him (curled up with neuralgias that came partly from *bhang* or *kiff*, partly from annoyance with me) evidently wondering why on earth he did not go and get cupped, since he was patently in need of it, but he was too contemptuous or fairly urbane to suggest it.

I took out a map. Mohammed did not like the map: he could not read and felt at a disadvantage. There was the identical hairpin bend! Borzo pointed. This was in the *dir*, or outer wall, of the Anti-Atlas, through which you climbed into the interior of the mountains—it was after this hairpin bend you entered the territory of the Ikounka.

I was a month with this *patron*. I was a guest not an employee, but I can say *I was with this* patron. As one of the household I suffered from his headaches and constant moral collapses beneath the pressure of the hostile filibusters. Business Ups and Downs drove him to bed often, he scuttled to a drug-cabinet, or a snuff-nest: every day he would sit in his office, his head buried in his hands. He must get married he said—a German or perhaps an English woman, the best for this business—he thought English—it was essential. All he had in the world was the cat, *Tellurio*. The animal was *Tellurio* after his youngest, and his fairest, brother—all of them killed at Caporetto, one after the other, Tellurio first (the youngest) and he would wipe tears from his eyes as he howled after his cat, "Tellurio! Tel-LUR-io!"

Of course, God knows if the man ever had a brother, much less as

129

many as he said he had; he had formed this habit, of sucking up to strangers by way of his dead family—all killed, all decorated!

In Barbary all men are Mohammeds, all women are Fatmahs. You may find this convenient to remember if you go to Barbary. There is no Berber you would not be safe in addressing at once as Mohammed. The Europeans say, "That Fatmah over there," meaning "That woman over there," just as the Americans say, "That Jane over there." But the monotony in the men's names is even more marked. I never met a Berber who was not named after the Arab prophet. It is just as if every Englishman were called Bill, and every Irishman Patrick.

This Mohammed belonging to the big grocer was a *Si*. "He is a Si!" the *patron* insisted, stroking the headache out of one damp temple. "Si Mohammed! Oh yes, he is a *Si*," said Borzo. "Mohammed is not a nobody you know. He owns three houses. It is three houses isn't it, Mohammed, you own?" Looking at him from a distance, with extreme laziness, Mohammed nodded.

"Yes, three," he said, one eyebrow slightly raised, in shadowy disdain, a little on the lines of an embattled infant. This particular Mohammedan was so extremely good-looking after the manner of Guevara—though with a lighter touch, not heavy and Sephardic, but lordly and lovely, in the way that must make us recall, when with the Berbers, the Tuscan and Roman *condottiere* princelings—that there was something grotesque about the title *Si* (that is roughly our *Sir*) and the slight pleasure, however languid, which he seemed to feel at the accolades of the preposterous Borzo.

I rushed to my window after dinner hearing loud cries, stamping and blows; and looking down into the dark lane I heard a heavy smack, smack, smack. It was the German chef. There he was in his white funnel cap. He was attacking with his fists a "native," whose eyes he was blacking, or *poaching* perhaps one should say, since he was a chef. Each smack of the fist as the chef *poached*, and *double-poached*, an eye, then another eye, was met with a bellow of Berber rage. (The chef received no blows himself; a "native" does not return a blow, that is an understood thing.) The dark figure fell; the chef kicked it, after which he returned to his kitchen. The native rose, and after blubbering out a plethora of curses in pidgin French, he rushed away into the night; but not before his Berber pal in the kitchen had hurried over to him, and scratched and cuffed him on his own account for some minutes.

This was the Tragedy of a Tart. It was the *Gâteau Maison* that was the cause of the assault. The chef had spent all day making the *Gâteau Maison*, building up the rococo glaciers of the elaborate meringue. A small one had been specially prepared for a magnate in the next alley. One of the two Berber kitchen hands had been instructed to carry it upon a plate into the next alley. But he had dropped it on the way. I had noticed before dinner as I went to the garage a fragment of the wrecked icing at the corner. I had not of course understood what it was. I had thought it was a wedge of froth from a gutter, with perhaps a paper frill from a box of dessert biscuits. That was where he had left it, where it dropped. The chef, walking down the lane—the Splendide-Astoria occupied all one side of this passage—to have a look over the gully at the end of it at the horizon of stony-road above us—the crest of our hill—and see if the hotel-car was coming along with the *Vigie*, the Casa paper, to see what crimes had been committed overnight worth a short gloat—chanced upon the icing, against the wall. He knew at once it was his cake. He recognized his handiwork, white-of-egg choked with dust, bisected peaches to confirm the dimensions of the accident.

I could see him, almost, hurl himself back upon his kitchen, in a swift scuttle of his carpet-slippers, his white head-dress on the back of his head, as always, like a drunken pope. The boy was not there. How natural to decide to avoid the first paroxysm of the chef's displeasure! At last however hunger brought the wretch back, and I should not have minded seeing the chef, in his clown's kitchen get-up, white in the face as his spotless apron, charge out of the kitchen at the first faint whisper of the prodigal without, hitting the Berber with great smacks of his pallid fists—oh that White Man's Burden! How the German understands!

I watched at my window—it is my business to know everything, to watch and to wait. Soon the cook-boy was back, shrinking against the wall, there was a writhing shadow. He was shouting in the dark lane, addressing himself to the door of the kitchen. Borzo watched from the front door, beside the kitchen door, also the housekeeper. The chef went out and drove off his kitchen hand, whose face was badly cut—he retreated howling.

"Chef est un con—chef est un con!" the boy roared and whimpered, as he quickly returned, the chef once more back in his kitchen. Suddenly Borzo, who had been holding his head and inhaling deeply his cigarette, darted over and caught him by the arm. They struggled for a moment, Borzo was so weak and small, then he dragged him forward and bundled him roaring like a baby into the front door. The boy slept in a store-room beside the office, behind a curtain. That no doubt would be where Borzo would be putting him.

That was an evening pregnant with minor disturbances. A little later I was in the office when a native soldier, in full marching kit, entered the hall and stared into the office glassily at Borzo. Borzo scratched his chin and looked at him. Then he said:

"What do you want?"

"Nothing," said the soldier.

Borzo got up.

"Yes but after all, what do you want! You say nothing. You want something. What is it?"

The soldier did not move.

"Nothing," he said as if in an angry trance.

After a few moments the soldier left.

Borzo shrugged his shoulders and buried his face in his hands.

"One is not allowed to serve them with drink," he said.

"Is it forbidden?"

"Oh rigidly," said Borzo. "It is expressly forbidden. You must under no circumstances give them anything."

Mohammed, who lived near the hotel, in one of his three houses, came in to receive his final orders.

The soldier returned, and asked for wine. Mohammed got up and led him outside, telling him where to go to get some.

Then two native soldiers came into the hall, of a different regiment, also in marching equipment. They asked for some wine at once without beating about the bush. When Borzo said he had none, they replied noisily and angrily:

"Si, tu en as! Si, t'as du vin. Donne!"

"Mais non, je t'assure que non. Ce n'est pas un café ici!" said Borzo.

"Si, c'est un café! Si, c'est un café!" exclaimed the soldiers.

"Je te dis que non! Ce n'est pas un café ici!"

"Une bouteille de vin!" said one.

"Du vin!" said the other. Both were drunk.

They soon left, muttering to each other in Chleuh.

"I don't know what's the matter with this place to-night!" said Borzo. "Everyone seems to have taken leave of their senses. That's never happened to me. I don't know I'm sure!"

Mohammed lifted one eyebrow and looked at the table. Trailing his feet languidly in his canary-yellow babouches, he left, and Borzo went out and looked up and down the lane. He then locked up, and the electric light went out. His light-plant in the garage fifty yards away kept the Arab neighbours awake they said, the motor had to be stopped soon after ten. We went into the restaurant, Borzo carrying a lamp, and there we had a drink or two, Borzo talking all the time in German, as he always preferred to do—about Germany, his favourite country. Every variety of Saharan winged insect plunged about the globe of the lamp. An enormous locust clattered from spot to spot, as Borzo groped his way in imperfect German from one street to another of nightmare cities of the Reich—in a purposeless wandering, clutching his head in both hands, as if attacked with a raging tooth-ache which had ascended to his temples, rocking from side to side in the lamp-lit court, while I dodged the rushing insects of the air. It was almost an Islamic Sensation! I left him about 11.50. He went to sleep in a chair in his best suit, as always, boutonnière and all, near the Chleuh kitchen-hand. There was no one sleeping in the hotel except us, there were the three waiters, there was the chef. Later on he got a lot of people suddenly—his hotel became renowned as the best res-taurant of the South, within a month. Quite likely now it is not there—Mohammed may have bought it cheap when Borzo crashed.

CHAPTER X

INTO THE TERRITORY OF THE IKOUNKA

Borzo's car was a large travelling saloon, it had no springs and when it was a bad *piste* the passenger was flung up to the ceiling, his head likely to protrude through a rent in the leather: but if, underneath, his foot, on the other hand, were not planted in the right spot it went down through a loose board. It was a car for Mr. Chaplin or for Groucho Marx, it was a true child of Borzo. Its doors opened, but only in response to extreme violence—then they flew open and hit anyone within reach in tit-for-tat savagery. We filled up with petrol for five hundred kilometres. But after fifty kilometres the car stopped. The chauffeur was very surprised as it slowed down. But as a matter of fact there was no more petrol. It had all run away. There was a *fuite*. I was not surprised at all, except that it had gone so far. By this time we were in the desert *bled*. Luckily a kilometre behind us was an important military post. A teaspoonful of gas appeared to be left, and a Berber or two pushed us, so we got back and some rough repairs prevented all the fresh petrol from running away. I bought petrol for another day's journey. Again we set off and were soon leaping along like a mechanical kangaroo. I could see nothing. If anything turned up—like a fort—I had to stop the car and look out.

Between Agadir and the Anti-Atlas it is mostly steppe. There is an argan wood, perhaps a kilometre across. Entering this there is a cactus hedge fifteen feet high: at night beneath the car lamps the giant pods of steel-blue are cut out in a fascinating sculpture. It is a submarine world: in old woodcuts it could have been used for the lair of the sea-serpent.

All the flooring of this scenery is sand, it must be understood, sprinkled with large stones usually—a *pierraille*. There is nothing resembling grass. It is as a land phenomenally waterless: in the interior of the Great Atlas you get clear torrents, very cold in the Saharan heat, reminiscent of Gavarnie.[1] Otherwise when a stream occurs, which is not often, it is the colour of the sand and earth—tan or ruddy. The desert begins here in any case: beyond Biougra there is a small village or two, but they are forts, and have no food-gardens to

---

[1] In the Pyrenees.

speak of—a few date-palms, great blue screens of cactus (*figuier de Barbarie*), black goats, camels and asses.

It is a question every traveller in a country of steppes of this order must ask himself—how the people manage to live, especially seeing how waterless it is. Mainly, in fact, they live upon their animals. That they are able to do because the latter are semi-wild. To take the camel: for six months of the year the camel does not work. He pastures. What however that term, "to pasture," means, in a sand and salt steppe, is something that absolutely excludes what the European thinks of when you say *pasture* to him. On the camel's customary "pastures" he has a considerable walk between any two mouthfuls—the little plants he finds are far apart, and they are not emerald green by any means. Sometimes they require his lips of leather to eat them at all. But the camel again is "much nearer to nature than the horse"; he is, in fact, an antelope, not so very different from the *addax*, and he had never become domesticated like the horse. When, in his brief stops in an oasis, he is locked up and fed upon grain and dates, he will, it appears, roar with indignation at these constraints upon his liberty and that unnatural food. He needs the nourishment that is found in the so-called "pastures," the "great spaces" of the desert, and it is the same with the small black goat.

Under these circumstances, if you see a domestic blockhouse in the middle of a steppe, you will know that however barren this landscape looks to you, that for the half-wild antelope with the hump we call a camel, or the black Berber goat, it is a "pasturage." These beasts, with a few pigs, and a corn-garden hidden by cactus hedges—melons, walnuts and dates perhaps, oil from the argan tree—keep a family or two alive (with every fourth year a famine). It must be remembered that the Berber, unlike the Arab, works. He himself is very near to nature, too, he can pick up a living from between the stones, convert the very salt of the steppe into a dollar or two, with those who need salt more than he, and any flesh he can catch for food has a bath of argan oil to swim in anyway; and actually too soap can be had if necessary, picked as it were with the argan nut, for the Berber women make soap from that.

The Anti-Atlas does not rise from the plain as a steep wall—or appear to rather—as happens with the Great Atlas. Here the *dir* is fairly deep. When you reach the foot-hills, coming from Biougra, you turn north in the direction of Taroudant, follow them for some kilometres, then enter a long valley, with several villages upon hills and a certain amount of cultivation. The Roman Peace of the French has allowed a steady redemption of land from the wilderness, where there is water, and the Soussi is far more peaceful by nature than the Northern Moroccan. The mountaineers are much less warlike than the Riffians for instance. So there is not a great deal going on in this long entrance-valley, but there are a few fields here and there, and terraces of grain or fruit well-laboured, up on the mountain-side, in the neighbourhood of the hill-villages and forts.

It was a long and rough journey into the interior of the mountains. We encountered the much-discussed hairpin-bend and rattled round it all right—the Berber driver had been here to take the sugar and tea to the fort at Aït Baha, to which I was going, to start with.

We now had entered the territory of the Ikounka. Their fortified villages and *agadirs* were visible from time to time. One I approached and made drawings of, as it had I think been one of those chosen by Dr. Montagne for illustration in his book. But at this point I shall pot for you that excellent study of the ex-naval commander (hated by all the British filibusters of these parts) to whose industry we are indebted for most of the more technical information we possess of the civilization of this part of Africa.

In the first place the name, *agadir*. This word *agadir* simply means *fortress*. It is called indifferently, it seems, *agadir* or *ighrem*. Thus the town Agadir means fortress, in reference to the large Kasbah on the top of the hill facing the sea—a conspicuous landmark, within and beneath which the original town was built. There are other *agadirs* in Maghreb, however, besides that particular historical town of *Panther* fame. Tlemcen was called Agadir to start with. Again Ajdir, the capital of Abd el-Krim's Riffian Republic near Alhucemas, is the same word: and Ajdir in the North-East of the Gzennaya tribe. All mean simply "fortress."

The *agadirs* of the Anti-Atlas are communal stores—*des magasins collectifs*. They are the last stage of an evolution that began, here and elsewhere, with the fortresses of the nomads. They started with caverns. The Touaregs still have such subterraneous hiding-places into which they lower themselves with cords, in which grain, dates and so forth are kept. A tribe of nomads would have something (however primitive their system of life) in the nature of a reserve store. However "nomadic," there would be a spot to which they annually returned. With the Touaregs it would be the recesses of the mountains of the Hoggar, for instance. Everything cannot be carried about, especially reserves of food. And in some cases in the Atlas, a pastoral unit would build a sort of fortress, in the most inaccessible place it could find, and leave it in charge of guards during its pastoral wanderings in the finest months.

Then there is the *transhumant* stage—the tribe which is nomad half
the year, sedentary half the year: half the year pastoral, half agricultural, or at all events a certain proportion of the year agricultural.
There is in fact every stage in between the "nomad" and the "sedentary." And a central store or fortress, for a reserve of provisions and a
surplus of goods, was as natural a notion as a "pirate nest" or
rallying-point for the Corsair, that Nomad of the Ocean.—So whether
as holes in the cliff, subterraneous caverns, or fortresses or embattled
store-rooms, where each family had its own particular vault, locker or
safe, the *agadir* is an institution that was a concomitant of nomadism—of the more prosperous and developed nomadism. It was a
small bank, if you like, of commodities, though later it has always
served as well not only as a store for food, but also for any articles of
value it was not desired to carry about, or which the family wished to
put in safe keeping.

In the North of Maghreb these *agadirs* often take the form of a
thatched village—built in the depths of a forest, or in the most inaccessible places of a mountain. This is a duplicate of the real village.
Silent and abandoned, with its streets and guarded approaches, beside the inhabited one—it is the shadow of the first one—reproducing
in every respect the dispositions of the other, as regards the huts of
the respective family units. But in the Sous this empty, this sham
village, has become *a fortress*. It has assumed proportions of which no
traces remain, at all events, in the North—though it may of course in
the past have existed as an institution but long have fallen into decay,
except for the few specimens left, in unsubstantial thatch.

To come more especially to the Ikounka, it is necessary to say,
apparently, that the Ikounka are a very unimportant tribe, belonging
to the Berber confederation of the Achtouken. Even their *agadirs* or
ighrems are not the most considerable or renowned. The reason Dr.
Montagne chose them as the objects of this special research of his was
owing (1) to the possession of a well-preserved, written, legal code for
management of their communal fortresses: and (2) owing to the fact
that their geographical position lends itself especially to study and
dissertation.

As to the Code first: it is a copy of (who has for "father" as they say)
a Code of the Ilalen, relating to the *agadir* of Ajarif. It deals mainly
with the questions of theft and of violence. If you accuse the porter of
the fortress-shop of breaking into your lock-up shop and stealing
anything, you have to prove it, or else pay a fine. If you make impro-
per proposals to the porter's wife, you have to pay a fine. If you find
clay in the wards of your padlock suggesting to the suspicious savage

mind that someone has been tampering with it, in order to obtain an impression of your key, you have to report it to the porter. If you dig a hole in the earth in front of the door of your neighbour's lock-up, causing rainwater to penetrate into his store and injure his grain, you have to pay a fine. If you draw your dagger within the precincts of the communal-fortress, such and such a fine. Abusive language addressed to the porter, such and such a fine. Neglect to turn up when warned for duty, in the fortress, such and such a fine.—They are concerned with very simple ordinances for the protection of property—to protect the porter from personal attacks or unfounded accusations, provide guards, etc.

The position of the Ikounka is however full of significance, and it is this that justifies the selection by Dr. Montagne of this unimportant fraction (one among fifty such) of the Achtouken. Their territory includes a valley called the *Imi Mgorn:* this means "The Great Entrance." This in fact the main opening in the Anti-Atlas—the natural path into the heart of it, to the valley of Aït Baha (to which I was going on this occasion) and so, higher up, through a passage between the Jebel Lekst and the Plateaux of the Ilalen, and eventually into the Sahara, by way of the oases of Tamanart and of Ifran. (This "Great Entrance" is however an entrance of which Europeans have not the *entrée.* Beyond the military post of Aït Baha no European is permitted to journey. He can go there only if his friends or his government are prepared to pay for him a very heavy ransom—or if he can successfully disguise himself as a Jew.)

It was this very dangerous position upon a passage through a mountain wall—leading from the Sous into the Sahara—that necessitated the intensive development and maintenance of protective armaments on the part of the Ikounka. [. . . .]

The Ikounka are not a very important *peuplade*, as I have said, and their villages are not impressive: even their *agadirs* are from the outside not much to look at. I say this to account for the fact, having come so far to see the Ikounka, fired with great interest by a perusal of Montagne, that having reached them I should neglect to go into their fortresses.

CHAPTER XI

BEAU GESTE OF THE GOUMS

Issuing out of the Ikounka country, still upon the plateaux inside the *dir*, not yet in sight of the central *massif* of the Anti-Atlas, a surprising village-block is met with. It is a village border-fortress, of an imposing sort, and the French have built their road to the military Post of Aït Baha past its gates. The approach to it is across terraces of flat stones, almost like a dilapidated graveyard, over which a prodigious steam-roller had been driven. Or it could be described as a natural Crazy Pavement, of cyclopæan proportions, laid down upon an irregular terrain, and so falling into terraces. Out of this enormous mountain flooring rose the battlements of the village. It had I dare say supported a thousand tribal sieges, and the *harkas* of more than one Sultan had probably invested it, or summoned its men out to join it. Its great gate invited the Battering-Ram. Its crenellations called for the stone catapult.

In Borzo's derelict "saloon" we charged across the Crazy Pavement and halted within snapshot of its walls, at my orders. A few tribesmen came up and gazed with awe at Borzo's car—their respect was not diminished by my hitting one in the face with the door, he having approached a little too near in order the better to observe me inside, through the glass, struggling to emerge. I *shot* out, as the door flew open, camera in hand, the tribesmen scattering—except the one that was knocked down. I fiercely snapped the embattled village six times and returned to the car. As however I had bought the Kodak at a second-hand shop (paying more for it than I should at the Kodak headquarters new of course) the shutter worked on the slow side, and I have a double image of everything in Maghreb in consequence. (My camera was a fit consort for the car.)

Rattling in every joint, we charged out of the village (I asked the driver to go quickly as we were late) and another long period elapsed during which I could see nothing, too busy with my experiences inside the machine. Anyone watching us from a neighbouring field would have supposed that Mohammed and myself were engaged in a death-struggle, as we clung to each other with both hands and were flung up and down and from left to right.

At last we reached a particularly lush plantation, where date-palms and bananas were joined by trees of a most extraordinary variety, for which, although I have described them carefully to an expert, I have not been able to find a name. It was a long elegant stem that rose to perhaps twenty or thirty feet out of a cactus-like plant. It had a bouquet at its summit.

Coming down beside this plantation, we found ourselves faced, at the distance of a few hundred yards across a valley, by the walls of the French fort, the residence of the commandant of the district. A few kilometres farther off was the ultimate frontier of the "Dissidence"— that is to say the territory of the mountain cantons that have not made their submission to the French. Beyond that line it is dangerous, if not impossible, to pass, as I have indicated. Later I asked the commandant what would happen if I drove Borzo's Tin Lizzie across that line. First of all, any road that can be described officially as "crossable" ends within a mile of Aït Baha. But allowing that it were possible to get the car forward at all, at the first village probably you would be stopped. You might not be attacked, that would depend upon the individual village. You would either have to go back or be taken before the Sheik. At all events, there lay the frontier [not] of the *Zone of Insecurity* (for a hundred kilometres we had been in what was technically that) but of that independent Berberdom—where all Europeans without distinction are regarded as interfering, dangerous enemies, and where, of course, the French exercise no control.

We stopped at the gate of the French Post. It was a large gateway in a high white wall. Within was a large preliminary yard, then a spacious Arab court, of the usual pattern. All we could see was the palms and the fountain, the covered walk all round the court, and Tricolour upon the main building. Mokhaznis[1] armed with rifles were at the gate.

Some way from the gate a stoutish man sat beneath a palm, reading a newspaper. He turned out to be an official. I was not quite able to place him in this system, he was in the service of the big grocer at Agadir, whose Mohammed I had taken; but he lived at this Military Post, where he had a large office, acting apparently as chief civilian, commissioner for stores, forage, etc.—I could not investigate too closely his functions, but he messed and was to be classified with the Non-Commissioned Europeans, those in command of the Goums or native soldiery. He was not of commissioned status. He was a grocer and stores manager I should say—a commissariat factotum.

---

[1] Moroccan auxiliaries.

By this time it was noon and exceedingly hot. As a pith-helmet was the sign of a filibuster, I had noticed, and as I particularly desired to distinguish myself from the British filibusters and avoid being lumped with the bulldog gold-diggers, I had no pith-helmet. My head-dress was black—"Enemy" wide-awake, reminiscent of *Richmond Gem* packets. It sheltered me: but it was so hot at present that I hoped the European under the palm would come over to the gate and welcome me rather than I have to go to him to put forward the claims of a community of skin. Mohammed pointed him out to us, as a fellow-servant of the same Provision-Merchant. At length I went along the road to where he sat and we had a civil chat under the palm.

He told me that the Berber Messiah would have to arise from the neighbourhood of the river Massa, according to the local belief. But first we discussed my letter to the Captain. The Captain was expected at any moment. He had gone over to the Souk, up the valley, two or three kilometres away, on the line of the "dissidence." It was an important market, requiring his presence, for it was the first time the French had attempted to levy taxes in that market. No trouble was expected, but we never know. When he had first come out here, the tribesmen had always arrived armed at these markets, and he would never come to understand how it was that he had not long ago received a ball in his skin. Like most *Vieux Marocains*, he was not enthusiastic as to the chances of the French to hold what they had got, for longer than fate willed, if as long. His attitude was I think that he had sat long enough beneath that palm—he had the feeling that he was *getting on*—the bearded mercenaries leaning upon their guns spelt not stability for him, but a sort of well-paid interregnum. All that dark "dissidence" but just out-of-sight, oppressed this typical, well-fed, English-looking Paleface.

We hung about at the gate. Then the Beau Geste note was heavily struck—from farther down the road two figures approached us, one booted and spurred, handsome and aquiline, the other in military flannels, and at once the atmosphere of the most African military service was imported into the picture. And I slowly discerned how in *Beau Geste* the reality was subtly falsified. For it is *not* the Foreign Legion, that is perfectly evident, that is in any way romantic. Nothing is more matter-of-fact—they are ordinary German foot-regiments and no more picturesque than a war-time *poilu*. It is the "Goumier" who is the true *Beau Geste;* for nothing is more dashing and *Film-fähig* than a squadron of Goums. And the white non-coms are, in appearance, all that the most romantic nursery governess dreams of after going to a performance of a film about the Legion.

141

The principal non-com of Goums (as they are always called) was an Algerian, a Jew I should imagine, and so more than ever like the real thing of the militant screen. He was debonair to a degree, as gay as he was brave, and as full of wit as a rather operatic uniform imposes, to ballast it, as it were, if only with airy nothings—to disinfect the fanfaronade. He was an excellent boy, of possibly twenty-one, of student-age—oh plucked from college to sit in a blockhouse facing the Jebel Lekst! Yet Arabic he knew as well as French as he said, beaming with ambition: "Etant si jeune, je suis pourtant un Vieux Marocain!"—"Although so young, I am all the same an *Old Moroccan!*"

These non-coms of this native militia occupied block-houses upon the line of the "dissidence," some miles away up in the mountains. That post at Aït Baha was their head-quarters. They relieved each other—I think every few days: it was the turn of *Beau Geste* to go up to the blockhouse now, after the siesta.

The *Goum* is an irregular soldiery. The Goums are more highly trained than the Mokhaznis, though the French military are of opinion that a really good Mokhazni takes a great deal of beating: and in fact, of course, all Berbers not only are so naturally warlike but are so often engaged in war, from boyhood on, that a few months of discipline turns them into perfect soldiers (whereas it takes four years of very hard work to make of the huge black lout from the Niger for instance a dependable *fantassin*).

Dependable, however, is not the word, it seems. For it is said that no Berber is ever *dependable*. After twenty years of service, he is still not dependable from the European standpoint. "Il faut faire attention," say the French—after however long a time! For they are unassimilable really. They are the *perfect soldier* certainly: but not quite in the European sense—never the perfect armed servant, or the automaton. So "Il faut toujours faire attention!"

Lady Dorothy Mills, in her book about Timbuctoo, says the French in the Soudan say the same thing regarding the Negro. "I have never personally come across dishonesty among the Negroes," she says. "I have also found a good deal of loyalty. But then my experience has been comparatively superficial and very brief. Most white Africans will tell you that the Negro has no abiding sense of loyalty or honesty; that after many years of seemingly both qualities he will let you down or rob you. And I suppose the white man who asserts this must have some sad and sound experience or reason for his assertion. Whether these regrettable lapses are the result of cold-blooded and deliberate depravity, or a sudden irresistible atavistic reversion to primitive instincts, I, of course, cannot say, but am inclined to believe it is the latter."

142

This is of course the *race problem*. A man can only be "loyal" to another man if he himself is very much of a *person:* this is rare, and still rarer must be the case where, given the necessary detached equipment, any case at all for personal loyalty exists. (Is not the idea underlying the term "loyalty," used above, that of the White Over-Lord? A Black Man *ought*—that is the idea—to sacrifice himself to a White. In practice of course he will do so just as long as he *must*, and for as long as it is convenient to do so.)

The differences between a French officer (say from Alsace or Normandy) and an average Ida ou Baqil, or an Ikounka, tribesman, are too numerous and important for the alliance to be in any sense *personal.* For the other each is a representative of a race, not a person. The *inferior* of these two abstractions can be "depended upon" so long as the race of the superior abstraction has its hands firmly upon the controls, and so long as no personal difficulty occurs to ruffle the surface of the abstract relationship.

We stood at the gate for half an hour. I never minded the heat— even at the gates of the Sahara, in a late month. The airmen tell you that the danger-line for the heat starts at about Port-Etienne, the Spanish Post in Rio de Oro. There—it is very sudden, they say—you feel it; you are not conscious of the change, that makes it odd, but you fly into a passion on the slightest provocation. If it is your first visit, when suddenly you are observed to lose your temper and begin shaking your fist in the face of your best friend, the old hands will all laugh at you in chorus, and tell you that you must *always* in those parts wear your pith-helmet. It is a standing joke, it seems, that collapse of the sweetest temper, where the sun-line begins.

But it is very hot indeed in the Sous; and by twelve o'clock it is far more agreeable to go inside, certainly rather than to grill in a gateway. The non-coms invited me finally to step inside. This was a special occasion and the Captain might be late—the Souk was at an end and he should have returned. We went into the court of honour. A raised pavement led to a fountain in the centre. As often as a mosquito attempts to breed (upon the water as they must) the fish snaps up his eggs. We went out of the side of the court, in to an extensive garden. Bananas had recently been planted: for the most part it was a North-African garden of large, scentless, bright, quickly-fading flowers. We walked across it, and there was a zoological garden, mainly composed of gazelles and mouflons. Beau Geste, most light-hearted of all renderings of French military life, offered his favourite gazelle, through the wire-netting, a cigarette, which it swallowed in a flash. Cigarette after cigarette vanished into this mouth; I gave it a packet,

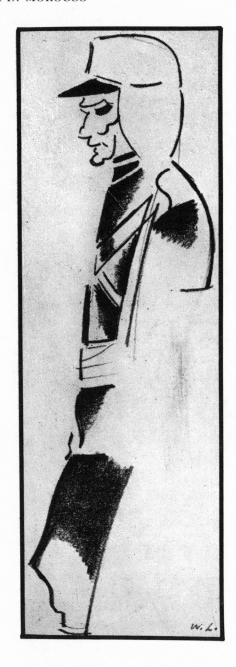

to show how much I appreciated tobacco-fed gazelles.

The Captain's house stood in the middle of the garden. We returned to the principal, official court and examined the civilian's office, the door of which opened upon its arcaded walk. After that we went to the rear of the official residence, to the Mess of the Non-coms, and had rabbit and champagne, Burgundy and duck, port and bananas. With the most perfect hospitality these excellent fellows—six including the grocer, who was the only civilian—gave me a wonderful lunch, not at the expense of the French Government, but out of their own pockets, since they pay for their own food, wine and coffee. A nicer lot I defy you to find—give me the *Goums* for hearty romance, it is a dud impresario I must say that could neglect them for the Legion! Beau Geste shone, he gave a really magnificent display of devil-may-care real-thingness. The gramophone, in this large twilit Mess where we were dug in from the sun, suggested the Western Front, and they had records even of the distant ditties that palpitated upon the air of the Menin Ridge or Chemin des Dames. We discussed everything from the Aïssaoua and Hamadsha[1] to the black banners upon the Mosque on Fridays. The annual feasts at Meknes, when the followers of Sidi Mohammed Ben Aïsa assemble from all over Barbary and tear living sheep to pieces with their teeth, also swallowing knives and forks, glass, screws, cactuses and so forth, is one of the big sights. Europeans are kept at a safe distance, on the roofs, because, when the Aïssaoua are at the summit of their frenzy, they are liable to fling themselves upon the White Man, and there are few "Old Moroccans" who have not some tale of being bitten.

Beau Geste on this occasion insisted that if a European was going into the streets he must be careful to wear light-coloured clothes. This is a fact—I have heard it often—no Jew can go out of doors at such seasons, it is more than his life is worth. But the Jew is recognized by his black costume. Hence *black* is to be avoided. Beau Geste insisted that a *black felt hat* would be quite enough—*black* in any form standing for *Jew*—it would be highly unsafe, and the Aïssaoua, foaming at the mouth, would rush you, and perhaps bite your nose off and swallow it raw. The Civilian bore this out. A *black overcoat* was fatal! He had known a case! His friend (he gave the name) had lost a limb, through being mistaken for a Jew—he was in mourning at the time for his grandmother. Their rabbis keep all the Jews indoors. They eat everything in sight. Every year at the time of that feast several babies disappear. *Whose?* Why the newly-born children of the Aïssaoua wo-

---

[1] Religious brotherhoods.

145

men. *Is that possible?* Is that possible indeed! I should say it is, since every year it occurs! Possible! Why, they would eat anything! They eat their children every year—at least half a dozen or so disappear every year. *Is that so?* That is alas so! There is no way of stopping it. They think that is the right thing to do. No one has ever *seen* them eating their children: but every year at the same time a certain number disappear.

Beau Geste confirmed this. They were brutes—they ate their children. What more natural? When later on I asked a high authority if the Aïssaouas ate their children, he said, "Oh not quite that—not their children." But they do eat animals—like lambs, pigs and chickens—alive. And as to the latter bird, they swallow a small one whole, with all its feathers. (Sparrows they will eat alive up to any quantity—they are particularly proud of not turning a hair at the *feathers*.)

As snake-charmers they do not of course confine themselves to "charming." It has always been quite an everyday spectacle in Morocco to see a snake-charmer—of the Brotherhood of Sidi Aïsa—bite off the head of a living cobra and swallow it, and follow this up by devouring the rest of the body, as a famished man might gollop up a liver-sausage.

I learnt the Captain had returned, and so with very great regret said good-bye to these delightful people. Beau Geste was my pilot to the main building—he showed me the whitewashed target on the outer wall of a shed where their levies were taught to aim straight—not fire of course but hold the rifle. A Mokhazni took me the rest of the way, round to the residence of the Captain.

Captain La Croix, whom I now had the pleasure of meeting for the first time, is a particularly charming and intelligent French regimental officer. He is a dark, large-headed, active man, and as he came quickly into the room where I was waiting I was astonished at his costume—the belted smock, of light fawn-coloured alpaca, reaching to his knees, his long black hair, and spurred top-boots, gave him the appearance of some contemporary of Tolstoï, gone-Moujik, yet exceedingly *soigné*—I recalled the accusations brought against Tolstoï that he dressed like a peasant but had his smocks made of the finest silk. He read the letter from the Colonel, I explained my interest in the fortified communal stores of the Ikounka. Upon his table, and in his bookshelves, I noticed André Gide, *Revolt in the Desert*, *General Bramble*, several books of Robert Montagne's, and many more that confirmed the effect immediately produced by this unusual personality, namely that I was in the presence of a person more capable than most of showing me all I needed to see; and, in the sequel, a delightful experi-

146

ence it proved to be, for all too short a time—in the company of this enlightened man, who spared no pains to show me over the most interesting parts of his domain—for he was for the moment the rajah of this part of the Atlas. As we came out into the garden before his residence we found several Chleuh gardeners at work:we met twenty men in file carrying pitchers of water—orderlies and sentries were on all hands, and the Kaiser himself could not have been surrounded with more homage than this French colonial captain, nor ever certainly have lived in so charming a palace even in the Ægean.

Preparations were required for a visit to the Ikounka fortresses it seemed—the Sheiks had to be warned. We got into the car. I was to go for a tour of inspection with Captain La Croix, who had to pay a visit to an outlying Post. Striking south, we were soon level with the walls of the Atlas. The inside mountains here rise to about 12,000 feet; they are very barren and sun-dried masses. We were to visit two Kasbahs—the first was the Dar Lahoussine. La Croix said he had the day before given the Caïd permission to absent himself for a couple of days to go and get in his harvest, so he knew he was not at home. It was a very big castle indeed, upon the frontier of the "Dissidence"—the mountains facing us were all "dissident." It was here that the former Sheik, a year or so ago, had caused a rising. When we walked up to the principal gate Captain La Croix had to thunder upon it for some minutes before it was opened. We climbed all over it, except the women's quarters. The next castle, seven miles farther on, was a garrison. Cavalry from Tiznit (under the command of one European non-com at the moment) occupied it. There was a look-out man in one of the towers. In the course of our visit the garrison were summoned to their stations. This stream of tribesmen rushing past us through the courts of the castle was a film-scene in fact—"the Attack on the Castle." I was drawing the stables at the moment and did not see them take up their battle-positions. On the way back to Aït Baha we observed two armed horsemen approaching, one behind the other, with sweeping cloaks descending upon the backs of their horses. As we drew abreast of them the leading horseman saluted, his mount rearing, his cloak flying—a gallant picture of the romantic heyday, by Eugène Delacroix.—It was Beau Geste, with his *Goum* orderly, going up to his blockhouse in the High Mountains!

If I did not start back at once I should not reach Agadir in time, so I agreed to return the next day as early as possible and Captain La Croix was to take me to Assads, where there was a very fine communal fortress, the best in the district. He had invited me to stop for the night, but for various reasons I thought I would go back, though I

147

should have enjoyed extremely passing a night there. At the end of a couple of hours of hideous travelling, the sun set, and Mohammed stopped the car. He went to the side of the road and to my astonishment I next saw him kneeling in the direction from which we had just come and prostrating himself. There was nothing hasty about his prayers. He may have thought that he was providing me with an "Islamic Sensation." But all day he had been very subdued, not having at all expected I think such a warm welcome for me, upon the part of the military. He was an Agadirite after all—he had become infected, Berber though he was, and local man, with the scepticism of the filibusters. Then he had hoped to take me to an *agadir* or two. Now he was drawing attention to himself I think—no one had taken much notice of him. (I knew I should have to pay another five francs for these prayers.) The chauffeur was not of high enough rank to pray, or in any case it was not necessary, and he had nothing to gain by it. We got in very late, but as the officers now used the Splendide-Astoria as a *popote*, dinner was never over till well after ten.

CHAPTER XII

VISIT TO A SHEIK OF THE ANTI-ATLAS

In a better car next day I was at the Gate at Aït Baha late certainly (Agadir would not make the way smooth to the difficult places, for author-trippers, who scorned the honest filibusters, and their straightforward romance, and jolly flag-wagging under the noses of the Frogs—tourists unduly learned, for outsiders, about the *leffs*[1] of the Anti-Atlas—the news spread among the chauffeurs that I was a friend of the French, and able to take care of myself: the car came late!)—but all the same we could get to Assads not much after the hour fixed, and I was delighted once more to be in the company of Captain La Croix, and to be able to pursue our conversation of the day before. I had found all he imparted to me of the greatest use. An intelligent man can tell you many things, of a certain order, that sometimes you may otherwise spend weeks in digging out of the halting lips of our average-sensual chum, Everyman.

We got at once into the car: a box full of carrier-pigeons was brought out by a Mokhazni and placed beside the driver (this time a Spaniard). We returned through the territory of the Ikounka, then—instead of turning south towards Biougra, turned north, and followed the *dir*. It was a track, or *piste*, all the way. At last we reached the hills, of a paler, more silvery sand, spotted with palmetto or cactus as usual. We passed two important palmeries. La Croix told me he had sent a Mokhazni over the mountains the night before on foot, to warn the Sheik of our arrival, and tell him to expect us for lunch.

After another hour we turned in towards the mountains and began to go up out of the plain. We now entered a sandy valley full of palms. It was very fertile. The corn-gardens were rich and closely planted, we passed at some distance a very large Souk, and next came in sight of a great village, whereupon we stopped. A small bearded elderly man, turbaned and small, leaning upon a rifle, rose from the bank at the side of the lane. He got into the car and a little later I found he was the Sheik, who had been waiting for us outside his village.

In the valley beneath us there was a stream, with plenty of water, and high date-palms crowded the bottom; upon either side of the

---

[1] Tribal confederations.

149

stream, in terraces, the food-gardens were packed. The village opened with quite imposing (always fortified) houses. We ascended and upon our left and right chains of asses and mules were treading the corn upon large circular platforms, and beyond that was a large white castle. This was not the castle of the Sheik, however, but of his brother. Not above a few hundred yards beyond was a second castle. This was our destination.

An untidy ramp led up to the great gate, crowded with people. We got out, the Sheik first: several tribesmen approached their Chief, and kissed his hand, going half upon one knee as they did so, and afterwards carrying their fingers to their lips, as if to say *hush!* and then retired, a pleased and dutiful look upon their faces.

Going into the castle, we were conducted through several passages and courts, and came out into a really cyclopean one, at the bottom of which were two large doors, horseshoe-arched, standing open. It was the guest refectory. Long and lofty, with the doors in the centre, it had a European table and two chairs, in addition to the divans, and piles of cushions and rugs. The Sheik had disappeared—it was his business to look over the dishes and see all was as it should be. His brother was much less negroid than our host (who was at least half black, woolly and thick-lipped, with a face that had its full melancholy share of the good-nature of the Negro—though he was a very quiet personage—mixed with a canny Berber owlishness).

Several Negro slaves blocked the door, in idle composure. For a few moments we stood there talking, when our host returned. Captain La Croix and myself seated ourselves at the table and coffee was brought to us, which we drank alone. It tasted so strongly of mint that we drank very little, but the Captain discussed with the Sheik regional matters. The Sheik did not understand French and they conversed in Arabic. Then we removed from the table, and all sat down at the far end of the room. There was a divan against the wall, but the thing to do is to sit upon the floor and rest your arm upon the divan, above more rugs, which you drag into position. I crossed my legs, my favourite position. The Sheik's trailed away lazily to the left.

A Berber manservant hurried in with a bowl of brass, and a brass coffee kettle: from the latter he poured water over our hands, and a second domestic offered us each a towel. The Sheik cleaned his teeth with his wet forefinger. I followed suit.

Tea was brought in, that dreadful hot green syrup, drenched in mint. You are supposed to drink three glasses. Then came a big bowl full of hard-boiled eggs. They are all small eggs, for the chickens, like the goats, are small in Barbary, and the thin layer of white is stained

150

an inky blue from the encroachment of the yolk. All hard-boiled Soussi eggs have a putrid taste. Is it the feeding of the chickens? That must be it, but I cannot tell you, as I forgot to ask someone not interested in their sale why all eggs were thus. A large bowl of peeled almonds was brought in. I ate a great many of these delicious nuts— whenever the Sheik looked up I took a handful of nuts. Honey cakes followed. They were damp and intensely sticky buns, I bit one and left it: but immediately afterwards large bulbous griddle cakes were brought in, punctured all over with air holes. All this food was placed in a small circular table—*in* because from above it resembled an up-turned sieve—it was upon stout legs perhaps six inches high. (The almonds were in bowls upon the floor, also the hard-boiled eggs.)

With the griddle-cakes were three small bowls: one contained pure butter; one pure honey; one butter, honey and argan oil mixed. You dipped the griddle-cake in whichever of these three sauces you pre-ferred. But the Atlas honey is supposed not to be very satisfactory owing to the habits of the bee, who feeds upon the flowers of the huge cactus called *figuier de Barbarie*. On the other hand, argan oil no Euro-pean will eat if he can help it. (For many purposes the *arganier* is a more valuable tree than the olive: but its taste for the European palate is so horrible, that it is difficult to market its produce in Europe.) The butter is very peculiar, but better than either the honey or the oil. So I dipped my griddle-cake in the butter.

Next came the *couscous*. This is the national Berber dish. Resolved at all costs not to be too intolerably conservative, I put my fingers into the *couscous* and ate some. *Couscous* may take almost any form, so long as it has a *base* of, not semolina, but *semoule*. This was a sticky rice-like paste, with the flavour of argan oil and rank goat's butter. After the *couscous* came a bundle of skewers, upon which were stuck black pel-lets of alternate liver and fat. We sat round this miniature table, the Sheik and myself upon one side, Captain La Croix upon the other, and luckily the Sheik who had been told I expect that I was a notable white *Taleb*, speaking neither Chleuh nor Arabic, allowed me to eat as I wished, and discussed matters of moment with his master. A dish full of the bodies of about a dozen small chickens, plastered with poached eggs, then was brought in, and the Sheik tore a leg off, offering it a little slyly to me. He himself put his forefinger into the inside of the bird under the breast bone, and prized it up: he picked the breast clean, and we dropped the bones into the receptacle that served as table—what I have compared to a sieve but upon legs.

Next came a mass of fragments of mutton and of lamb mixed. Noticing that I was turning over the pieces with my thumb, the Sheik

151

smiled encouragingly and plunging his hand in up to the wrist, as if it had been a lucky dip, groped about inside and then pulled out a little hard lump of mutton, a tit-bit his practised fingers had been able to fish out by themselves. This he offered to me with a nice smile, faintly insisting that it was a good morsel. I thanked him and bit all round it. I knew from all accounts and all precedent that this tired, black-blooded, sympathetic, almost timid elder had shot and poisoned a quantity of people in order to have more and still more of such good things of Berber life as we were now called upon to sample. This was the Fat of the Land. From a village notable like any other, he had assumed the title of *Amghar*, and fortified his house so heavily that soon it assumed the aspects of a fortress, and he had egged on his brother to do the same lower down the valley. Then he had made war upon neighbouring villages and next seized power in the canton. That is how you become *Sheik*, and that is how probably he had done it. His last step would be to run the *agadir* or democratic fortress-store of the little republic of which he had become the tyrant. Why he had not done this I did not like to ask.

But there are alternatives to this way of becoming Sheik. He may for instance have been the Sheik of the Maghzen—the Chief chosen by the central Arab Government to represent the canton.—A tribe is composed of a conglomeration of what are called *ikhs*. An *ikhs* is a patriarchal (agnatic) family, composed of the descendants of a common ancestor, with whom are incorporated strangers who have married into the *ikhs*.

In any tribe of the Anti-Atlas, made up of a greater or lesser numbers of *ikhs*, or patriarchal groups, usually the members of the *ikhs* which has been there longest (in fact at the foundation of the tribe) are the most influential. In so far as one can speak of aristocracy in such a case, these members of the Founders' Family constitute the "nobles," and their leaders or elders have most say in the deliberations of the council of the tribe.

But if the Sultan, or the "Maghzen"—the Cherifian Government—are appointing a Sheik, they invariably choose him from amongst one of the "oldest families"—one of the families that are of the original founders of the tribal unit. And of course the Sheik of Assads may have reached his present eminence in that way, though even then a rare amount of intrigue and a good deal of arsenic must accompany the emergence of such a tyrannical personal power as that possessed in the present case.

The Sheik now produced his long reed pipe with a small clay bowl—they look like very rakish cigarette-holders—for *kiff*-smoking.

152

Kiff is usually hemp and tobacco mixed. He had a very quiet smoke so that there was a dreamy interval while the tea was brought in: this his brother, the other Sheik, prepared, over by the door. We each got a glass, and then began in every corner of this cavernous feudal apartment a sound of long-drawn-out relishing and lip-smacking: the brother, from over by the door, had a noisy deep-drawn sip: the Sheik at my side responded: Captain La Croix gave a good deep *aah!* of appreciation, and other drinkers at the other end of the apartment joined in—the effect was of contrapuntal *Amens:* so we went on for a few minutes in complete silence, until the first glass was finished. Then the Sheik filled another pipe. When the third cup of tea had been drained by the Sheik and Captain, an attendant came in bearing a large barber's squirt and rapidly approaching the latter deluged his face, hair and body with rose-water. He did the same with the Sheik and myself. Meanwhile a brazier had been brought over and placed beside our host: this he poked up a little, blew upon it, threw upon the coals some fragments of what I suppose was gum-benjamin or aloes, and a delicious smoke was produced, which the Sheik as far as possible caught in his clothes, and invited me to do the same. I opened my jacket, and buttoned it up upon as much of the incense as possible.

This terminated the meal; and Captain La Croix indicated to the Sheik that as we had not a great deal of time we had better start for the fortress overhead. (The *agadir* could be seen from the courtyard outside the room in which we were eating, immediately above us, and from the *agadir* you could look down into the castle.) So we all left the guest hall, the luncheon over.

CHAPTER XIII

THE *AGADIR* AT ASSADS

In the huge cavern of the entrance, the sun blasting down outside so
that we all stood in an opaque shadow, which ended abruptly, were
gathered the two Sheiks, slaves, Captain La Croix, his Mokhazni, and
tribesmen. Out of the lofty tunnel that led to the stables was brought a
large white horse, with the swagger saddle of Barbary, high-peaked,
and, Graham tells us, a torture to the civilized horseman, and Captain
La Croix leapt upon this dazzling steed and moved out into the sun-
light. An enormous mule followed upon the heels of the white
charger, and that was for me: then came a sensible little ass for the
wise old Sheik and a mule of far more reasonable dimensions for his
brother. I attempted to get hold of the donkey: but laughing with
much respectful mischief the Sheik pushed me out of the way and got
on himself. I had to have the giant mule. With palm-fans in our
hands, and attendants on foot to push us up if the mules stuck, we
started, passed once more the fraternal castle (watched no doubt by a
hundred Fatmahs from the lattices and portcullises) and entered a
wilderness of rocks and argan trees. Above our heads, upon the
summit of a steep hill, was the famous *agadir*, which the Colonel from
whom I had received my permit had assured me was the finest in the
whole of the Anti-Atlas.

It took us a half an hour to reach the top: it was an exceedingly
steep, winding ascent, far too steep in fact for anything but a donkey.
La Croix was obliged no doubt to go up upon a charger for administrative reasons, but it must have been uncomfortable.

The hill was high, sharply pointed, and very neatly turned by nature, at least as observed from a distance—it could have been flattened
into a big pyramid easily, except that, at the back, it grew into mountains behind it. Its tip, its small horns, were the round towers of its
citadel: and the walls of this citadel were softly rounded too, and
continued down the side a little way, merging into the body of its
rocky spit. It was like a neatly cut tip to the hill, smoothed round and
roughly polished—the perpendicular ferrule, say, of a steep parasol.
And the very topmost top of the hill were the flat roofs of the towers
of buildings. From this little platform you could look down plumb
into the interior of the castle of the Sheik No. 1 (observing all the

goings and comings of its occupants) and also a great panorama of the *Azaghar*, the Plain of the Sous, was inclined for your inspection like a rich saffron carpet, to the north-west.

We all passed under a large thick-gated arch, beside which was the entrance to a tower. We were then inside the outer shell of the fortress. The rocky track continued inside this arch, still no better than the bed of a torrent, and led to the main entrance of the inner fort.

Throughout, the ramparts were exceedingly solid, built of stone and concrete. Beneath the winding archway of the main entrance the ground still mounted, a few stone steps added at the top. There you reached a small court, with a tower at one side: it was a well, surrounded by the high circular battlements, and this was the porter's quarters. The porter and his family live in the *agadir*. He has the right to use the cistern of the fortress to water his animals. He is called the *amin*.

Upon this occasion the Sheik asked the porter if he wasn't too old to continue in his duties (to which the veteran replied with an emphatic negative and some hearty remark that made them all laugh good-naturedly) and I gathered he had occupied the position for some time, though apparently they are as a rule engaged by the year. I asked the Chief how long the *agadir* had been built. A consultation ensued between himself, his brother and the porter. Captain La Croix said a dispute had taken place—they were unable to decide, but that all were agreed it had been built "in the year of the great wind."

It seems the Berber of the Atlas has little idea of time, and relies mainly upon such methods of computation as the above. The reader may recall the story in the Arabian Nights in which a wanderer returns to his native city and as he enters it feels so elated to be home once more that he addresses a poor woman and her child who were resting just inside the gate. "What a delightful child!" he exclaims. "How old is he, madame?" The woman replies, "He was born, sir, in the year of the great Fart." (This was the year, in which the traveller had himself left the city. And, it may be recalled, the reply depressed him considerably, owing to the fact that it was he, as it happened, who had been responsible for this particular historical milestone.)—No Berber knows, it seems, how old he is, except in relation to other people, and even then they are apt in the end to forget who came upon the scene first.

From this sunk court—which is very intricately built, and the details of which could only be explained by the use of a plan—you enter the main court (which is a short street) of the *agadir*. This is a mass of deep lock-up shops, three storeys high. There are not above a hundred chambers all-told in the *agadir* of Assads: some of the largest *agadirs*, or *ighrems*, of the Anti-Atlas, contain as many as two or three hundred. But the Assads Shop is one of the best built and is in perfect preservation.

What is perhaps most striking, externally, about this strange shuttered street is the enormous rough-hewn wedges of stone which protrude everywhere, thrust into the face of the masonry beside the doors or above the lintels, to serve as steps, up and down the fronts of the buildings of this concentrated village-street. The Chambers are narrow and deep, the entrance six foot high, but in width not above four feet, penetrating to a depth of perhaps as much as fifteen feet. In the doors a small hole is cut sometimes, large enough to admit a cat. Mice are attracted by the grain, and in all the *magasins collectifs* cats are used to keep the mice in check.

As regards the best position, from the standpoint of the tribesman, the middle chambers are preferred: the lowest of all are apt to be damp, being next to the ground, the uppermost are apt to suffer from leaking roofs, and the occupant of a top chamber is compelled to keep the roof in repair. One of the forms of theft most carefully provided against is that effected by making a small hole in the ceiling of a chamber and so causing the grain in the room overhead to pour down into your own. On the other hand, should rodents make holes in the wall, it is the duty of the occupier to repair them. Lastly, any door can be pulled down that is proved not to be rat-proof.

Every possible misdemeanour is provided for, and in some cases the fines imposed are rather curious. Here, for instance, is one of many such provisions, taken, in this case, from the Code of the Fortress of the Beni Bahman, but the laws governing the supervision of these shops are much the same throughout the Anti-Atlas:

> He who fornicates with a she-ass inside the *agadir*, in view of the porter, or in view of any other witness (in whose testimony reliance may be placed) will pay a fine of 2 *dirkem* to the Oumanas, and 3 *sa'as* of corn to the She-ass.

(It is interesting to note that the above crime is punishable with death according to the Koranic, the Arab, code. Often there is, between the Berber and Arab view of the same matter—as the respective punishments in the above instance demonstrate—a critical difference.)

Leading out of this main court, which is also a village-street, is a narrow passage, two flights of steps, and then a subterranean passage or tunnel with shops on either side. Passing along this burrow in a crouching position, you cannot stand upright, you issue out, at the further end, upon the top of the outer ramparts.

Access to the roofs is gained by means of the trunks of trees, into which steps have been cut, which serve as ladders. Captain La Croix released the carrier-pigeons from the inner gateway, with a message for Aït Baha: they went down into the valley and then rose, disappearing over the crest of the mountain that lay south of us.—After more green tea, however, in the gateway of the *agadir*, we started back for the castle below, and after a little more conversation with the Sheik, we left Assads—the two Sheiks and their followers lying upon the shoulders and necks of their horses or asses, in those attitudes which betoken more than virtuosity as horsemen—that treating the animal as an arm-chair, or better, as a convenient farmyard gate to lean upon—which, in fact, denotes an absolute solidarity with the animal. The last view we had of them was of this mounted group in the open space in front of the first of two castles, lying about upon their mounts as they politely waited for our car to disappear, or wheeling in a lightning right-about, to disappear with the abruptness of a Djinn, flashing behind a cactus-wall.

CHAPTER XIV

THE SOUS

("Distant and mysterious, home of the Mahdis and Pretenders")

The Sous is referred to by Dr. Montagne as "the distant and mysterious" Sous—"the home of the Mahdis and of the Pretenders, of the religious reformers and of the Taleb magicians"; and it is the country of origin of all the snake-charmers—the "Soussi" are the poets of Morocco—its acrobats have been signalled in Chicago and all the great cities of the West: then the Chleuh and especially "Soussi" is said to be of all the Moroccans the one with the best business head. But above all the Sous is the great messianic territory selected by prophecy as the birth-place of that ultimate Man of the Hour—the Deliverer that is to come.

"The Sous" is unfortunately a rather loose term; it suggests sometimes a very extensive territory indeed, sometimes a quite small one. A map of some sort is of course essential, if you are to follow even a short discussion of what shall be intended by "Sous." Assuming that the reader has an idea of the main features of the geography of Morocco, I will define, before going any further, what is most generally understood by "the Sous."

The administrative district of the Sous, under the "Makhzen," comprises much more than the mere valley of the Oued Sous. When you are speaking of "the Sous" you can, and people often do, understand only the Plain of Taroudant and the neighbourhood of the river in its lower course. But the more general significance of the term "Sous" is all those purely Berber and Chleuh-speaking mountain territories reaching from Telouet, the Glaoua headquarters, in the High Atlas, as far as to the Atlantic, and from Marrakech to the Oued Noun. This is the region in which the dialect termed "Tachelhait" is spoken.

The reasons that have caused the central power of the "Makhzen"—that is to say the Arab Sultans at Fez—to settle the limits of this administrative territory in this way can be brought under two or three heads. First, the territories in question were roughly the South por-

158

tion of the Cherifian Empire. A line from Demnate to Mogador—that of the northern *contreforts* of the High Atlas—would give the frontier of this great division of South and North. Secondly, "the Sous" as understood in this way, conveniently establishes the limits of the main mass of the independent, never properly reduced and subjugated, part of the Berber World. The Chich (that is more or less definitely Arab or else Arabized) tribes in the Marrakech Plain, serve to limit this purely Berber World upon the North: the Arabized Saharans limit it upon the South. The line of oases or "palm-gardens," of the Dades and Upper Dra in the South is conventionally the southern limit of Barbary proper: though in fact the nomads beyond are much more Berber than anything else, however much superficially Arabized and Islamized they may be, or so almost all the authorities upon the Sahara tell us.

When however in a café conversation a filibuster, or an airman, refers to "the Sous," in a loose way, he does not mean anything so inclusive as the Demnate-Mogador, Telouet-Agadir territory. He simply means the Valley of the Sous and as much to the south of the Oued Sous as would take you to the desert, fifty kilometres inside where Tiznit stands. (In the map you will see at once where Tiznit stands—there is nothing near it.)

But Tiznit, and Ifni (the "Santa Cruz de Mar Pequeña" of the Spaniard) on the coast, are in what is usually called "The Spanish Sahara." And the airmen (and usually also the filibusters, who take their cue from the airmen) call everything indiscriminately "Rio de Oro" that is south of the Sous, and north of Podor, in Senegal.—Having settled these points of popular, as opposed to technical, nomenclature, you will be prepared for what I next have to write about—namely one of the most intensely mysterious countries in the world, "Rio de Oro."

Tiznit is 100 kilometres south of Agadir, in what is called the Spanish Sahara: and already halfway to Tiznit the desert begins. The walled oasis city of Tiznit stands in the commencement of a desert that is continuous (as steppe, mountain, or "erg") as far as the River Senegal. Tiznit is the *clou* to this geography. You may take Tiznit as a limit.

This desert that begins just south of the Oued Sous is several times the size of Morocco. It has never been properly penetrated or explored by Europeans. It is inhabited by what are certainly among the most savage people on earth—the Mauretanian nomads. And a big section of it is occupied by what is technically (and strictly on the map) a Spanish possession, called the Rio de Oro.

160

The Rio de Oro proper is an absolute desert. It is sand and steppe, nothing but that: 500 kilometres North to South, by 300 kilometres West to East, roughly.

It is an almost complete *terra incognita*, as are the other deserts in which it merges on all sides. Gautier, one of the great French experts on the Sahara, says of it: "There is not, in all the Sahara—the Libyan Desert included—a section about which less is known than the Rio de Oro."

Upon this desert coast the English established themselves in a place called Cap Juby. There were driven out (without regret, I should imagine). The Spaniards now have a fort or Kasbah there, which is also (or was until recently) a penal colony. Besides that (and this is the most important thing about it) it is a station of the French Aéropostale Service.

All that we know of the Rio de Oro has been learnt from the aviators of the Aéropostale Service. And occasional Spanish airmen who have ventured down there will have the same story to tell. While I was in Morocco the Rio de Oro was always in the news. The following typical report appeared for instance in the Casablanca Press at the end of July:—

DES INDIGÈNES DU RIO DE ORO TIRENT SUR UN AVION ESPAGNOL

Las Palmas 22 Juillet.—Un avion qui inaugurait le service aérien entre la Péninsule et Las Palmas, aux Canaries, ayant été contraint, en raison du brouillard, de survoler, à faible altitude, la zone insoumise entre Agadir et le Cap Juby, a été attaqué par des indigènes qui ont tiré plusieurs coups des fusil contre l'appareil, dont une vitre a été brisée par une balle qui n'a heureusement atteint aucun des occupants.

L'avion a pu poursuivre sa route et atterrir au Cap Juby, où le pilote a fait son rapport au commandant de la garnison.

This is a thing of weekly occurrence. Airmen (French or Spanish) who for one reason or another get too low, are fired on, that is invariable: if they are forced to land, they are either killed or held to ransom. There is no exception to that rule.

Airmen who have landed in the Rio de Oro and have come back to tell the tale (and usually an airman is not killed, because the ransom for a good airman is substantial) always remark how, descending in a completely empty desert, within ten minutes or so "les Maures" or "los Moros" are there before them—there is a sudden dust and there are the wild horsemen, their rifles pointing at the intruder—or they come up on foot, as it were out of the ground.

One French airman who was held a prisoner for some weeks came back with his nails worn to the quick, where he had been forced to dig and scrape in the rocky soil with his bare hands—when, the night arrived, his nomads camped—to make the hole for their camp-fire, to boil their tea. He suffered greatly from hunger and thirst—he got hardly anything to eat or drink; and until his release he was treated as an ordinary slave of the band who had taken him. The largeness of the ransom expected does not much modify the treatment of their prisoners by these particular bandits.

CHAPTER XV

THE "BLUE MEN" OF THE RIO DE ORO

An Aéropostale pilot, stationed for a long time at the Air-station at Cap Juby, was, I found, an inexhaustible store of information regarding the Mauretanians. They are the famous "Blue People," or Blue Men (*les Hommes Bleus*) whose "Blue" trail lies all over the history of Maghreb. The airman said that numbers of them come up to the Spanish fort to trade, or to receive presents. The Spaniards (who are extremely afraid of them) give them presents even if they bring nothing with them to sell, which they accept fiercely as a tribute, without thanks, or with loud curses if they do not think much of what they have been given. They allow the Spaniards to remain there—they are on sufferance: the Moors remark contemptuously that the Spaniards do not give them any trouble. My French informant told me that not only do the Spaniards give their Mauretanian "subjects" no trouble, but are so terrified of them that the officers will not move more than a few yards outside their fort, from year's end to year's end. It is incredible, according to his view of the matter, how abjectly they are the prisoners, in this small and mournful fortress, of the nomads outside its walls.

If you go outside the walls (as the braver of the inhabitants of this strange capital of empire do, from time to time, to stretch their legs) there are certain rules that have to be observed. One of the most striking is to do with what the German *Korpsbursche*[1] would call "fixing." You must not under any circumstances "fix" a Mauretanian "Blue Man." It is quite essential to remember that for these most fanatical of all Moslems, your glance is a serious defilement. Also, no doubt, upon your emergence from the fort, you are identified with the strange terror-stricken garrison within. Anything that could be even remotely interpreted as taking a liberty (an insolent *sans façon* on the part of the member of a community only tolerated on the condition that they adhere to this dishonourable seclusion) must at all costs be avoided. But should they find you looking at their faces, much more should you seem to *stare* at them, that is quite fatal: immediately

---

[1] Student corps.

163

the muzzles of all their rifles rise, focused menacingly upon the offending person—to teach manners, at least, to the unclean one who has ventured to poke his nose outside his prison. At their feet you may look. Out of sheer contempt, that is allowed. Your head bowed, therefore, you may slink outside the ramparts of the fort, while a downcast eye, fixed upon the exceedingly filthy blue feet belonging to these lords of the desert, will not attract a bullet. But even then it is only a bastard "Maure," the dregs of Mauretania, who ever comes near the fort. What a situation, seeing the legendary Spanish pride—and what an odd *reductio ad absurdum* of the arrogant European idea of a Conquering White Race! The fort at Cap Juby might almost be maintained there by the unsuccessful Spanish in order to revenge themselves upon the rest of "progressive" Europe, by disgracing as it were the still active White Empires. "You will *all* sooner or later come to this!" the Spaniard it may be sardonically is saying! Such at least is the picture that all bring back from a visit to this peculiar colony of Spain's.

In 1850 the first and last European to cross Mauretania died (from wounds and exposure) at Mogador. It is the only territory of any dimension in the world where, definitely, it is quite impossible for the White Man to go. No Paleface can walk into it and walk out again, without paying a crushing ransom, becoming a slave, or being killed.

The cause of all this is not however the feebleness of European arms. It is a result merely of the competitive susceptibility of European nationalism. Rio de Oro could be wiped up in six months or less by the French, without any trouble whatever. But Rio de Oro is "Spanish." If the French invaded Mauretania, the nomads they were driving before them would all pass over the imaginary frontier line of this desert-colony of Spain's. "International complications" would immediately supervene. It is, in an even more aggravated form, the same sort of difficulty with which France is confronted at Agadir.

Some years ago the Spanish Government was on the point of ceding Rio de Oro to France. Then suddenly the French Aéropostale Service was established. From Toulouse to Dakar this service is bound to pass over the Occidental Sahara—the "Spanish Sahara" as it is called: and the only intermediate halfway stop between Casa and Dakar is Cap Juby. The Rio de Oro has to be *survolé*—there is no alternative. But thereupon a new situation arose. The Rio de Oro, as an aeroplane route, acquired a value that it had not possessed as a mere desert, one evidently irreclaimable by man. The Spaniards, just on the point of parting with the Rio de Oro for a song, jacked up their price, and stood out for a sum that seemed to the French negotiators exorbitant.

164

They broke off the negotiations. There the matter has remained ever since.—Yet for the perfecting of this extraordinary French colonial empire the Rio de Oro is of critical importance. And the non-possession of it by France may one day—who can say?—be in the nature of a military disaster.

Under these circumstances—and this is a fact of contemporary history, or geography, of which the majority of people are quite ignorant, I find—a vast territory, nearly the whole of the Occidental Sahara (North to South, from Tiznit to Podor—West to East, from Cap Juby to the Saoura) is an impenetrable blank: it is a No Man's Land: and actually Georges Hardy and Gautier, in their recent books, which set out to bring the topography of the Sahara up-to-date, have to leave huge question-marks upon their maps.

Before the French occupation of the Sahara, the "Berabers" of Tafilalet, were the recognized masters of the oases of the Palm-road across the desert to Timbuctoo. The Berabers have been more or less driven off these routes: but they have retired into the regions west of the Saoura—the regions, namely, that we are talking about, the most general name for which is Mauretania.

Under the heading "La Mauretanie," Gautier writes as follows:

> The extreme Occidental Sahara to the west of the Niger and of the Saoura is an immense country, about which there is very little to say. . . . Thanks to the explorations (already far off) of Lenz and of Foucauld, thanks to expeditions on the part of the Camel Corps, one has a sort of idea of its general armature: the Eglab *massif*, bombilation of the pene-plain, with its ceinture of elongated *ergs*. In the south, upon the borders of the Soudan, we have information regarding the Mauretanian Adrar—a red-terraced plateau, devonian or silurian, very like the Touareg plateaux of Tassili, of Mouidir, or of the Ahnet. But the interesting part (of Mauretania) from the human standpoint is precisely that that is least known. (*Le Sahara.*)

It is surprising to learn again that no geographer is on firm ground at all in dealing with what would seem so accessible as the Saharan edge of the High Atlas. And it is even more puzzling when we are told that all the information we possess regarding this region dates mainly from what explorers of forty or fifty years ago have left us. I will however continue my quotation from Gautier.

> At the southern border of the High Atlas, on the Moroccan (or western) side, we can only barely guess the nature and position of the great oases. That of Tafilalet is certainly a little universe to itself: its ancient capital, Sigilmassa, played a great role in the Berber Middle-ages. But the only information we have upon Tafilalet is that of explorers who

165

passed through it rapidly, often having to conceal themselves (Rohlfs, de Foucauld, Harris). In the opinion of de Foucauld—without whom the greater part of the Sahara at the foot of the Moroccan Atlas would still be a blank upon our maps—the oases of the Dra are the finest of all the Algerian Sahara. But that is about all we know.

To come upon this kind of geographical *blank*, or semi-blank, only a relatively short distance from places that anyone, with the necessary permission, can with perfect security visit, demonstrates the difficulty of the task with which the French have been confronted. Also, I think, it does tend to justify the cautious and "indirect" (political, rather than military) approach of Lyautey. Another thing that I think is suggested by these facts is how precarious European control in fact is. The Great Caïds of the Atlas play somewhat the same role as the Princes in India. For a French Imperialist, like Lyautey, the High Atlas was seen in terms of the Great Caïds of the Atlas, because the risks and difficulties were to him but too apparent. And if you are going to be an imperialist, whatever we may think of the sort of intelligence that goes with imperialism, it is better to be an efficient one than the reverse.

But Gautier quite correctly says that the most interesting of these *blanks* is that to be found in the part of this territory nearest the Atlantic: and once more in this connection, *Atlantis* appears upon the scene: for, if the Rio de Oro ever submits to European penetration, it is more than likely that the whole *Atlantis* problem, resulting from the troublesome passages in the *Critias,* will again be forced upon the scientific world.

> It is above all upon the Atlantic Coast where problems of high importance await a solution. There is one such problem, a matter of physical geography, that is of world-importance: namely the question of *Atlantis.* The text of Plato is very vague: but geologists and zoologists admit that recently there has been a continental sinkage in the ocean-bottom. Upon this question it is possible that a detailed study of the coast will bring to light most interesting confirmatory facts. (*p. 217, Le Sahara*)

What Mauretania means for the "man-in-the-street"—the European colonial, the "Vieux Marocain"—is simply a country where any European entering is immediately caught, slaughtered or ransomed. It is a sensational frontier for Morocco to have, all said and done, at its southern extremity. The deserters from the Foreign Legion always escape into Mauretania: they are immediately caught, and the nomads, that is a recognized thing, get fifty francs for a Legionary. It is not much. But it is just worth "touching." So they bring him in. But they have not always the time to spare, and then it is said they kill him. None of these people are ever seen again: some may be held as slaves—they are usually good strong German peasants. (As a rule the Arab or Berber has valued the Negro much higher than the European, as a slave. In the market Cervantes would fetch far less than Uncle Tom.)

There is a good café story, told by the Airmen of the Rio de Oro, of one particular Legionary caught by the Mauretanian nomads, and who subsequently, as a slave, had an unusual destiny. This fine fellow had had enough of it, he deserted, he hurried over into the Rio de Oro. Immediately he was sighted and caught by nomads. They looked him over. They went through his pockets, and there they found a photograph. Before the War, it seems, this strapping German had been a private in the Prussian Life Guards. In the photograph he occupied a highly-favourable foreground position. He had on a magnificent helmet with eagles sticking out of the top of it. He dwarfed all the other persons in the photograph. Clearly, he was the most important person there. Clearly, he was no ordinary man. This was a most important capture!

His captors had a consultation. They came to the conclusion that they had captured no less a person than the Emperor of Germany. This in their opinion being the case, they put the photograph away in a safe place, gave the ex-legionary a severe beating, and put him down the well again, with a piece of bread and a date or two. This they repeated during a period of two weeks. Then, to his intense relief, they stopped, and did not put him down the well any more.

The reason for their behaving in this unpleasant way was that, believing him to be the Emperor of Germany, they were afraid of his escaping. In consequence they thought it best to break him in at once. Their reasoning was that he would be so relieved at being no longer flogged and put down the well, that he would, when comparing it with what he had suffered, be quite reconciled with his lot.

They began travelling round: and wherever they went they showed other nomads (such as they regarded as safe and not likely to steal or take him by force) their valuable booty. They would show the photograph and him together. And it was universally agreed that it was indeed the German Emperor, and they were very much envied for the possession of such an unusual European. They would still occasionally put him down a dry well when one was handy, to be on the safe side.

At last, after some weeks, they parted with him for a very substantial sum. The nomads who had bought him started restlessly off, and again for some weeks he was tramping the steppes at the heels of his wild masters. Then they reached a *ksar* or oasis, and he was sold once

167

more—this time for much more money. When he changed hands, he was always *sold with his photograph.* So he went on changing hands, as people got to hear of him, and fresh most tempting offers came in all the time. His price soared and soared, until at last a tribe nearly bankrupted itself in buying him, and he became its most valuable possession—a sort of a Koh-i-Noor,[1] worth all their camels and horses rolled into one. Then they sent him down, under a heavy escort, to the coast at Cap Juby, to realize on him. The idea was to enter into negotiations for his sale with the German Government, or otherwise to get in touch with a millionaire amateur, likely to wish to acquire a German Emperor.—When they showed his photograph to the Europeans, however, they were received with shouts of laughter of course: and they nearly shot one or two of them in their indignation. They could however get no offers, and at last came down from the sum fixed—fifteen thousand pounds sterling—a thousand or two. They were convinced these Nazarenes were bluffing them. So they sat down and waited.

But this part of my good café-story goes on for a long time: it is enough to say that at last, nervous and shaken in the belief as to the value of their capture, the Moors got down as low as a thousand pounds—by this time loathing the sight of this honest German face. And the end of the story is that, convinced of their terrible mistake at last, they sell him for forty francs to a good-natured airman, and take their departure, only saved by those words of sovereign efficacy *"It was written!"* from blowing their brains out where they stood.

This is a typical Aéropostale yarn of the *Rio de Oro.* And in the Sous, amongst the Legion or amongst the filibusters and mongrel pioneers, or the "Vieux Marocains," hundreds of such tales circulate. You meet here a pilot who was surrounded by nomads when his machine came down, or there a Legionary will turn up who shows you a letter from Germany from a comrade who claims to have got through by the good offices of a homosexual Sheik. There are many tall stories. But in the South of Morocco the words *Rio de Oro* brighten up any company. All the tongues start wagging together at *Rio de Oro*—this vast No man's Land is like a dark, always stormy, uncrossed ocean, whose sinister sand-billows lash the south of the Sous, and whose neighbourhood breeds numberless stories of adventure.

Since my return from Morocco I have not met a single person who had ever heard of the Rio de Oro. Say "Rio de Oro" anywhere in England—except perhaps within the doors of the Royal Geographical

---

[1] Crown jewel.

Society, or it may be the Foreign Office—and those monosyllables pregnant with adventure will fall upon uncomprehending ears. "Rio de Oro?" the person to whom you say it will repeat. "*Rio de* what?" For everybody it is a *great blank*, just as it is a great blank for the cartographer. But he at least can tell you where it ends, and what is its latitude, and how it stands as regards the meridian of Greenwich. No one else—outside of Africa, or the Aéropostale Service—has ever heard of it.

Yet there are only two places in the world to-day where no moneyed legginged globe-trotter (prancing forward with pistols and puggaree determined to write a book) is refused admittance by the inhabitants. Tibet is a mere tourist centre. The Borneo Headhunter would not hunt the head of a horse-fly if you paid him. All the Pacific and Patagonian cannibals have become vegetarians. There are only *two* forbidden lands. One is in equatorial or sub-tropical South America. The other is the Rio de Oro.

CHAPTER XVI

THE SAND-WIND OF THE COAST OF ATLANTIS

The Rio de Oro would be nothing to us but a big resonant meaning-less name—the label for an enormous nothingness, which, whatever else may be there, contains neither the waters of a river, nor the glint of gold (the parched fringe of it is dangerous, like something incandescent, dangerous to touch, but only *a frontier*) if it were not for the airmen. It is because it lies beneath the air-route of this most romantic of all services that we hear so much constantly about it. It is never off the lips of the airmen; between Toulouse and Patagonia, it is the sector of their flying route most beset with dangers. It is not only the nomads underneath, always waiting to catch them, but the violences of its atmosphere. The latter matches its human representatives. The red Sand-Wind of the desert is a fitting elemental mate up above, for the savage wanderers that infest it down below. It is one and all these things that make up this dark entity, with its big rolling name—Rio de Oro.

For the first time in the Earth's history we have to take into count a new territory—namely the upper atmosphere: when we speak of an ocean or of a desert, we have quite probably to think also of that other waste above it. Formerly, in speaking of a great plain, we were apt to have to refer to the mountains that enclosed or ended it: and in speaking of the people who dwelled upon it, it would be our business also to refer to the people of the mountain—the one without the other, that would be an incomplete picture.

But now, higher even than the mountains, we have to take into our conspectus that new, very solitary, not by any means numerous, people, who for all practical purposes live in those superior altitudes. So when we are speaking of the nomads of the Rio de Oro, the fact that there are *other* nomads higher up cannot be ignored. Indeed if they were forgotten, they would at every moment make themselves felt, and disturb the symmetries of the scene, recorded however ably. Saint-Exupéry has expressed this *air-status*, as it may be called, with great effectiveness—in his extraordinary book, *Vol de Nuit*.[1] I will

---

[1] Translated into English as *Night Flight*.

170

quote the passage where I think he has done this for us: the city to which reference is made beneath is a South American city however.

> Three pilots . . . hidden by the night, meditated their flight (*méditaient leur vol*) and, towards the immense city, would descend from their stormy, or peaceful, sky, *like strange peasants come down out of their mountains.*

These "strange peasants," this novel race of the upper airs, cannot be left out. But to eliminate them from the Rio de Oro would be particularly vain, for this is one of their chosen fields. When you say Rio de Oro—*en connaissance de cause*—you say *air* as much as you say *earth.* The "Airmen of the Rio de Oro" are to-day as much a part of this Rio de Oro, as are the famous "Blue Men" themselves. And it was my privilege while in Morocco to meet one of the most unusual of this new tribe of the sky—one of the most outstanding Air Men of the Rio de Oro. I refer to Mr. Antoine de Saint-Exupéry. Having undertaken to tell you something about the "Blue Men" of the deserts, I must also touch upon the men up above them.

Around the *Vol de Nuit*, and the *Sand-Wind* of these deserts, collects most of what is melodramatic in the Air Life of the Rio de Oro—and also startlingly beautiful (for what is more beautiful than the records brought back to us by men who have lived amongst clouds and storms?).

The French Aéropostale Service linking Patagonia and Toulouse—the establishment of which is one of the heroic events of the last decade—instituted the *Vol de Nuit* (otherwise the Air Service would have lost to the liner and railway train by night what it gained from them by day: it was a question of life and death for the interests of the air).

Antoine de Saint-Exupéry, in his book *Vol de Nuit* (it was published in 1931), shows us the Air Man, and more especially the Aéropostale-man, as no one else will ever be able to do (for it was the first months of that service that were the most glorious). André Gide, in his excellent Introduction to this important little novel, says of it with great justness: "Le héros de *Vol de Nuit*, non déshumanisé certes, s'élève à une vertu surhumaine. Je crois que ce qui me plaît surtout dans ce récit frémissant, c'est sa noblesse."

Noblesse, in a way we cannot use that word in English, is the term indeed that we need to describe the mind that is revealed in *Vol de Nuit*. All that is *base*—to use another word that accommodates itself with a bashful awkwardness upon English lips except where money is concerned—is ignored (though one knows that in a highly-capitalized

171

undertaking of this sort the life of the pilots would scarcely be a matter of anxious concern to the *Direction*). Nothing but the loftiest of principles finds a place in this nobly-conceived and admirably-written air-epic—this, as Gide says, "frémissant" sketch.

But if all the Aéropostale Air Men were dipped in the rare epical emotion pervading *Vol de Nuit* (and that I am persuaded must be more or less the case) then the deserts and the upper atmosphere, suspended above the Rio de Oro, would be a superhuman tract (and I believe it is). At least as fanatical as the inhabitants of the tracts beneath (of the men of the Saguia El Hamra—Ouled Ma'gels or Reguibats—dipped for their part in the inky indigo of their cottonades) must be the fanatics of "action" to be found above. They "act," these extraordinary Air Men, "as if there was something that exceeded in value human life," just like the "Blue" mystics beneath them in fact—though whether that something be any sort of "Allah" I cannot conjecture.

But *Vol de Nuit* must certainly be read—although it does not deal specifically with the Air Life we are called upon to consider here. I have read no book that imposed the same conviction of the high values involved in the psychology of human flight—in its first and epical period of course. Here is another specimen (inadequately translated, I am afraid). "In any crowd of people," reflects the hero of *Vol de Nuit*, "there are men, not evident to the casual observer, marked with no sign, but who are prodigious messengers."

A consciousness on the part of those here written about, that on account of the intensity of their experience they are marked off from other men, is stressed throughout. If all Air Men felt like this (perhaps it is lucky they do not) we should speedily have an Aristocracy of the Air. (I suspect in this case Saint-Exupéry lends to his more prosaic companions in some measure the romantic elevation of his own nature.) The Superman of this brief novel goes for a walk—but with the full consciousness of the fact (and properly so) that even *on foot* he is not as other men:

> He thought how, turning about their *kiosques à musique*, the little bourgeois, of little townships, lived a life seemingly dumb, but sometimes in fact heavy with human drama. . . . His own ill instructed him in many things: "That opens certain windows," thought he.
>
> Then about eleven o'clock . . . he turned in the direction of the offices of the Company. Slowly, with his shoulders, he divided the stagnant crowd about the mouth of the cinemas. He lifted his eyes towards the stars, which shone in the narrow lane of sky above him, almost effaced by the electric signs, and thought: "To-night, with my two Mails in the air and on their way, I am responsible for an entire sky! That star is a

sign! It is searching for me in this crowd of people, it picks me out. That is why I feel a little foreign, a little solitary."

A musical phrase came back to him: it was a few notes of a sonata he had heard with some friends the day before. His friends had not understood: "That art bores *us*, and it bores *you*—only you do not admit it."

"Perhaps . . ." he had replied.

He had felt solitary in the same manner as again to-night, but very rapidly he had understood the richness of such a solitude. The message of this music came to him, to him alone among this average-mankind, with the softness of a secret. So with the sign of the star. He was being addressed, among so many people, in a tongue that only he could understand.

That (the speech of the stars) is the tongue of the "strange peasants" coming down out of the cloud-caps and precipices of the heavens!

So much for the peculiar nature of these other men of the sky: but there is something odder than this duplication of the desert (which has to be reckoned with, as I think has been shown). It is this. On occasion *the desert itself* levitates. It rises bodily into the air for thousands of feet—what is its maximum I do not know—and provides an almost solid surface, far above the inferior plain, as though to afford an absurdly physical basis for this mere metaphor of mine. It is the *Sand-Wind*—that is what this agency is called. It is by means of the Sand-Wind that the desert has this strange power of levitation. At the bottom of its scorching depths there are still the inferior nomads, with their ears and noses full of red-hot sand. On high are the Air Men of the Rio de Oro, in their roaring air-skiffs, dashing along a burning reddish surface—the roof of the storm, in a fresh mildly sunlit world. In the best-known popular account of what occurs, it is described as follows: "We were in fact flying above a surface at once dense and vague, impenetrable, flat as a superficies of worn metal. This had nothing in common with those cloud-seas which I had often traversed in the higher atmosphere, and which the light, according to the time of the day, transforms by magic into snowy mountain ranges, cascades of coral, or blocks of fire. The matter that this time I gazed out upon, stretching to infinity, from South to North, from West to East, was of a neutral colour, and of so compact a grain that the shadow of our machine fell upon it with the utmost definition. It seemed as if all of a sudden an *ideal plain* had come into existence beneath us, situated between us and the real plain below."

This is from the *Vent de Sable* by Joseph Kessel, where he is describing a six-hundred-kilometre journey on the Aéropostale Route between Cap Juby and Villa Cisneros, the two points held by the Spaniards in the Rio de Oro.

Mr. Kessel's book is not a good one—it is not a book of the high order of *Vol de Nuit*. But it is about the Rio de Oro and it describes the life of the Air above the Mauretanian wastes.

Anyone who has encountered the "Sand-Wind" elsewhere, will, by trebling its density, be able no doubt to picture this peculiar form of storm, proper I believe to Rio de Oro. In late July there are sudden and alarming spasms of red sand-storm in the plain of Marrakech, for instance. Hot as is the sun (it reached 125 degrees in the shade this summer during my stay) that is nothing to the breath of the sirocco Sand-Wind. You see a red cloud behind the palm-gardens: then the palms begin whirling suddenly in all directions, as they are struck, their lofty india-rubber trunks dashing their plumed crests against each other: the sun vanishes in the red whirlwind, then the blast hits you—you find yourself wrapt by the Sand-Wind. Your face and hands are pricked and scorched as if you were standing in front of a formidable furnace, in the bombardment of hot particles.

Mr. Kessel's account of the flight to Villa Cisneros is a little disagreeable and silly (with that sort of feminine thrillishness and volubility that spoils all the more popular French literature—and from which Saint-Exupéry is so conspicuously free)—it is in fact too much so to be translated intact. But I will give you the gist of it—it is a first-hand report of this very special order of burning fog and storm in one.

Mr. Kessel's journey began in the face of the mild threat conveyed by a slight sand-fog. "The morning had been foggy," he says, "or, rather, it had been *sandy:* for the fog which covered the coast was formed of solid molecules, which the desert blew out over the Ocean." But the fog cleared up: about noon they got away, and should have reached Villa Cisneros in about four hours of normal flying.

Mr. Kessel, after peering down idly at the inhospitable desert for a while, composed himself, inside the *carlingue*, to listen in to the radio-messages. Then rather suddenly he realized that the air had become *fresh*. "We must be pretty high up," thought he. But, looking out, his view "was blocked by some novel element, close beneath the machine." This novel element was the roof of the Sand-Wind.

They had gone right above it, and there it was on all hands now, nothing else was visible at all: it was the surface of a new, less palpable, Earth.

But, in such a case as this, there was a rather alarming side to the experience. It was already four o'clock, and they should in the normal course of things have already reached Villa Cisneros. This artificial plain of torrid sand in-flight invariably moved *ocean-ward*. Often it would stretch out from the coast of the Rio de Oro over the Atlantic as

174

far as the Canaries—re-establishing, in its semi-solid form, the land-bridge of the Lost Atlantis. First confronted by the compact columns of sand, stretching between earth and sky, the pilot has rushed up the side of them and surmounted the body of the storm or wind-fog or whatever it is. But now, since there was no limit to its extent it seemed (and it might stretch for a thousand miles to St.-Louis-du-Sénégal, as often happened) between then and sunset he would be compelled to dive into the burning red darkness underneath, and go and hunt blindfold for Villa Cisneros somewhere at the bottom! That was the alarming side to this otherwise even and agreeable flight, in a pleasantly fresh atmosphere.

The *Vol de Nuit* above the Andes, when the pilot is attacked by a cyclone among the highest-peaks (which start to vomit a grey snow) in Saint-Exupéry's book, is a splendid achievement: and Mr. Kessel is not able to write things like that: but all the same he gives a quite creditable journalistic account of this plunge, as the sun is setting, into the heart of the Sand-Wind.

For three hours they had flown without any point of reference, in an abstract world of fluid sand. Where were they? Were they bearing inland over the Rio de Oro, towards the wildest depths of Mauretania? Were they over the ocean? Had they passed Villa Cisneros, and were they on the road to Port-Etienne? With these queries revolving in their respective heads they plunged down into the Sand-Wind.

"A suffocating breath rushed into my throat and parched it, a sort of minute hail scorched my skin: and the light that reached us was yellow and sulphurous, decomposed and filtering—sub-marine and subterranean at once."

Down into this they dropped at top speed—they had been at a considerable altitude and this descent was steep and rapid at first, then they changed to a gentler angle of flight.

The Radio bellows in Kessel's ear that a message has come through from the plane that had just left Port-Etienne. The Sand-Wind is there too!—They continue to descend into this uniform "dark, torrid, and powdery poison." Then, all of a sudden, rushing up at them from beneath, are the foaming waves of this most permanently bellicose portion of the Atlantic Ocean. They charge the first enormous foaming roller. Columns of mustard-yellow smoke—which is the bottom of the immense pit of the Sand-wind—whirl in the midst of the glittering spray. They are up and over the edge of the wave. And then begins a sort of switchback—in order not to lose touch with one element, at least, suggestive of the nearness of the shore. The roar of the waves,

Mr. Kessel assures us, overcame at times the sound of the motor. Then, when least expected, a cliff springs up out of the water: with a jump the plane clears it, bending upon one wing, and then everything disappears—they are once more in the abstract heart of the Sand-Wind.

Soon they are back again however above the breakers: and then an incredible tacking operation starts. "This coming and going . . . was of the same order of sensation as that encountered in an anxiety-dream. Everything about it, besides, partook of the colours and outlines of nightmares. The steep coast-line surged up with a terrifying rapidity—there it was, hollow, grained, ill-omened: and it vanished again as quickly as it had come. It appeared mobile and murderous."

Meanwhile the motor got red hot: whether Mr. Kessel is inventing it or not, he describes the plane as growing tired and heavy and no longer vaulting up the cliffs quite so energetically as at first. Then they get into a zone well-known to all the airmen of the Rio de Oro for dangerous atmospheric displacements, in the neighbourhood of the earth: the traveller (Mr. Kessel) and the wireless operator are shot about like bullets in the belly of the plane, as the machine flounders and trips in these treacherous inequalities of the air.

However, I have followed far enough the adventures of Mr. Kessel, at the bottom of the Sand-Wind: he did survive to tell the tale—at length they groped their way back to Villa Cisneros.—You see what the Sand-Wind is by now, at all events. So much I think we have gathered from Mr. Kessel. It is a moving block of desert: and it is always moving out from the coasts of the Sahara over the Atlantic Ocean, which (many people would have us believe) not unlike itself, a fluid block, is superimposed upon the twilit depths of the submerged Atlantis.

CHAPTER XVII

THE BLUE SULTAN

Looked at purely from the standpoint of the politics of to-day and of to-morrow, the "Blue Men" are important people. For the conquest of Maghreb by the European is rather a pacification (even an extreme form of *entente* between the French upon the one hand, and the Sultan, and still more the Caïds, upon the other) than a final military overthrow.

Should Morocco (as a consequence of some great dispute between the nations of Europe, or for any other cause) begin to slip out of the hands of the European, one of the two places where the clutch of the Nazarene will first loosen is the *Blue Belt*, in the extreme south. The other is the Riff, in the extreme north. These, for the French, are the two danger-spots. [. . . .]

Prior to the Fourteenth or Fifteenth Century the Sanhadja and Touaregs were all one large and powerful family of *veiled, nomadic* Berbers: they occupied the whole of the Western Sahara, from the Atlas to the Niger, all the plains of Rio de Oro and Sous. They were camped in the plains at the doors of Rabat.

Then powerful tribes of Arabs came, or were dispatched, down into the Rio de Oro. They defeated the Veiled Berbers. All the Veiled Berbers, except the Touaregs, became subject to the Arabs. And at last they became so ashamed of *the Veil* (or Litham) which they came to regard as a symbol of inferiority and servitude, the emblem of a defeated race, that they left it off altogether. They became fanatical Moslems. They even learnt to speak Arabic, and quite forgot Berber. In this way the Berber World of the South was cut in two or rather three. The Berbers in the Atlas (High and Anti-) remained independent, and Berber. Those in the Occidental Sahara became Arabized; and the Touaregs (still with their veils) became isolated from the rest, in the depths of the Sahara.

The Arab domination lasted long enough to blot out the Berber tongue, to suppress the *Veils* worn over their faces by the "Blue Men," and to inject them with a violent, mystical, Islamism—long enough to make the Rio de Oro, in fact, "the intellectual centre" of Islam in Maghreb. But the Arabs did nothing more than that with their power:

177

they confined themselves as usual to being politically destructive, and to saddling another race with Allah and all the highly political, proselytizing, mumbo-jumbo of Islam. Then they degenerated. They lasted 300 years at most. By the Eighteenth Century the Berber had driven them out of all their strongholds, one after the other.

If a certain amount of Arab blood has passed into the "Beraber" or "Blue Men" of the Rio de Oro, here and there, how much is it? Very little, Gautier and most authorities think. The most famous Arab tribe in the history of Morocco is the Ma'qil. It is the Ma'qil who subdued the Sanhadjas. It is they who colonized all the Moroccan Sahara. Ibn-Khaldoun, the best of the Arab historians, writes: "The Ma'qil came into Maghreb with the tribes descended from Hilal, and it is said that at that time there were fewer than 200 of them."

There is apparently no reason to regard these figures as an exaggeration: and so, as they were constantly engaged in battles with the Berbers (and that does not lead to a waxing, but to the reverse, in the numbers of a people) it is reasonable to assume that there is not so much Arab blood as all that to account for in the Moroccan deserts, and in fact that most of the "Blue Men" are also of the most true blue Berber race. Even many of the so-called "Arab" tribes, such as the famous Beni Hassan—or even Ouled Ma'qil, all that is left to remind us of the Ma'qil—may not be, or have been, Arab at all: "On aurait tort de croire," says M. de la Chapelle, "que les tribus dominantes soient toutes d'origine arabe": but all—"*tous*, suzerains et vassaux, ont abandonné le voile, devenu l'emblême de leur situation de vaincus."

The Berber Renaissance, as this movement of revolt against the Arab has been called, culminated in the Sixteenth and Seventeenth Centuries in the combination of the Atlas Berbers and those of the Sahara. Between them (and abetted by the Touaregs) as the so-called "Berabers" of the Sahara they came to dominate all the Western oases: and finally the remnants of the independent Arab tribes vanished altogether.

This Berber Renaissance came to its culminating point only as it were yesterday. The great Kasbahs of the Atlas, the founding of Smara,[1] the great movement northward of the "Blue Men" of Ma el Ainin, were the last expressions no doubt of this last powerful ferment of the Berber nationality.—And then came the European, with his cannon (and if it had not been the French, it would certainly have been the English or the German—far more destructive, in all probability) and the curtain was rung down upon the Berber Renaissance,

---

[1] City built in the central Rio de Oro late in the Nineteenth Century by Berbers under the rebel leader Ma el Ainin.

and perhaps upon the Berber history-book altogether. At Sidi bou Otman,[1] Berber history encountered another dimension, as it were. In the very midst of their tradition, full of the old Almoravidic dream as ever, up from their tents in the desert came the "Blue Men" as convinced as ever of their mission, since another purgation of Islam was due, and another dynasty (of lean men instead of fat) was about to be founded. And then the French shells burst among them, and that exploded at the same time that old Berber dream.

But from 1880 to 1910 Ma el Ainin, in ignorance of this new dimension (the *mechanical*, that is, superseding the *human*) prepared to become an Almoravid in due course, when the call came: had his city built, and got everything ready for the moment. Alone amongst the Mauretanians, his father's family had retained the veil, as an emblem of sanctity—it was (although he did not understand that) a *Berber* emblem too. All the stage was set. Maghreb was again menaced by the Nazarene: it was misled and betrayed by impossible sultans. In 1910 he invaded Morocco. And like his son two years later, he was immediately routed, and he died upon the spot. His age was seventy-two. That I should call a rather sad destiny, for obviously according to the old system of Magic to which he belonged he was intended to be Tsar of Maghreb, from Tangier to Timbuctoo. It is sad, like the untimely vanishing of the Red Indian. The Magic of the Machine is a magic that should make those that handle it more afraid of it than they are; for Machines are far more terrifying than Djinns. But that in any case is how that great Marabout ended his days, and the "Blue Men" under the leadership of his son, El Hiba, have seemed, politically, to come to an end, too.

The French Administrator will assure you that *les Hommes Bleus* are as dead as mutton. Merebbi Rebbo?—why what is he but a poor devil who travels about from *ksar* to *ksar* trying to raise money! And no doubt the French Administrator's account of the matter is perfectly correct, providing the "Blue Men" are not taken up by some hostile Magician of the Machine—capitalized and modernized. Is this possible? I do not know at all: all I know is that the Blue Men are being eyed with a compassion that is suspect by Filibusters with more rifles and other armaments than they know what to do with (a hiatus in supply and demand). Politics I know nothing about. But I expect if one cared to delve under the surface that a hundred political currents could be found—perhaps even good healthy subterranean rivers.

---

[1] Site of the defeat of the then "Blue Sultan," El Hiba, by the French in 1912. El Hiba was followed as "Blue Sultan" by his brother, Merebbi Rebbo.

CHAPTER XVIII

ARMS-SMUGGLERS AS VEILED MEN OF THE SOUTH

The "Blue Men of the South" occupy the territory from the Sous to Senegal, if by "Blue" is meant the wearing of blue garments, and generally it is. The peasants of the Sous wear clothes that are blue, and no other Moroccans are distinguished by costumes of that colour. But the consistent and deliberate staining of the skin with the blue dye from imported cottons is peculiar to the Mauretanian nomad, "the Blue Man" of the Rio de Oro. There, and in the Soudan, even the face, hands and feet are brought to a deep blue *patine* with the indigo of the *Guinée* cottonade, well sunk into the dark enamel of the unwashed savage hide. (Neither Tourareg nor "Blue Man" of the Rio de Oro ever uses water to clean himself, the former regarding the use of water for that purpose as peculiarly disgusting, and rather unlucky.)—The Mauretanian, when buying a cottonade, wets his thumb and runs it over the surface of the cloth to see if the dye comes off well. His one desire is to be absolutely as blue as possible. That is the real "Blue Man" then—bearded, blue-dyed, wild-eyed and every inch a religious fanatic. These "Blue Men" are to be met with in every Souk of the Sous, and are of course even more often seen in the oasis city of Tiznit: and they are radically different in appearance, that is certain, from their sedentary "Blue" brethren—some more, some less: the farther you penetrate into the interior, the less like the Berber of the Sous they become, no doubt.

Merebbi Rebbo, the "Blue Sultan," may or may not be plotting a rising: what is certain is that he is recognized as "Sultan" and as spiritual suzerain by a number of dissident tribes, unfriendly to the French—for instance the Aït ba Amran and the Ida Oultit. The true Blue Belt begins roughly at Tiznit. The Aït ba Amran, a very powerful "Blue" unit, outside the French imperium, a coast tribe, would be an important unit, of shock-troops, in any thorough-going "Blue" revolt. Where Merebbi Rebbo actually lives, namely at Kerdous, is Igezzoulen, if that means anything to you. It is situated on the mountain of the Ida ou Bakil, about level with Tiznit. It is said to be a place of some importance. But no European has ever seen it. It belongs to that large impenetrable district of mountain fortress and *ksar*—upon the edge of which much farther to the east, are for instance the

180

French outposts at Tatta, where at present fighting is proceeding. (For a hundred kilometres, even, upon the near side of Tatta, you can only make your way under armed convoy, and the convoys are frequently attacked.) As to the regions of the *ksars*, and "Palm-gardens" east of Tazerwalt, it would be quite impossible to visit, for any European—far less easy to-day, in fact, than in the time of Foucauld. A very desperate sort of filibuster, travelling in howitzers, or in the high-explosive-line, might get there, but no one else.

You cannot go to the territory of the Aït ba Amran, nor the Ida Oultit. Nothing beyond or around Tiznit is safe, unless you are engaged in the contraband trade. Only the road between Agadir and Tiznit is all right, and after dark that is not safe they say, not so much because of robbers from the mountains, as owing to the crossness of the smugglers, who of course do a roaring trade after dark.

The French are completely documented, it is unnecessary to say, upon these unapproachable, "dissident," tribes. They know all about them from their native agents and spies of course. In the *Documents et Renseignements de la Direction Générale des Affaires Indigènes*, for example, you can find out all there is to know about most of them. Lieut.-Col. Justinard (who was for four years at Tiznit) has written a very interesting brochure on the Aït ba Amran. According to Lieut.-Col. Justinard, the Aït ba Amran "continues to proclaim the sovereignty of Merebbi Rebbo (that is the 'Blue Sultan')—welcoming him when he goes into their country." And he adds: "In the event of an advance by the French troops, it is probable that the tribes of the Aït ba Amran would confront them, in a solid and resistant block: but their resistance would not, most likely, last very long. We (the French authorities) entertain such close relations with so many of them, that, at the propitious moment, there would be no absence of intermediaries to arrange for their submission."

But this would depend no doubt upon many factors from outside the region involved, and outside Morocco altogether: also upon the nature of the appeal of the anti-foreigner agitation in the Blue Belt, and what support the tribes immediately supporting the Blue Sultan, in the Western Anti-Atlas and the region of the Noun, received from the still "Bluer" desert beyond. In this connection it is necessary to remember that *all* the tribes of the south gave their support in 1912 to El Hiba, when he was proclaimed Sultan at Tiznit, and placed himself at the head of the "Crusade of the South." In the words of Lieut.-Col. Justinard: "All the sub-tribes of the Aït ba Amran, as all the people of the Sous, *without distinction of 'leff,'* grouped themselves behind El Hiba."

There is always the "Crusade" factor to be reckoned with, also the dislike for all that is foreign, which is fairly powerful, and the promise of loot.

But the dislike of foreigners is easily brought to a head by *foreign* agitation—as the Germans during the War kindled the anti-French emotions of the Sous and the Noun. During the European War the Germans pointed to their alliance with the Turks to show what a Moslem-loving lot they were, and they succeeded in thoroughly stirring up the Aït ba Amran and the rest. A landing was to be effected upon the coast of the Aït ba Amran below Tiznit. This *coup* was of the same order as that planned by our friend Spilsbury, Mr. Cunninghame Graham's "Clubman-filibuster."

All I am saying here, then, is that the northern part of the Spanish Sahara is an ideal spot for an unlimited number of *coups de main*. It possesses a deserted coast, it is outside the French zone, it is only Spanish in name. It is as completely isolated as it is possible to be. Filibusters are as irresistibly attracted towards it as fashionable people are drawn in train-loads every spring to the Côte d'Azur. As there is no substitute on earth for Cannes and Monte Carlo, so there is no substitute for the Southern Sous.

Saint-Exupéry told me a story of a "Blue" rising, but I am not clear whether it was the one of 1921, or a later one. He said it was a much more recent affair. At all events, the "Blue Sultan" had raised his head again (the head which is the only Berber head perpetuating the tradition of the veil) and the "Blue" dissidents of the Anti-Atlas began massing. A little prematurely one over-zealous faction attacked a French outpost in the mountains: and the first thing that the French Commandant at Tiznit heard was that two or three Mokhaznis had been slaughtered, and a European Corporal had been boiled alive. The entire tribe had gathered round a large iron cooking-pot, brought to the boil with pine-faggots, and then thrown the corporal into it. Twenty seconds after he had received this startling intelligence, the Commandant at Tiznit was at the telephone, and not very much more time had elapsed before, at the military flying-ground at Agadir, the planes were being loaded with bombs. Another half-hour or so, and, while the tribe in question were still dancing round the unfortunate corporal in the iron saucepan used for cooking sheep, a rain of bombs started to fall upon them from the sky. Many were killed. Every morning for a week the planes made their way to the territory of the offending tribe, and dropped bombs on it. At last a deputation waited upon the Commandant at Tiznit. He sent them away without seeing them. Next morning the planes came back and dropped another hail of bombs.—Day after day the elders of the tribe waited upon the Commandant at Tiznit. He saw them at length and said, "Do you think it is a nice thing to boil a corporal? What have you come here for? Aren't you ashamed to show your faces? I refuse to see people who boil corporals! You must not come here any more—I shall not see you if you do!" And the next morning the planes went up and dropped bombs as usual. The spokesmen of the tribe continued to wait upon the Commandant at Tiznit. At last he saw them again. "What do you want now?" he asked them. "We want to offer our submission immediately," they said. "We wish to become your allies! You keep on dropping bombs, we cannot get on with our work. Our fields and villages are ruined."

"What! Be friendly with people who boil corporals!" the Commandant exclaimed. "I've never heard of such a thing! Nothing is further from my thoughts than being friendly with people who make a habit of boiling European corporals!—I would far sooner have people of that sort as *enemies* than as *friends!*" But the spokesmen of the tribe kissed his booted knee and implored him to make peace and to stop the aeroplanes. Then the commandant considered a moment, and he spoke as follows: "Listen! My spies tell me (I am very well informed!) that there is a meeting to-morrow of representatives of all the Blue tribes. I tell you what I will do. I do not wish to have you as *friends*— Heaven forbid! But after the tribal meeting to-morrow come down here and tell me what has been decided upon by the assembled chiefs. And do that every time there is a meeting. You get me?—oh unworthy boilers of unfortunate corporals! I shall know whether you tell me the truth of course. I am excellently informed! Should you try that on and bring me incorrect information, planes will come up at once with more bombs than before. Now go, and may God be with you *never!*" In this manner the French were promptly informed of everything that occurred: the rising was suppressed.

This is a typical military café-story: it no doubt represents a state of affairs that is fairly constant for these regions.

The outward and visible signs of all this ferment is the frequent capture of people smuggling arms. On July 9th, for instance, the *Sud Maroccain* published the following report:

CONTREBANDE D'ARMES

dans le Sous

——

Une affaire de contrebande d'armes, sur laquelle on garde le plus grand secret, a été découverte, ces jour derniers dans le Sous.

Les Affaires Indigènes de Taroudant étaient avisées que des dissidents s'approvisionnaient en armes et en munitions dans les Ida Indouzel. Une surveillance fut organisée et elle permit de surprendre des indigènes sortant d'une maison avec deux animaux chargés de cartouches. Un officier qui se trouvait au Souk Telata des Manaba, aussitôt prévenu fit une perquisition dans la maison, ou l'on trouva un gros approvisionnement d'armes et de munitions.

Après des constatations le Caïd Mohamed ould Malek ainsi que son neveu auraient été arrêtés.

This was July 8th, 1931: but two weeks before that, on June 24th, a far more spectacular seizure of arms was effected, this time just outside Agadir. No smuggler in his senses would go by road when he could with perfect ease get his cases of arms in by ship. But why these particular consignments had come by road, was, I heard in the case of the July 8th seizure, because the arms were destined for the immediate neighbourhood of Agadir. They were for people in *pays soumis*, in short.

In the affair of the "Portuguese navigator," the arms would normally have gone by sea (to Ifni, or elsewhere, upon the coast south of Agadir): only the "Portuguese navigator's" ship was being repaired. The reader was almost at once, in the case of the "Portuguese navigator," transported into an atmosphere of romance. "Veiled Men"—the Bluest of the "Blue"—stalked into the story; which only serves to show the type of romantic mind of which we have to deal with in the personnel of the Contraband Traffic. They see themselves as the heroes of a Hollywood Crime Film. For, as far as one could gather, it was quite unnecessary to dress up in that way.

This must have been at the suggestion of some public-school-boy-minded White, or Pink, filibuster. For to what Berber would it ever occur, of his own accord, to dress up as a "Veiled Man"? A "Veiled Man" is for a Soussi simply a dirty indigo savage: and in the second place no "Veiled Man" is ever seen anywhere north of Latitude 29 or 30, or at least very rarely, and the smugglers would merely be drawing attention to themselves by this fancy dress.—No, the "Veiled Man" touch betrays the handiwork of the romantic European, and I should not be surprised if the European were ultimately found to be an Anglo-Saxon! For what other European, except the Englishman, has that childish passion for *dressing himself up as an Arab*, to which I already have drawn attention? None. No other European sub-race has ever sunk so low, culturally and intellectually, as the Anglo-Saxon: none, for instance, could have been responsible for the orgy of schoolboyishness and Victorian-housemaidishness (of the Dime-novel order) exemplified by Hollywood, in its Detective Stories and Boys' Own Paper type of Strong Silent Film, could it? The arguments that point to the hand of a romantic Anglo-Saxon are irresistible! On the Van Dine principle, upon the mere evidence of style, and craftsmanship, the moment I saw "Veiled Men" I thought "*Ha Ha!* A rat, a rat!—I see my Anglo-Saxon's hand in this!"

However, I will give you a few of the bare facts: they will help to throw a light on how the country must be honeycombed with confederates of this trade, all busy passing on boxes of cartridges to each other. The "Portuguese Navigator" said that he was a simple sailor who had been commissioned to land a specified cargo, at a certain place upon the coast beyond Agadir. As however his boat was *en panne*, he had gone by car instead: and if anybody (since he was himself the merest sea-captain) Ahmed ben Lahouissine now—*he* was the culprit! Ahmed was a most prosperous Chleuh, with many automobiles, residing at Casablanca. But the latter, namely Ahmed, was profoundly astonished and a little hurt when arrested. The man they wanted was obviously Zeroual, he said. So all the detectives hurried out into the *bled*, where Zeroual lived. But Zeroual bolted himself in. They saw him peeping at them through the shutters. When they prepared to break in his door, Zeroual opened it suddenly and expressed his very deep astonishment and dignified displeasure at their extraordinary behaviour—he had remarked what they were doing through the shutters, yes, that was true, and indeed had been at his wits' end to make out what they wanted! However, he thought if they would have a talk with a Chleuh grocer called Ahmed ben Hajim they might find out something: for meanwhile Lahouissine (who was there) had reminded Zeroual how the latter along with himself, both *Veiled* like "Men of the South," had paid frequent visits to Ahmed ben Hajim. So Zeroual had to say at last something or other and he said he thought the latter might be worth hunting up.

But the cases of Arms-smuggling follow each other with such rapidity that the last is soon effaced in the mind of the public by some new affair: also, in order to make way for B and C, A is frequently dropped altogether in the newspapers. So with this case of the Chleuh grocers and chauffeurs, dressing themselves up as "Veiled men." I have never heard what happened to all these "Portuguese navigators," Chleuh "grocers," and native garage-proprietors. I regretted this very much. They all seemed to fade out suddenly.

Romantically disguised in the Blue Veils worn by the Almoravid warriors, on their way to found the Moorish Empire in Spain, these people would have made a fine police-court group. But whether the matter became too intricate to report, or was shelved in favour of more recent cases, no more was heard of this particular band.

I think I have said enough to bring up-to-date the tales of Filibusters in the Rio de Oro, and show how Captain Wyndham, in his Tall Ship, *The Lion*, of London, and the "Clubman-filibuster" of the Naughty 'Nineties, is unworthily, but extensively, followed. The "trade" invented so long ago by Captain Wyndham still flourishes, upon all that desert coast from Agadir to St.-Louis-du-Sénégal. And it can readily be seen how to-day Major Spilsbury would be meeting the Blue Sultan at dead of night (both disguised as Blue Men of the South, in heavy indigo *lithams* over their mouths and noses) in some noisome alley in Safi or Mogador: and if stopped by a French policeman the gallant major would merely curse him for an interfering (and quite impotent) ruffian, and remind him, with several more "round" oaths, that no British Subject can be touched by the police in the dominions of his majesty the Sultan of Morocco. As to the "Blue Sultan" why (the indignant major would shout) *he* was his Touareg batman of course! That is how the thing would be done to-day.—But as it is, the social changes in England, the steady impoverishment of all true blue "Clubman-filibusters" of the Spilsbury type, means that filibusting, the world over, is the poorer too. It has "lost caste." It is no longer a profession for a gentleman, since there are no *true* "Clubmen" in it now—only perhaps a few members of the R.A.C.!—A squalor, a drabness, a communist anonymity, has settled down upon the "trade" of Captain Wyndham, of London—towering in his Tall Ship, in the centre of those "Spacious Days," able with luck to "see Marlowe plain," though too old to hope to gloat upon the calves of Essex!

KASBAHS AND SOUKS

*The Berbers have always been a
powerful, formidable, brave and
numerous people—a true nation like any
other in the world, such as the Arab,
the Persian, the Greek, and the Roman.*

—Ibn-Khaldoun

EDITOR'S NOTE

The following section prints excerpts from the surviving typescript of *Kasbahs and Souks*, found at Cornell. The typescript comprises chapters 11-14, part of Chapter 16 and all of Chapter 17 of the projected book. Chapter 15 and a portion of Chapter 16—in all 19 pages—appear to have been used for an article sent by Lewis to *The Geographical Magazine*, London. "Herewith your typescript back," the magazine's assistant editor, Archibald Lyall, replied to Lewis on February 21, 1935. "I was most interested to read it, but I fear it is a little too learned, historical and scientific for the public to whom we hope to appeal."

The chapters of *Kasbahs and Souks* which survive in typescript, some 70 pages, seemingly came from the last third of the projected book. They are entitled "Berbers as Dolmen-Builders," "South and Sous," "Ksar or Tent," "When is a Nomad Not a Nomad?—the Dual Soul of Maghreb," and "The Souks of the *Pays de la Peur.*" Among the illustrations planned by Lewis for the book were diagrams designed "to make clear the essential similarity of the Kasbah and an important Manhattan skyscraper."

The paragraphs in *Kasbahs and Souks* comparing the Berbers and the Norsemen should be read in conjunction with another spirited account by Lewis of the Norse marauders. This occurs in *The Mysterious Mr Bull* (1938) as Book I, Chapter 5, where he describes the Vikings as "ferocious, seagoing, playboys. . . . But these big bloodthirsty Scandinavian schoolboys, fair, flaxen and fierce, with unwieldy big pink bodies, and a fixed idea of cut-throat fun, never tired of bludgeons and battle-axes. They were the sinister Peter Pans of the land of frostbite and white-nights."

The two magazine articles are blended here into a selection from the surviving typescript and this should give some idea of what the book might have been. The evidence is that "What Are the Berbers?", first printed in *The Bookman*, December 1933, constitutes the chapter, possibly the two chapters, immediately preceding the surviving block of typed material. "The Kasbahs of the Atlas," from *The Architectural Review*, January 1933, is inserted at a point which seems appropriate.

Only half the extant typescript is used, since the rest sees Lewis becoming involved in somewhat tedious discussions of the history, and historical literature, of Barbary and other issues. The excerpts included represent him in an engagingly ebullient vein. "The Kasbahs of the Atlas" is printed complete but a portion of Part I of "What Are the Berbers?", including copious quotations and material duplicating *Filibusters in Barbary*, has been dropped. The titles of the articles are retained in the text but the other material from *Kasbahs and Souks* is arranged under headings inserted by the Editor and for this reason these titles appear in brackets.

Finally come some salient points from "Poor Brave Little Barbary," an article published by the *Daily Herald* of London on October 10, 1933. Lewis wrote more than once for the Left-wing *Herald*. The title of his Barbary article was a play on propaganda glorification of ravaged Belgium in World War I.

WHAT ARE THE BERBERS?

I

ARE THE BERBERS "LITTLE BLACK CELTS"?

In writing a popular account, a little touristic, of the hinterland of the great Barbary coast-towns, you find that your first job of all is to explain how few Frenchmen there are in these "French Possessions," and how few Arabs in this until recently Arab country. Something very summary indeed to start with of course has to be set down—calculated to shake the reader's confidence in his easy assumption that he knows without being told who it is lives in Morocco. But at that stage you just say *Berbers*, and leave it at that, as though it were perfectly evident who the Berbers are. But in fact nothing is farther from the truth.

The Berbers are what a newspaper would call a "mystery people," like the Basques. No two authorities are agreed as to who or what they are. Some assert they are this, some that: they have been said to come from such opposite regions as Persia, the Baltic, and the Bermudas—from India and from where they are at the present moment.

The Berbers occupy the largest area of any race in Africa. From Tangier to Timbuctoo, from Larache to the Libyan Desert, it is the Berber with whom you have mainly to deal. The great majority of the inhabitants of Maghreb or Morocco are Berbers (certainly not Arabs, who are less numerous in point of fact than the Jews, or at present than the population labelled "European"); yet if you are to understand this part of the world at all, sooner or later you will have to address yourself to the question as to what manner of people the Berbers are: everything hinges upon that—at all events the sort of question that interests the more intelligent traveller or that for matter mere newspaper-reader. And what must be considered a most important secondary question is to what extent they are nomadic or the reverse: and if nomadic, what that may signify exactly.

The former problem, for it is that, will be the first to which I shall turn my attention: I shall attempt to give you some idea of what researches of ethnologist or historian have brought to light. But before doing so I shall be so bold as to place before you the results of my own unaided investigation with the naked eye—of far more value in such a case than the microscope—and I believe, where the evidence is so conflicting, of first-rate importance, supplementary to the gropings of the often almost eyeless historian: provided of course that the eye brought into action in this informal field-work is in the head of a trained observer. In my own case the organ of sight can be said to answer to that description I suppose: for the kind of art that I have always practised, the art of design, founded as it is—like the severe linear art of the Renaissance Masters or the Greeks—upon a constant, in the truest sense scientific, study of Nature, qualifies me far better than many professional ethnologists to pronounce myself in a matter of this nature. The painter is in a sense the perfect *naturalist.* And it is impossible, possessing these qualifications, to remain, week after week, in the presence of a certain people—brought in contact with scores of them from morning till night, noting their gestures and expressions, instructively registering all that the most accurate, "pin-point sharp," camera-image would register—without coming away with a bag of impressions forcible enough to entitle you to generalize as to what breed of man you have been with. Without undue effrontery I believe then I may offer my private, unbiased, unprofessional opinion at the outset.

It is perfectly clear that the Berber people—the Riffs, Hahas, or Chleuhs—do not belong to the Semitic race, like their Arab overlords. This much is established by mere eyesight at once. But a great authority on Morocco, namely Budgett Meakin, has stated, once and for all, what my eye confirmed for me, and what on behalf of my eye I now endorse. In his admirable book *The Moors,* you will find (page 415) the following passage:

> There is a strong supposition that the mysterious Iberians in the peninsula were of Berber stock, and I am inclined to believe, from internal evidence, a theory which at first sight struck me as very far-fetched, that they were closely allied to the "little black Celts," the genuine Celts being a tall, red-haired people. If so, they were ancestors to part of the population of the western parts of Cornwall, Wales, Ireland and Scotland, to say nothing of Biscay and Finisterre, and the builders of those rude stone monuments which exist as well in Barbary as in Britain. Professor Brenton makes out the Etruscans to have been Berbers, and Professor Keane holds the Berbers to be of Caucasian stock.

The so-called "little black Celts" are indeed the people who always come to mind when brought in contact with these swarthy, lean, mountain and desert races, with their bony and thin-lipped profiles, dark, deeply-set eyes, looking out upon the world with that burning

191

and abstracted stare which is peculiar to this type in Wales or in Ireland. Even in their worship of loyalty (so that they excuse their factiousness upon the ground that *it brings out the virtue of faithfulness!*) they are reminiscent of the Celt—the Celt in the grand style, of course, the Ossianic Celt. In their unalterable belief in friendship too, and in the vast importance they attach to it, in spite of stabs-in-the-back which abound, and arsenic in their tea and slippers, which is a matter of routine—in spite of being such *bad* friends more often than not themselves—in the teeth of their own treachery, too, in short!

In Henri Basset's *Essai sur la Littérature des Berbères*, this point is insisted upon, where the author is writing of the Chleuh poetry: *nothing* relieves its more than Celtic gloom, haunted as it is as though with the recollections of a Golden Age—even love as a theme not taking the place it should, when it occurs being only brought in as it were to swell the tide of squalor and calamity. Two things alone redeem this settled distress—friendship and memory of home.

"The sweetness of friendship, its power, the joyous devotion of friend to friend, have inspired the Chleuh poets with some of their most touching verses. The power has been theirs to make plain to us, how a true friend can be saddened at the sight of the tears of his friend, and how, to comfort him, nothing seems too difficult or bitter:

> The ball whistling from the ambuscade, what is there that is more
>   bitter?
> The tears in a friend's eyes, they equally are very bitter.
> The rose-laurel it is bitter: who that has ever tasted it has found it
>   anything but that?
> As for me, for my friend's sake I took it into my mouth. I found that it
>   was sweet."

Everything hinging upon sentiment and upon impulse, in beautiful theory at least, going with a quick and infinite slyness of disillusioned wit—that is a "Celtic" trait if I am not mistaken. Then there is a great deal of the "Celtic Twilight" in their most everyday habits—as when you meet two tall, willowy and beardless braves, inanely wandering along together, holding each other by the little finger, brilliant blossoms dangling in the hands that are disengaged: indeed all that matchless air of infinite wandering indolence that reminds one of the cadences of Mr. Yeats's *Wanderings of Oisin* more than anything else: all that great unworldly air—it is characteristic of these people as it is of the more familiar "Celts," so it is not idle to note them in this connection. It has this practical effect, upon the political plane, that they remain aloof from the fussing invasions of the hordes of breathless Europeans. They are not at all impressed. The sudden hotels, banks, docks and cafés spring up out of the ground: but they are arrogant and indifferent, in the midst of all this passionate, undignified bustle; and they display no desire, which is significant, to get out of their *jellabas*, turbans, or *chequias* and put on a *complet*, such as they could buy in any of those huge French stores named CHEAP, that is "Bon Marché." [. . . .]

II

ARE THE BERBERS ATLANTIANS?

The south of Morocco and the Rio de Oro are, for the "Atlantis" fans of course, of critical importance; for it is there that the great submerged bridge across the Atlantic Ocean starts, upon the African side—the Canary Islands being crests of the mountains that were overwhelmed, according to their way of thinking. And indeed it is difficult, when one is in this region, to resist the suggestions which upon all hands assail one. One learns for instance that the argan tree—that is the giant Moroccan olive, peculiar to Maghreb—is only found in Morocco and in Mexico. And a hundred other puzzling facts crowd upon one's attention, in support of these fanciful Platonists.

There is for example the obsolete Guanche tongue, first cousin of Tifinar, formerly spoken by the blond Berbers of the Canaries. Again, cave-burial, of the same type as practised by the early Berbers, was perpetuated by the Guanches up till the Fifteenth Century. Every variety of cactus, the so-called "Barbary fig," the "euphorbe," etc., sprouts in fantastic exuberance all over these desertic landscapes. And you have all round you a scenery that, did you not know you were in Africa, would make you suppose you were in the middle of a Mexican steppe. Even the vast conical straw hats, hung like Christmas trees with trinkets, and sustained with coloured cords, worn by the *bled*-dwellers, is that Mexican headgear proper, one had always thought, to the *mesquite*. The *Mexican illusion* is perfect in every respect, where things and not people are concerned. As it is, you observe with astonishment a figure from a Maghreb Miniature riding through a Mexican landscape bristling with cacti, and dyed red to suit the Navaho! But what value are we in fact to attach to these analogies?

Mr. E. F. Gautier will tell you, and he is the supreme contemporary authority upon the subject of Maghreb, that this desert land has borrowed everything that it possesses. All its Mexican plumes are borrowed. Even its orange groves, its *mandariniers,* hail from China; and its eucalyptus it has got from the Australian bush, only a half a century ago!

Whereas the landscapes of Gaul must have been much the same (so he says) as the present day French country-side, the landscapes of Maghreb at the time of Jugurtha must (he asserts) have been *toto cocle* different from those of to-day. The giraffe and hippopotamus have left it, but the cactus and camel have been brought in their place.

"What," Gautier exclaims, "in the present-day landscapes of Maghreb, is the most characteristic vegetation—that that more than any other, no painter would omit? Why beyond any question the gigantic *hampes* of the aloe, or the pachydermic absurdities of the cactus! But both aloe and cactus are *American plants;* they were imported by the Spaniards three or four hundred years ago."

But were there really no cacti in Maghreb four hundred years ago? There is no corner of this country anywhere, from north to south, that is not overrun with these gigantic vegetable objects—these "pachydermic absurdities." Is it possible, that from Larache to Figuig, and from the Tell or Tunis to Agadir, the Spaniards are accountable for all the Barbary figs, cacti, euphorbes, etc., to be found so much at home, in such great numbers—even allowing for the rapid powers of reproduction of these useless, colourless things?

However that may be, the *Mexican impression* remains. Also the all-important *argan* (the staple tree and source of revenue—soap producing and bearer of a richer oil than the European olive of the inhabitants)—the argan still remains to be accounted for, and a quantity of other "transatlantic" plants and animals.

But that there was once a land-bridge of some kind across the ocean to the shores of America is not disputed. In that respect a number of specialists, such as the biologist, are in opposition to the historian; so you do not have to be an Atlantis fan to concede the ancient causeway to Mexico. The only question really is how big the bridge was, if it bulged, I suppose, and became "continental," how thickly it was peopled—how sudden was its submergence.

I do not add to my other high-spirited heresies a belief in Plato's continent. I only think that because the historian knows nothing of this past, and professionally is bound to be hyper-cautious, that is no reason to suppress and sweep aside the many puzzling facts connected with the great Flood myth that has haunted the mind of humanity for so long (and which, however extensive, a flooding of the Euphrates is inadequate to account for). I refer to the facts that give colour to the Platonic account of Atlantis.

The most obstinate Atlantis fan is not so far as all that from the matter-of-fact assumptions of the latest science. It is not unlikely that some day or other, in some form, however modified, what the Egyptian priest of Sais told Solon [in the *Timæus*] will emerge in the discourses of geology, and the other sciences concerned. The signs upon the surface of the earth and the animals that scuttle in its crevices will whisper the same tale as the disdainful priest, who mocked at the Greeks and called them children, because they had never heard of the greatest catastrophe in the world.

The great authorities in Maghreb up to date are not encouraging however and have set their faces with one accord against all cock-and-bull stores of a Golden Age buried beneath the waves that roll between the Rio de Oro and the Rio Grande. Mr. Stéphane Gsell is a model of caution as befits a great historian. Yet when he is doing his best to put this matter of the origin of the Berbers in its true light (Vol. I, Book II, chapter vi, *Histoire ancienne de l'Afrique du Nord*) he finds himself constrained to examine, before anything else, this historical Old Man of the Sea, the *Atlantis* theory. No historian can ever forgive Plato for that myth or whatever it was of his; he can never feel quite the same towards Plato as any other man—there is a gulf fixed between Plato and every true historian—the unplumbed, salt, estranging sea of the engulfed Atlantis of the *Timæus*. Oh, why did Plato do it! the historian appears to say, and he cannot ever understand; but in that specialist's mind of his it reacts upon his whole system of philosophy.

Often as it has been refuted, up it has sprung again, a phœnix of a belief; Gsell will not hear of it; but he finds it necessary, as I have said, to parade his refutation of it in front of any other, in his final examination of Berber origins. "Atlantis was mentioned by nobody except by Plato, and by people who had read Plato (Tertullian for instance)," he points out; and he adds that "it is impossible for the historian to take into serious consideration Plato's assertions." He is cross with the geologists and the zoologists. "Let geologists and zoologists by all means demonstrate," he grumbles, "that in a very distant past, America and the north-west of Africa were joined together by a continent; that successive cataclysms broke up this gigantic bridge, then caused it to disappear altogether, except for a few debris—Madeira, the Azores, the Canaries, the Cape Verde Islands. They are at liberty to maintain that the latest phases of the collapse of this continent or bridge occurred in a period sufficiently recent for men to have been the witnesses of it; that the channel separating the Canaries from Africa is posterior in date to the Quaternary Period." Let them do this by all means, but do not let them talk about the *Timæus*—do not let us hear the name of Plato in this connection, or of his cock-and-bull story about Atlantis! Please let them spare us *that!* Such is the attitude of Mr. Stéphane Gsell.

In conclusion, what we must at least allow regarding this theory is that it cannot be ignored: when you are dealing with Maghreb and its rather mysterious inhabitants this prank of Plato's exacts attention, and requires to be elaborately refuted, before you can go on to deal with anything else. It would be as unscientific, I think, in the present state of our knowledge, to dismiss it as to embrace it. So when the solid red block of the Sand-Wind reaches out over the ocean, from the Rio de Oro to the first island-peaks of this persistent dream, do not let us quite banish the suggestions that this spectacle conjures up.

["THE BERBER BUG"]

If Gsell is hostile to the Atlantis-fans, he is indulgent—as far as his extreme prudence will allow him to be, even favourable—to the belief that sees in the Berber (who is after all, until he gets sun-burnt in the *bled*, as white-skinned as us) a member of the European family. "It is permissible to add to these," he says, at the end of his enumeration of points that may be regarded as fairly established concerning them, "the resemblance between certain constructions of unmortised stone—on the one hand dolmens in Africa: upon the other hand, dolmens found in the West of Europe, dating from the third millennium." [. . . .]

There are a great number of investigators who have come to the same conclusions regarding the megalithic remains of North-West Africa (Henri Martin may be cited): it seems to be beyond question that the same people raised the stones of Stonehenge, the *menhirs* of Brittany, and the uncouth steles and assemblages of uncut stones in Maghreb. Little dolichocephalic brunettes are responsible for the erection of all these big stones stuck on end: and the Toursha or Etruscan was according to at least one authority a *big dolichocephalic blond*, and this big horn-headed golden-haired Paleface was the blood-brother of the same-looking men in Maghreb, or the Guanches of the Canaries. But the Berbers remain, for the historian, a "mystery people," in the same category as the Basques and Etruscans. [. . . .]

I shall have occasion to return to this question, which is, of course, of great importance, for there is a bug in all men that represents their heredity, and which make them behave in such and such a manner and no other (up to a point, and making due allowance for the heightenings and modifications brought into play by what we call "genius").

The Berber bug is not easy to define, it is contradictory, made up of grace and savagery, of industry and indolence. There is a proverb current in Maghreb—it runs thus:

> Never sit when you can lie,
> Never stand when you can sit,
> Never walk when you can stand,
> Never run when you can walk.

197

DESERT SOUKH

This is the handiwork of the Arab rather than the Berber, I should say. All are agreed upon one point, namely that the Berber, in contradistinction to the Arab, is positively fond of hard work, and hard manual work. [. . . .]

Descriptions of individual Kasbahs or fortresses—how they dominate this valley or that, how many towers they have, how many slaves, or how many women are secreted in their walls of mud-concrete—that would be not much use to you, unless you understood the meaning of those crenellated apparitions—understood in what they have their roots. How did the Berber come to live in a mammoth fortress? And *who is* the Berber, too? That is what it is desirable to know.

And as to the Souk: as we find the Souk today (usually not much more than a sort of Stonehenge, in the midst of a desert, or standing gaping like a jaw full of hollow teeth in an empty countryside, two rows of vacant cells facing each other, or else here and there become a city-Souk, fortified into a big mud-metropolis, with a Pascha in a Palace to look after it and collect taxes) that is another aspect, simply, of the same thing. It is the wilderness and insecurity that decides the form of both Kasbah and Souk. [. . . .]

The history of the Sous (of Old Sous, as well, Sous el Acksa) has been unfortunate: always the Berber energy has been undermined and brought to nothing by the confusing presence of the Arabs, and their imposed religion. Islam, and all the religious machinery of subjugation the Arabs brought with them, was a more powerful instrument of conquest than the sword. By bringing *Allah* upon the scene, in short, they always are able to get the better of the Berber, who has not taken the precaution to provide himself with a first-class God of his own.

It was the same with the Spanish Conquest as with everything else. The Arab was always at the Berber's heels, Koran in hand, to steal from him anything he won, and stamp it all over with the catch-words of Islam.

"All writers are agreed in saying that the first man who entered Andalus with hostile intentions and deeds was Tarik the Berber," the Arab record says. "As long as Mohammedan Kingdoms existed in Spain, there was a constant and bitter feud between Arab and Berber," says Meakin. "The Arabs had themselves to blame . . . it was by Berber arms that they had conquered Spain." But, that once done, they acted as if their role had been the major one: and Meakin quotes R. P. A. Dozy to the same effect: "[*The Berbers*] . . . *were the veritable conquerors of the country.* Musa and his Arabs had done nothing more than pluck the fruits of the victory won by Tarik and his twelve

199

thousand Berbers over the Visigothic army . . . when it came to dividing the fruits of the conquest, the Arabs appropriated the lion's share."

I have been insisting so much upon all these facts connected with the struggles of Arab versus Berber, partly because what is most interesting politically about Morocco at the present moment derives from this hereditary disposition of the extra-Moroccan, the Saharan "Berbery", to take the lead, and to supply (or threaten to supply) the great religious chiefs, for the liberation of Berbery from the successive yokes of the civilized world. Marrakech always is the earliest capital, within the borders of Morocco, for the first concentrations of these fanatical waves. [. . . .]

[THE POLICEMEN OF THE DESERT]

One of the two great dates, from the standpoint of the outer world, of the history of Maghreb, or still better of Barbary, is 1300. That is when the Saharan Merenides built their pirate fleet. The epoch of the Corsairs began.

Upon the ocean these Barbarians or Berbers expressed themselves in the most perfect manner yet, it would seem—for sand or sea was all one to them. As Saharan bandits afloat, naturally they could but behave according to their nature. They behaved as if the sea had always been their element: Norsemen could not have been more at home on it, and, being upon it, could not have been more conspicuously lawless and piratic. They soon knew all the trade routes and the times of passing of the fleets of the civilized powers, just as they had always known the itinerary and time-tables of the trans-Saharan caravans. They became the great and menacing factor of Chaos upon the ocean. That they remained for half a millennium.

Give the Berber a waste—a sandy one or one of salt water, it is immaterial—and he will be entirely *chez lui*. In their nature, like the early Celts and Germans, these people despise trade and agriculture. They cannot see why, when you can plunder, you should do what they for their part always got Negroes to do. Indeed, the Touaregs, the purest Berbers of the Desert, who still exist in the old manner of the Veiled Men who were the Almoravides, have a saying that I think I have already quoted: "With the plough enters in dishonour."

But the Touareg, the essential Berber, prefers not to be called a Brigand, especially by unsedentary persons like himself. "Empire-builder" he thinks would be nearer the mark. The Soudanese Touaregs, for instance, objected strongly to being treated by the newly-arrived French as "bandits", infesting the desert routes: and when on one occasion a French officer stationed at Timbuctoo hurried after a caravan which had got away by night without paying the "droits du marche" exacted by the French *Fisc*, the Touaregs of Timbuctoo laughed a great deal, not by any means up their sleeves though doubtless in their veils: they waited, guffawing in their *lithams*, and when the little Frenchman got back with the money, they exclaimed, with some finger-wagging equivalent:

"You brigand! Oh you highwayman! You ought to be ashamed of

yourself! But there, you're just the same as us! When we hold up a caravan we are only exacting a 'droit de passage,' or tax—just the same as you!"

What after all could be more just than that! The Touareg had put his finger on the spot undoubtedly. The Normans were pirates to start with. They were the Corsairs of their day: they were dreaded just as much as was the Berber afloat of a later age. Where the dark animal-prows of their shore-hugging warships or war-canoes were observed off any coast, the "sedentary" bourgeois crossed himself, and followed the course of the sea-vulture with an anguished attention. *"Libera nos a furore Normanorum!"*

What is all white colonization however but brigandage? The French officers who have magnificently captured Morocco for the French Republic, are many of them descendants—purer probably than any left in England—of those Normans who drove on and led forward the sleepy English to the great Britannic achievement, the archetype of all colonial brigandage—namely the painting of the world-map a pillar-box red. Where the Touareg winks at the French officer, and claims him for a fellow-robber, he is fundamentally right. He could do the same with the white "Pukka Sahib", or the Empire-building Briton following in Rhodes' footsteps further south.

But the Touareg, the white suzerain of the Desert before the coming of the French, even if he were not the intelligent person that, according to all accounts, he is, would be bound to be better provided with arguments upon this point than upon any other man: for the relationship involved in the above story from Timbuctoo (identifying the role of the French desert-police and Touareg or Beraber, over against the peaceful caravan) is the main fact in his existence. The pros and cons of the Tent-versus-Oasis, and how it may be best arranged that both should live, a little bitterly, one for the other—that has always been the great problem of the Desert. None the less it does the Touareg great credit that he sould have thought it out so thoroughly.

By the blackmail of tax and toll the professional bandit of the Sahara has lived, preying upon the sedentary Haratin populations of the Oasis, and the traders of the caravaners. But the important fact is that the bandit was an institution, of the same order as a "robber baron" of the Dark Age in Europe, or as the Bank-Baron today. He was not, or is not, an irresponsible outlaw: he is an armed ruffian with whom a pact must be made. He polices, against graft, the trade-route: he is a very violent and high handed policeman. Generally he is reputed to have kept his pact. Each oasis has always had its armed nomad to protect it against other nomads. For this it paid the nomad heavily, as the Speak-easy proprietor pays the Gunman. But it would have paid still more heavily if it had *not* paid, and attempted to live *without* a protector! How can you expect the Sahara Desert to be more orderly than the United States?

In the Dark Ages France was a desert of sorts. Walled cities occurred at regular intervals. Near the city in most cases would be a "frowning" castle. In the castle lived a "robber"—that is some adventurer, or hereditary bandit, and his armed band, who kept other bandits at a respectful distance. Or at the start the armed adventurer, at the head of an armoured gang, would single out some important river-crossing or mountain-pass. There he would entrench himself—en-moat himself—in a private fort, and take toll of all passers-by. He was technically a "transhumant," for he would rove about the country, always however returning to his *agadir*—his moated Kasbah.

There are different kinds of armed parasites in the Sahara, however. Some move about more than others. Some are the more definitely accredited police of such and such an oasis, or groups of oases. Some prefer not to be tied down in that way. It is a matter of taste: it takes all sorts to make a world.

One of the most intelligent of authorities upon the Sahara is undoubtedly Mr. E. F. Gautier, whom I have had occasion to quote several times already. He gives an excellent account of the "Berabers," or Saharan brigands, hailing in this instance from Tafilalet, and operating upon the Touat route, that joins Timbuctoo and the Atlas.

This fine hard-working body of high-principled brigands had for a considerable period given every satisfaction. They had assured the safe-conduct of caravans of slave-traders, or of those transporting northwards musk, amber, ivory, gold-dust, salt or ostrich-feathers. They had their beats. They had their *esprit de corps*, and great professional pride. Now when the French arrived upon the scene they soon saw through the French, as they would have (even more easily) seen through the British. Sunday morning service, with the chaplain in a white *jellaba*, would not have taken them in! They simply regarded the French, and with considerable reason (just as did the Soudanese Touaregs), as rival gunmen. And in that spirit they received them, disputing this desert highway with them inch by inch.

The Frenchman, this armed interloper, was attempting to wrest from them a universally (the desert over) recognized right, an immemorial one: and the Beraber treated him as—a highly enterprising outlandish bandit, come on a super-*rezzon* or raid—with just that touch, no doubt, of rather noble indignation that one racketeer of

203

very old standing would betray at the sight of another racketeer who was a common or garden (if dangerous) upstart, butting-in without warning, without a shadow of excuse. There must have been that touch of scandal and outrage—the French were not quite gentlemen. The Beraber, after battle after battle, fell back into the still unreclaimed tracts of the Rio de Oro. There he is to this day, still very angry. Or he took service with this new Saharan super-policeman doubled with gunman, the French Republic (just as the Sikhs or Gurkhas went into the service of the English).

The *respectability* of the "Beraber," of this "brigand" of the Desert, is the thing upon which we have to insist (just as, in times to come, the *respectability* of the British brigands who were—and still are—the suzerains of half the earth, will be insisted upon, by the really scientific historian, no doubt). Gautier says of the Berabers: "These are in fact seasoned bands—far more truly a corps of regulars than the so-called army of the Sultan: composed of picked men like the crew of a corsair, cemented by the discipline of the caravans, the memories and traditions of many interior expeditions . . . they are *professionals* of war—something in the nature of an equivalent, in the Sahara, of the barbaresque pirates of the Mediterranean. Armed with good carbines, they are the equals of no matter what regular troops in the world."

But the respectability of these desert *banditi* becomes still more marked when they become semi-sedentary, as is apparently fairly often the case. When they *sit down*, or half-sit-down, to their parasitic role, then their law-abiding, regular, and unimpeachably respectable character *saute aux yeux*. It becomes perfectly obvious even to the most narrow-minded observer.

In the walled oasis in the border region of the High Atlas and Anti-Atlas, facing the Sahara, a most harmonious and fraternal condition exists, indeed the sedentary oasis-dweller asks nothing better, it would seem, than to have these muscular parasites officially attached to his person. There, in the Upper Dra, the collaboration of *Ksarian* and Nomad is, according to all accounts, nothing less than idyllic.

The *ksar*—or small walled Saharan City—surrounded by the tents of its lords and masters, the Sanhadja nomad, is the place to look for armed blackmail under its most respectable and august guise. There the swarm of desert gunmen indeed comes into its own, and at the same time rests on its laurels, in a sense. It is, so to speak, the Lotus-Land of the Bravo. There, at last, without actually going out of business, he can be at rest, without *razzia* or *rezzou* to drag him out of sunny contemplation—day in day out (without even lifting a hand or

204

displacing a muscle)—of the delights and advantages of brute force. "In other places," says my authority, "the suzerains (for the most part Arabs or Zenatas) established themselves in the midst of their conquests by the enslavement of the Haratin: or else they continued (in spite of them) to roam the desert, and their function in that case remained negative. The village buys each year their promise not to molest it: but this promise, even, is not always very strictly adhered to. . . . The 'debiha,' or protection, only concerns the inhabitants of the *ksar* travelling across the lands of the nomads. It does not include the *ksar* itself."

But in this region of the Oued Dra (of which the *ksar* of Nesrat is typical) it does really seem that a *fusion* of *Ksarian* and of Nomad has taken place. Both have obligations and rights, mutually recognized. It is a perfect working arrangement between these two hostile principles. The Agricultural Age and the Pastoral Age have come together and have settled down—if it can be said that a nomad has "settled down" at all: here at all events he comes as near to "settling down" (to being "sedentary") as it is in his nature to be, and without losing (that is the danger he must always guard against) his ferocious and redoubtable qualities—those that secure him the suzerainty over all those too firmly wedded to the soil, his traditional prey.

The reason for this may be that the Aït 'Atta are members of the great Berber tribe, the Sanhadja, and, unlike the Arabs, more nearly related to the negritic Berberized Haratin, or mixed Berber and Haratin, populations of the *ksar*. However this may be, the latter (the sedentary *Ksarians*) can own property, they cultivate the land, they are answerable for the commercial and industrial side of this particular community: whereas the former (the Sanhadja Nomads) pasture their flocks, form escorts for caravans, and guarantee the safety of the *ksar,* for which they exact a payment which, according to the standards of blackmail of this highly dangerous desert, is said to be exceedingly fair and reasonable. In case of attack, they man the *ageddim.* An *ageddim* is an isolated tower, about 30 feet high, built on some strategic point outside the oasis. They protect the irrigation works and fields in case of inter-tribal disputes, firing upon any person or persons approaching the borderline of the city under their charge. On the other hand, in some cases the vassals, that is to say the townspeople, are not allowed to make war upon another *ksar*, without first consulting their nomadic lords and masters. But there are *Ksarians* who have this right, and fully exercise it. They can do in fact almost anything they like, including fighting, provided they pay their taxes and acknowledge their particular nomadic parasite to be their sovereign lord.

205

The Nomad however, that is understood, would be no further use to the *Ksarian* if he ceased to be fierce, and also passably nomadic. Even the police force *within* the *ksar* is chosen for its ferocity. The *Jem'a el 'Amma*, or popular assembly, chooses its policemen, to keep order within the walls, [from] "among the most turbulent of each faction." In that way "the terror they inspire" makes it easy for them to keep order—the more terrible they are, the more effective is their police-work. But *outside* the walls, and face to face with the wild nomadic world bristling and darkening on all sides without the oasis, these "turbulent" qualities of the accredited bully cannot be too exaggerated provided they are accompanied with a nice sense of honour of course, and that with the bandit in question his word be as good as his bond.

The analogy between the "Berabers" or Touaregs and the White Europeans requires, I am sure, no further emphasis. The "empire-builder" is now generally conceded to be a colossal brigand, merely—a parasitic policeman upon the grand scale. And I believe it is quite true to say that if the White Europeans who overran the world a few centuries ago, with all the wonderful destructive resources of science to back them, had not possessed such an unsuitable religion as the Christian (unsuitable for a cut-throat and armed parasite, that is understood), that then the White Man, armed to the teeth, would be living to this day in perfect harmony with all those defenceless masses of mankind, that he describes as "natives." And, is it necessary to add, the world as a whole would be a far more peaceful place than it is at present.

Had the Beraber, or M'quil, bands sung sentimental hymns wherever they went: had they confessed incessantly to the people of the Oasis, with tears in their eyes, how wicked they were to oppress them: and then had they of course been at pains, as well, to arm the inhabitants of *ksar*, or of oasis, with Lebel rifles of the latest model and other weapons—*then* I daresay the Desert would soon have been in an indescribable uproar.—But I do not of course wish to be offensive and only point out this quite obvious analogy in passing, so that I may throw into a bold relief the nature of this cat and dog association—where, as throughout these barbarous countries, the soul of Anarchy and the soul of Order are embodied to perfection in Tent and in Oasis. [. . . .]

[BERBERS AND ARABS]

The Berbers have never been unmistakably masters in their own country. Even the Almoravids were conquerors in the name of a foreign cult, namely Islam. How has that come about?

The Arabs have always been their enemies. Yet even the great Arab historian Ibn-Khaldoun, speaks of the Berbers in the following terms:

"The Berbers have always been a powerful, formidable, brave and numerous people: a true nation like any other in the world, such as the Arab, the Persian, the Greek, or the Roman."

In spite of these great qualities, they always have been politically occulted. Even when paramount within the borders of Maghreb, for centuries together, it was as "Arabs" that they ruled. The Merenides, for instance, one of greatest dynasties in the history of Maghreb, were Zenatas, that is to say Berbers. Yet "the Zenatas," Gautier writes, "once arrived at pre-eminence, behaved as all other Berbers have— they blushed at the mere thought of being Berbers, they were ashamed of their origins." They pretended to be Arabs.

The Arabs, on their side (borrowing from the Romans) called these people *Berberi*—one can imagine with what nuance of second-hand contempt—*Barbaric* savages! And that is the name that has stuck to them. Even today a Berber, who is used to urban life and its civilized standards, has to swallow before he can utter the words (in reply to your question) "I am a Berber." It is difficult in the same way as are the words "I am a peasant," on the lips of an ex-ploughboy, or Shropshire Lad turned Cockney.

But Gautier I think does not anywhere make proper allowance for this central fact: namely that the Arabs had put their religion across, and so handcuffed and chloroformed the Berber. The insidious potions of a violent proselytizing theology more than account for the behaviour of the Zenatas. It was Allah, not Ocbah in short, who got them between the wind, once the Berbers had accepted Islam, and agreed to genuflect six times a day in the direction of the Red Sea.

The Arabs were "the Chosen People," and they never allowed the Berbers to forget it! (Oh how all-important, politically, to have a God of your own, gentlemen!—and not to have one of foreign make, imposed on you lock, stock and barrel, along with all the compelling theurgic machinery that goes with such an importation! How often this sort of debtor—that man *in debt for his religion*—must find himself

207

tripped up, or between the Devil and that deep sea that is a God who is never quite his own, but *somebody else's!* To which the Arab would doubtless reply, "More fool you for not having the gumption to manufacture one!")

When the Merinides became all-powerful Sultans [in the Thirteenth Century]—the Umbrella over their head, the prayers said in their name in all the Mosques—it was only elementary policy to give themselves out as not so much Arabs, as *Cherifs*—as enjoying direct authentic descent from the Prophet. It was *Islam* that imposed this upon them, and, of course, the exclusive, fanatical, character of that particular creed.

Nowhere, I think, has this been sufficiently insisted upon. Certainly Gautier has neglected it.

So all the great things the Berbers have done, they have done in the name of the Arab God. And from that it was only a step to doing it *as Arabs.* And that must after all be the main reason why the Arab has got the kudos for anything done by the Berber; that seems patent enough.

The Arab, it is true, not only got old Allah across and fixed him fast upon the back of the Botr or the Beranes, where he could never shake him off: he also taught him Arab arts and crafts—pottery and poetry. But after all the Berber didn't gain much that way. The Romans and before them the Carthaginians had done as much for him or more: and the Berbers were not such "barbarians" as all that. In the terrible resistance they put up (under Koceile and their sorceress-queen Kahena) against Arab invasion—in the Seventh Century literally wiping out (as in the Battle of the Nobles) not once, but repeatedly, the armies of the Arabs, and chasing them for two thousand miles, as far as Egypt—they were acting in concert with an organized and highly civilized power, that of Byzantium.

Everything, I think, points to *religion* being the key to this part of the mystery. (The Romans, like the French today, were "civilizers," were pagans, not religionists.) The strength of the Arabs lay in that.

On the other hand that does not entirely resolve the difficulty of why the Berbers have not got more out of being a "powerful, formidable, brave and numerous people" than they have. The presence of "a dual soul" is certainly somewhat at the bottom of it—that is the explanation of Gautier at all events and he is a person of the utmost good sense. It is because of *the dual soul of Maghreb*—the *nomadic* and the *sedentary.* That is why Maghreb was never one.

The imported religion—and such a religion too, one of the most ferocious and fantastic engines of mass-bigotry that the world has to show, anywhere in its well-stocked Chamber of Horrors—*that* gave them one "dual soul." And the fact that they have from earliest times been half nomads, half "sedentaries," did not make things any better—that bestowed upon them a *second* "dual soul" as it were. And perhaps, after all, of the two dualities in question, the second was the more important. That is perhaps why, in spite of being so "brave and numerous" ("like the Greeks, or the Persians"), they never in fact became "a nation" at all.

Indeed (to show how the "double soul," twice-over, worked) their great *national* upheavals have always been in the name of religion rather than of race. These spasms have been a sort of civil war, about the Arab Allah. They have always taken the form of a tribal *ruée*. Maghreb having been split up into these two parts—*one* that wandered outside the sedentary fold, and *the other* that sat down like a good boy inside it, and cultivated its garden—these "national awakenings" have invariably taken the painful and destructive form of the former flinging themselves upon the latter—on the ground that they were not religious enough. When the Desert Puritan had done his worst—founded yet one more desert dynasty and ruled for a century—the country fell apart again. It was never in order to be a "powerful, and redoubtable nation" that they took up arms: only to see which was the more outstanding Mohommedan, *not* the better Berber.—So they have always remained "brave and numerous"—as a race they are quite a distinct one, of fine physique, and seem to possess extraordinary qualities—but they have never been "a nation."

On the other hand, the Arabs have been a *nationality*—a very successful one, "like the Greek or Persian." And yet they too are divided into "sedentary" and "nomad", as much as are the Berbers. And indeed, as Nomads, they are a much more extreme type, it is generally held.—Gautier describes them as something like *the perfect nomad.* But it makes no difference, it didn't stop them from being a nationality. Allah, again!—So (leaving Allah out of it) are the Berbers perhaps too homekeeping on the whole? Are the Berber nomads not out and out nomads enough? Or the sedentaries not stationary enough?

Without answering this at once, it can be asserted with great confidence that there are no flies on the Berber Nomad: as a Nomad—"Beraber" or Touareg—he is a match for any armed vagabond in the world. Everyone is agreed that he is as much at home in his tent as an Englishman in his castellated suburban home—lawnmower, wireless set, five-foot of sooty rockery, privet hedge and all.

In spite of all this, the Berber is not the Arab. It may not be much to boast about, but the Berber is more like a European. He would *build* if he had a chance—not only dolmens but Houses of Parliament. *Underneath* he is bourgeois, whereas the Arab is not—scrape the fat Pascha in his palace and you discover the outlaw of the steppes. Scrape, on the other hand, the Berber and you might find at last something like a crop-headed Prussian court-official.

The Berber respects the law: he could make a citizen if allowed to. But the fact is he has been prevented for so long—all his more respectable instincts have been discouraged and dashed for so many centuries—that he no longer believes, it is to be feared, in respectability as practicable, at all events where he is concerned: the fatalism he has accepted at the hands of the Arab caused him to take it for granted that he must hasten from pillar to post and so he does.

It has been the Berber destiny to be exploited, not to be the exploiting one—although "brave" to a wonderful degree, it appears, and (as an exploited race) "formidable." [. . . .]

[THE BERBER AS "EUROPEAN"]

The Berber nature is like the European nature, as I have more than once hinted. And above all there is nothing *abstract* about it. Your Berber possesses that *personal* standpoint that endears. This is, who can say, a failing: but if so, it is a *European* failing—that no one can deny. Gautier for instance admits that the Arab is capable of essentials, in the sense that should he fall into religious strife it will not necessarily be about the personality of this gentleman or that, but really about *an idea* of sorts, even if not a very important one. Not about *a person* merely, at all events. "Not so with the Berber!" however, he says. No! "Whether in Christian Maghreb, or in Mussulman Maghreb, the only great religious convulsions that have shaken the country to its depths have never had anything to do with an aberrant conception of the divine. *There is there an indigence of ideas, and a passionate attachment to persons*, which is typically Berber."—And that, as a rule, is typically European too.

Donatism [in the Fourth Century African church] was not a heresy—it was a schism. But—still more European than that—it was actually a proletarian revolution. All the violent separatism of the average European, the "clannishness," distinguishes the Berber soul: all the pagan instincts are his at bottom—he is not really even a religionist. Why, when he wishes to have a religious war, he cannot even think up a point of dogma to have it about! He has to fall back upon the personal appearance, or the personal sanctity of such and such a person, or similar childishness. Indeed, he far outdoes the European, so it would seem, in all the most European of lovable shortcomings. He is warlike without purpose, impulsively personal without critical faculty, godless except for superstitious considerations. And, if he has not made *work* into a religion, he is by no means averse to work, as is the Arab, and could quite well make it into a sentimental cult one of these days, if his masters put it into his head to do so. But no Irish or Scottish factiousness could make a more undisciplined brawler than is the Berber, as quick to rush to his weapons apropos of nothing, as he is to put them down again and forget about it.—But I need not pursue the catalogue of these analogies, it is sufficient to say that the Berber inclines far more, in the matter of the more intimate springs of conduct, to the Occidental than to the Oriental. He is a fierce, rough, painstaking, home-loving, obedient, romantic, orderly, pathetic, chivalrous, easily-duped, Barbarian—if it is to be a Barbarian to be like this—attached to the things of the physical world, repelled by the abstract.

As to his "nomadism." The Berber is, I believe, a nomad, for physical reasons. Just as a nation with a long line of sea-coast is perforce a nation of *sailors*, so it is fairly obvious that a nation living upon the borders of the greatest desert in the world is perforce a nation of *nomads*.

But the Berber is not a true child of the desert I should think, if whatever we are told of the Touareg is true—and it must be true, for all people who knew them tell the same story. Such different people as Mr. E. F. Gautier and Lady Dorothy Mills describe the Touareg in much the same way. The latter for instance writes: "The Touareg is a born filibuster who loves fighting for its own sake, who is drunk with his own beauty and cunning and rapacity, and who, perhaps because he does not take life seriously, seems to get more out of it." (*The Road to Timbuktu*)

Even love, among the Touaregs, seems to have a strongly European character. "Love amongst this 'primitive' people," says Gautier, ". . . has a familiar air of gallantry, which in fact seems to be a caricature of our own. . . . *Le Flirt* is the grand preoccupation. This presupposes naturally cultivated, independent women, who are not absorbed exclusively by household cares.—Marriage occurs late, and is not a rule of life at all: the impenitent bachelor, of ripe years—the old maid—these are Western atrocities that can be met with among the Touaregs. . . . In order to understand the extreme oddity of this sort of affair, you have to remember that, elsewhere in the world, the Mussulman family invariably takes the form of the harem."

If you take the Touareg as the extreme example of Berberism, then, he does not seem a true child of the desert, for the desert does not seem to have had quite the effect upon him that you would expect. He seems to have treated the desert more as if it were the sea. Not "to take life seriously"—one can understand the sailor being like that, not a hermit of the desert. This lighthearted "filibuster" of the Sahara—with his paradoxical "old maids" and "old bachelors," and anything but "primitive" sexual habits, with his unlikely "sense of humour"—he produces an impression altogether the diametrical opposite to the Arab.

No wonder the Berber made such a wonderful sailor, in his other role of Corsair! The Touaregs always sound like buccaneers. They are the Norsemen of the African steppes. [. . . .]

All the Berber's weaknesses are engendered upon that hearty (Graeco-Roman) obsession for the purely concrete and the physical.

The intensity of the "inner-life"—the cultivation of those tracts within our nature where sensation is transformed into idea—is where a number of nations outside the European family have in the end the whip-hand of this Graeco-Roman schoolboy, too exclusively married to sensation. The European "individualist" has, it is true, been a spoilt child of fortune. But Europe—like "Barbary" or Berbery—has never been able to organize itself. It has not been given it to sink its tribal differences to a common end. And as a consequence today it looks as if its "Great White Day," as D. H. Lawrence called it, were at last to end.

We are, of course, *nous autres Européens*, complete barbarians, and those of us who affect to believe they are not so, are the most barbarous of all: for it is a thing that cannot be altered now, it is too late, and the most civilized thing to do is openly to confess it. How like, even, our history is growing to theirs! Sir Richard Burton, who was most intelligent, makes some very good remarks in his Introduction to Dr. Leared's book *Marocco and the Moors*. Here is an excellent passage, and very much to the point (this Introduction is dated Oct. 1, 1890):

> The Moors (are) a savage people, sharp-witted withal, who have studied and deeply appreciated the wild and reckless havoc which "Civilization," *versus* Native Rule, has wrought and still works in the Nile Valley. But these "Barbari" are fighting a losing fight. The time is coming when France and Spain, the Powers most interested in the matter, will, by perpetual pressure, get the better of some softer-headed "Caliph of our lord Mohammed, enthroned by Allah his will;" and the steam-whistle on the Tangier-Fez railroad shall destroy not only "feudalism," but fanaticism and privacy, lethargy and independence. Nor will the European occupant, after the danger and damage of defeating a nation of *fous furieux*, of fanatics brave to desperation, find great difficulty of securing his conquests. The invader has only to follow the frontier-policy of ancient Rome, ably imitated by the modern Briton. He will buy Maroccans to fight Maroccans; pay them liberally, officer them ably, and arm them efficiently. Wild races always and everywhere prove how greatly gold downweighs patriotism.

These "Barbarians" have lost their fight, as Burton foresaw would happen, and in the manner that he predicted. Gold everywhere has spoken: and Barbarians have been bought to fight Barbarians, and have conquered them. "Wild races always and everywhere prove how greatly gold downweighs patriotism"—and somewhat less "wild" races of Barbarians prove it, too, every day. I am of the opinion that the Berbers should have considered themselves rather lucky to have been "conquered" by the French. I can imagine many conquerors less pleasant than Lyautey, as I have already remarked. [. . . .]

213

[KASBAH-ART]

Now I am able to complete what I have to say upon the subject of the Kasbah-art. The Berber is anything, I should say, but in a position of abject submission to a High God. Even, I should guess, he is essentially the reverse—the true worship of the Berber peasant being the saint-cult of the Koubah, rather than the more abstract devotions indicated by the mosque. And in his Kasbah-art he seems to have put at the disposal of Man, and brought into the service of his personal egotism, all the resources of a monumental aesthetic developed originally for some far more abstract and lofty purpose. The effect is rather that of a cathedral organ being employed to accompany a Tango. These towers that are pharaonic *pylons* may be partly responsible for this sensation, which forces itself upon one's consciousness. But there are other factors as well, such as the alarming scale of these structures.

A parallel to these contradictory sensations is to be found in a sense in the New York skyscraper-architecture. For example, a colossal caricature of an Anglican church was the form several of these monstrous American buildings took: it was as though the New England architect, when he sat down to think out what shape he should give this prodigious block of masonry, had been unable to visualize any very large building that was not a church. Or it may, of course, have been the Magnate or Corporation that commissioned him to do it.

But this explanation of the Kasbah is entirely in harmony with what I have been supposing to be the true inner nature of this gifted "barbarian"—having this little *Renaissance* all on his own account, in the seclusion of the African Atlas, palace after palace springing up to house the Borgias of this epoch of princely *banditti*. The Berber is, as much as the European at his worst, in fact frantically *physical*—he is in love with force and power. And as to "individualism," no one can say, on that head, that he is a step behind no matter whom you may mention. As many as *fourteen times* he apostasized from Islam. Today he is only a Moslem out of habit, no doubt—and he might as well be that as anything else. His heart is more in the great Confrèreries, with their magical basis in a distant pre-Islamic past, or in the pagan deities that survive, their sanctuaries masquerading as a maraboutic shrine. And this quick-witted "Barbarian," of great personal charm, is capable, in the most ancient form under which we know him (namely the

Touareg), of precisely that *detachment* and *objectivity* that every European observer has remarked as belonging to him. As Lady Dorothy Mills has put it: "he does not take life seriously." As Gautier has put it: he "has a sense of humour."—But those are the great European virtues, are they not, which are at the basis of pure science and of pure art (two things which are far nearer together than is popularly imagined, of course).

In the Kasbah-builder all this can, I think, be divined. Such lofty and imposing structures, outside of Europe, have rarely occurred in response to a profane demand. Even the Borgias did not have vast temples built to glorify their temporal tyrannies. It is really probable, therefore, that, without knowing it, the Glaoui, the M'Touggi, and the Goundafi have achieved something a little unique. In conclusion, outside antiquity, or since the Renaissance, the rude productions of the contemporary Berber genius are, for the artist, the most interesting things to be met with this side of China, I should be inclined to say.

THE KASBAHS OF THE ATLAS

The great Kasbahs of the Atlas are a formidable explosion of Berber power; as far as we know (in this land without records, monumental or otherwise) its greatest. Most likely they will be its last. At grips with the great Kasbahs we shall find out all there is to be known of the essential Berbery, or Barbary. They are barbarous, if you like; but outside of China they are the greatest expression extant of the human being at this stage of the cycle of Earth-life.

All these great castles are in the High Atlas, in the Anti-Atlas, or in the mountains or plains of the South, or Sous. But the finest by far are in the High Atlas. And the workmen who are employed to build them all belong to one tribe, the Aït Ya Ya, living in a valley upon the Saharan slopes of those mountains, which wall in the desert on the north-west.

The oldest of the existing Kasbahs of the Great Lords of the Atlas, dates, I believe, from, at the most, eighty years ago. By far the greater number, however, are much more recent than that. As to the "Lords of the Atlas" themselves, they are also of very recent creation. They are self-created. Of the present reigning families of the High Atlas, namely the Glaoui, the Goundafi and the M'Touggi—only the M'Touggi dates from more than a century ago.

These enormous structures, called *Kasbah* (meaning fortress), must resemble the Pelasgian fortresses encountered by the first Greeks to invade Hellas. They are truly *cyclopean* in appearance, in spite of the fact that very little stone is employed in their construction. When in ruin, they remain as gigantic blocks, not of granite, but of mud. They have, all of them, the air of belonging to the civilization which had its headquarters in Crete and are of a truly grand and massive beauty. Often of very great architectural resource, most elaborately grouped, towers behind towers, their structural repertoire is suggestive of a civilization of the first order, in the background, rather than of a rustic tradition, however elaborate; they are, many of them, upon the boldest and vastest scale.

Who are the Kasbah builders? is one of the first questions that presents itself to the European artist. Well, it seems that they are certainly not gentlemen with brass plates upon the doors of their professional premises. They are nomads, of a rather special order— they must take cases of tools about with them on their donkeys, and today most probably picture-postcards or dog-eared snapshots in

217

their pockets, of the best castles they have built, and perhaps tattered testimonials in their Berber wallets or handsome vanity bags. They are simply Berber workmen who wander about offering to build castles for anyone who requires such a luxury, or if the client only wants a little mosque, or a fairly strong little fortified residence, suitable for a modest marabout, without much following, why, then *that*! The trades of architect and of master-mason are essentially nomadic, and these two trades are identical, and no doubt nomadic plumbers move along with them too—though *Carver and Plumber* may be a trade designation and these functions devolve upon one and the same person, for all I know.

"Le décor berbère a bien pour qualité propre la grandeur," say Terrasse and Hainaut; and certainly nothing could be more unlike the structureless confections of the Hispano-Mauresque than the type of these Kasbahs of the dictators of the High Atlas. It would, I suppose today, be generally conceded that Hispano-Mauresque—that is to say the architectural tradition responsible for the Alhambra (though not for the fountain of lions, which was a rebel gesture on the part of one of the last Moorish kings of Granada, restless under the barren rigours of the Koranic compulsions, which stamped out organic form, and put a *Verbot* upon life altogether, and for which, of course, the body of a lion in stone would be a trespass)—most people would even be eager to concede that this Hispano-Arabian pastry was the reverse of a great art-form. We have at present (how thankful we should be for this small mercy) the *monumental* appetite! And Hispano-Mauresque is the opposite of monumental: it is a feeble and unenterprising architecture; the dull shell is provided, and then the interior-decorator and the birthday-cake carver are let loose on it, and these minor personages are relied upon to drench it in ornament, and make it look as if it were a great swell after all, and a match for the most impressive monuments of any civilization whatever.

Luckily, here at least, all fashionable thought is with us: it is almost, if not quite, fashionably correct to prefer the monumental beauty of the Berber Kasbah, to the tiresome surface elaborations of the Arab-born Hispano-Mauresque. I took full advantage of this fact not to stop and write a chapter on the city of Fez in my book *Filibusters in Barbary*: and I am able to inform you without danger of incurring your contempt, I know, that while in Fez I visited *no* Merdersas—or any Merdersas anywhere else. A mosque is for me a stork's nest, nothing more. As such it serves its purpose. I confess that I am unable to understand why such an intelligent "author" as Mr. Richard Hughes should import a mock mosque into Wales, as I understand that he has, along with some friends, and why it should amuse him to dress up as an Arab and, I suppose, go and shout from the top of it.

But if the Berber tradition is an ancient one, how did it withstand the assaults of Arab taste? In the first place no doubt the absence of the written word (except for Tifinar there has never been in Berbery anything but the spoken language) has been the most powerful factor of any in mummifying a tradition that may be coeval with Knossos, or the early history of the Nile Valley. But the Kasbah art is also a part, essentially, of the scene in which it occurs. The walls of the Kasbah are made of the surrounding earth. When the Kasbah is a red Kasbah, the valley in which it stands is a red valley. With its tower of mud-concrete it is a puissant organization, and it owes its organization so much to the earth in which it is set that it has the air almost of some colossal vegetation, sprouting in this element of rock or mud. Its summits are spiked like a cactus: its flanks are marked and patched as if it were a rectilinear stump of a cyclopean cane, or a people of such stumps, webbed to each other by big pitted and spongy battlements: or sometimes the roofed towers, with their flat mud hats, blunt-edged, and with the thick blurred shadows of their eaves, appear like groups of some toad-red fungus.

Battered into impressive vertical planes, with its portholes or pencil-like slits high up, the earth of the mountain does not become rock, it becomes pocked and scarred. It is only battered into an imperfect concrete. By nature it is horizontal. It can only become a cliff—an elegant fragment of cliff—with difficulty. Its surface, where the water has splashed upon its declivities, is soon mottled like the face of a tawny cheese.

Near the tops of these feudal pinnacles of mud a system of rather Mexican ornament occurs. These are the rectilinear abstractions of the Berber rug, sometimes with disks, expanding stars, or framed diamonds. Often in an open space there are noughts and crosses, or else figures reminiscent of the Tifinar alphabet.

But no one could rush into these mountains and settle there, quarry out of the earth stiff ramparts of *pisé*, and produce great plastic fortress-prisons, lettered with coarse hieroglyphs, that so astonishingly belong to the Atlas as these Kasbahs do. They are the wild fruit of these particular short scorched plains or volcanic gorges; as they descend towards the Sahara from the central crater of Sirwa, the Kasbahs become more and more magnificent. The *ksar* of Ouarzazat is probably the culmination of this great out-cropping of the life—of man and of nature—of the High Atlas.

The Kasbah is as much a work of nature as a hive or ant-city, in one sense then. Only a people like the Berber, who know nothing of anything but nature, always in the company of the sun, the rocks, the

219

desert, could have produced them exactly as they are; they are so fine, in the first place, because of this great air of having been done unconsciously—as the animal, or as the human genius, functions. But also they could not have been produced without the existence of some very splendid tradition of building. In the past, in a world no doubt less primitive than this, these great habits of building had their beginning.

The first architectural oddity to strike the observer is the strange appearance—that is like a trick of perspective—of all these towers drawing together as they rise into the air. This in fact is the case: the flanking towers are tapered from the base up. In some cases, in the course of an ascent of, say, forty or fifty feet they may lose as much as a quarter of their girth. This obliquity of the Egyptian pylon, recalling immediately the ancient temples of the valley of the Nile, is probably a first clue to the ancestry of these buildings. The diminishing silhouette of the pylon (only two or three times as high)—in place of the sharply-projecting cavetto of the former, if the tower is high, there is a combed and martial crest—is found again everywhere in the heart of the Atlas.

In various places upon the rocks of the Saharan Atlas, or that eastern part of it which has been accessible to the European, designs of animals are seen. Near Figuig, for instance, there are two rock carvings of a ram, with the solar disk between its horns flanked with the uræus.

In Karnak, Gautier tells us, and in the temples of Upper Egypt, it is impossible to see the criocephalic Ammon-Ra, represented so often in the wall paintings, without immediately being struck with the analogy between Ammon-Ra and the Ram of the Atlas. "It is exactly the same profile of the same head," he tells us, "bearing the same disk, similarly flanked—the solar disk, in short. A necklace adds still further to the resemblance."

And *Ammon* is the god of the Saharan oases. So it is natural enough that his image should be found at Figuig, the gate of the Sahara. Ammon is not a very old god. The cult of Ammon-Ra dates from the eighteenth dynasty (that is to say, roughly 1,500 years before Christ). So we are well inside the temporal frontiers assigned by history to the Berber races.

Nowhere else in the world, as far as I know, is there any monumental building of this order, with a façade of dual towers, tapering in the manner of the Egyptian pylon, and producing exactly this effect, except the Kasbah of the Atlas. And in spite of the Libyan Desert and the Sahara, the Atlas is, after all, the next-door neighbour of the Nile, in the same way almost as it is the neighbour of the Niger. Between

220

the Eastern and Western Soudan and the Atlas there is nothing but the desert routes—a dream a few days long upon the back of a camel.

The resemblance has also been insisted upon between the Berber Kasbah-art and the Soudanese *Tatta* or Mosque architecture, of Timbuctoo, for instance. But I think this applies much more to the *nouala*. That is obviously the same thing as the Congo hut. Or it applies, of course, to the architecture of Tiznit, the desert city to the south of Agadir, built where the steppes of the Rio de Oro begin. Tiznit and Timbuctoo are in many respects interchangeable. The principal mosque of Tiznit, bristling with spikes like a hedgehog, the Brodj el Rhemis ramparts, could take their place among the spiked sugar-loaf effects of Timbuctoo without anyone remarking their intrusion, I should think.

The Kasbah itself is, in principle, a simple structure of four gigantic walls of mud concrete, at right angles to each other. Inside, the quadrangle so contained harbours the house of the chief, his stables, stores, barracks and so forth. At each corner (or only at two of the corners) are the pylon-like towers. That is how the Kasbah *starts*. When the local cantonal President first starts upon his career of *Amghar* it may be more or less that. But this fortified quadrangle No. 1 has built up against it a quadrangle No. 2, probably larger, or perhaps smaller, upon a higher or lower level than itself. Just as a Berber workman shuns a perfect symmetry on all occasions, and no two sides of a porch or two towers are exactly alike, so he would never dream, if asked to add a second towered quadrangle to the first, of making a facsimile of No. 1. There are no *facsimiles* in his repertoire. Besides, when a super-Kasbah, of towered quadrangle upon towered quadrangle, begins piling itself up, the particular purpose of each fresh monumental accretion has to be taken into account. The Sheik, or Caïd, has increased in power; he has an extra two dozen women, say; guests are more numerous and frequent; a hundred more black slaves are used in farm work; his armed guards have increased in numbers. The new buildings take the form implied by these new needs. But there is, of course, no end to the variety of circumstance dictating the growth, embellishment, or strengthening of the fortress. If it is to become a super-Kasbah, it rapidly becomes a kind of town, of the order of Animiter. It is the first stages of Babylon. Turkish-bath architecture is imported into it (as also, in fact, too, Turkish baths).

That, according to the standards of a classic art, or the most perfectly adjusted and organized civilization, this method is unsatisfactory, is true enough. But this is a *barbaric* creation, admittedly, of the same kind as a Shakespearean play: its canons are romantic ones, or those of expediency, realized in the midst of a social chaos.

[KASBAHS AND SOUKS—
A FORTRESS MENTALITY]

The monumental profanity of the Berber stamps him (I think I have sufficiently demonstrated that) as belonging rather to the Occident than to the "Orient" (as conventionally understood). The Berber egotism, careless of the jealous eye of God, indeed an utter stranger to such an "Oriental" notion, lifts himself higher into the air, in his imposing towers, than any other "savage" we have ever heard of, in a manner that would bring a cold sweat for instance to the superstitious Punic back: employing all the monumental architectural ordnance of a great religion to celebrate the *hubris* of a petty chief.

There is, it is true, another "savage"—one more truly savage than the Berber I think—whom you might claim to have even outdone him, and that is the American: and, as I have already said, the Atlas architecture reminded me more of New York City than of anything else. And in New York a young Middle West puritan—he was a taxi-driver—some years ago prophesied to me that the wrath of God would one day make an end of New York City—it was *far too high*, he informed me: casting his eye up into the heavens, in the direction of the ecclesiastical pinnacle of the Woolworth Building, he assured me that it had not been intended by Man's Maker (who had deliberately made him of a certain size, fixing about six foot three as the limit—he suggested that a giant of say eight feet, or even a man of six foot seven, was already taking heavy risks)—Man's Maker had not intended Man to build himself these giddy towers!—It was the echo of the booming of the Hebrew prophet in the mouth of this youthful Anglo-Saxon savage.

We can now turn to another aspect of the historical, or psychological, problems posed by Berber Architecture. The answer to all our questions regarding the nature of the "nomadism" of the Berber is to be sought in these immense strongholds.

I will put this answer in a nutshell. Here it is: *The only terms upon which a Berber can stand still, much less lie down, is to build himself a fortress.* This is an absolute rule for the whole of Maghreb. Berbery is indeed the *Bled-el-khouf*—the "Pays de la Peur."

There are only two sorts of Berber—the Berber incessantly on the move—the "nomad": or the Berber who lives in a towered and battlemented stronghold.

You can drive for hours in the Valley of the Sous, or anywhere in the South of Morocco, without ever seeing any dwelling (outside of a *nouala*) that is not a stronghold. The policing of the North by the European has here and there brought about modifications: but in the South there is no exception to the rule.

To drive through fifty kilometres of country in the fertile Valley of the Sous is to pass along a chain of village-fortresses. The cities are all walled cities of course—Marrakech, Taroudant, Tiznit. In Marrakech until six years ago the gates of the native city were shut at sunset. Still the gates of Taroudant and Tiznit are held by an armed guard.

But how much the Berber must desire in his heart to settle down, *to be at such immense pains to do so*! He must be one of the most authentic of "sedentaries" to build for himself these impregnable shells, rather than just wander off with a few goats and live beneath the stars—*à la belle étoile*—and spare himself all the hard work and anxiety of being a "sedentary"! For at the best of times he does not get much out of being "sedentary." Every fourth year is an agricultural catastrophe; and generally speaking he has to fight nature tooth and nail for every drop of water he gets.

What a bourgeois! And of course what amazing strength of mind and profound pig-headedness! He will be "sedentary"—when all the world is nomad! Everywhere in the midst of deserts, nowhere more than a few hours ride away from the greatest waste in the world, he sets his teeth and digs himself in. But these are only the most energetic and intelligent Berbers, we must assume. More than half of the Berber world is still in a state of nomadic flux. These are doubtless the great crowds of "Barbari" who have thrown up the sponge, and embraced forever the nomadic condition. But even in that the Berber displays his typical obstinacy. For, once he has made up his mind to drift hither and thither, nothing will turn him from his restless aberration!

The Kasbah, the really prodigious one, is the ultimate expression of the great sedentary resolve to stop in one place at all costs—and, of course, to lay in a store of the goods of this world, to rise above the nomad plane. But it is in vain. For living under such conditions is like having to plough a field in armour, or cultivate a garden which is under shell-fire night and day. It is not as though, here and there, at long last, the man could come out of his stronghold and work in the open unmolested. He has never been able to do that. His fortress is also an oasis. For a few yards round it there is cultivation. Then there is a big blank space, a few fields, and then another fortress. Sooner or later comes the limitless desert, and with that you get the *ksar*, with the nomad gunmen camped against its walls.

DESERT SOUKH

The reason for this sad state of affairs (and that it is sad all the Berber literature testifies) is no doubt largely geographic. The Sahara, and the saline and steppian character of Maghreb itself, are responsible. And the Arab, too, has borne his part.

All that is not *Kasbah*, or fortress, is *Souk*. These entrenched and fortified villages, with their watch-towers always manned (as much a matter of course as a look-out in the crow's-nest of a ship)—always at war with each other or preparing for war, must nevertheless buy and sell, in a simple way. The men must get their hair cut, or be bled or branded: and the women have to be constantly adding to the mass of rough jewelry with which they are already everywhere overwhelmed, or they require an amulet against the indigestion, caused by *couscous* or too much cheap green tea. Rifles and knives are necessary. Donkeys and camels have to be sold.

In a more peaceful country these requirements would be met by a "market-town." Upon some naturally central spot a small township would spring up, and there, once a week, the villagers from the surrounding country would meet and engage in a little barter and gossip.

This is not at all what happens in Maghreb. All villages there are fortified, barred and bolted: and no village would dream of consenting to a horde of people from other villages pouring into it once a week, however much they paid it for the privilege.—This is the "Pays de la Peur!" Such a "market-town" would be inconceivable. How much the French occupation may modify all this it is impossible to say: at present the Berber is still distrustful of this Roman Peace, and adapts himself to it gingerly.

So, seeing that they cannot meet in a fortified town or village, what they do is this. A certain number of villages select a deserted and unprepossessing spot, for preference in the middle of a stony desert. There they build a sort of empty shell-village of low stone huts, with no doors. Usually this village takes the form of a street, the rows of gaping cells facing each other. Sometimes there is more than one street: sometimes only a one-sided street. This they call a *Souk* (pronounced "sook").

For this strange place they next find a name. They call it, not Stonehill Market, or Market-Hungerford, or Market-Gallowshill (though it usually would live up to some such name as the latter, being almost always suggestive of the most gloomy possible associations)— they call it just Wednesday, or Monday. It is an abstract trysting place. *Souk-el-Arba—Souk-el-Thnine*: the Souk of Wednesday, the Souk of Monday.

To these Souks, until very recently, everyone would come armed with rifles, and of course daggers. (Every Berber carries a dagger,

225

hung upon a cord which passes over his right shoulder: it is the equivalent of the sword of the European gentleman and is today in the nature of an ornament. The Jew is not allowed, or was not until recently allowed, to carry one, not being a "gentleman.")

So this is the invariable rule of the Souk—it is a rough, miniature, open, village, left empty, except upon a specified day.—The Souk in this sense is the only place in "Barbary" which has not defensive fortifications of ramparts and towers.

But there are the Souks of the city. That there are so few cities in Morocco is the result, of course, of the conditions described above. For no village ever becoming a town, or common centre, it cannot obviously become a city.

A few very great and powerful conquerors, like Tachefin, have founded a city. Marrakech was his. And, as I have said, it was a monster Souk. It was a tribal place of rendezvous—a *market-city*, which Tachefin was powerful enough to guarantee as *safe*. It was not a Souk that six days out of the seven was empty. Mud huts gathered round it: craftsmen were installed in it. It was a permanent Souk.

The extreme paucity of cities is one of the main characteristics of Morocco. To use Budgett Meakin's enumeration—"There are only three inland cities properly so called, Fez ... Marrakech ... and Mequinez (Meknes). With these exceptions the only great centres of population are on the coast." There are nine of these: but they are much smaller, and owe their existence today largely to Europeans. In the South of Morocco, however, there are only Marrakech and Taroudant.

The Souk (the Souk of the *bled*) explains this entirely.

Accompanying this chapter are drawings of Souks of this order, as seen upon a day when there is no market. The stone hovels are built by placing one boulder upon another, until a rough cell about five feet high, and of as much depth and width, is built. Often there are other small buildings as well, perhaps covered, with a walled-in court six feet across: a café that would be. Also every Souk has tripods of rough-hewn poles, which resemble a stunted gallows-tree (as if in readiness to dispatch batches of dwarfs). These tripods are for the butchers.

If you examine these gaping cells of rough stone, you will generally not find so much as a bead, a bone or a thread left there from the last occasion upon which they were occupied. But in one or more of the cells you will find a black sprinkling of blood. This you will suppose is where the butchers have squatted. But such is not the case. It is the place where men have been "cupped" or bled. Every Berber is bled about once a month by the barber-apothecary, or whenever he has a headache. Whenever a Berber puts his hand to his forehead and remarks that he has a headache, you know that he is reflecting that it is about time he was bled or cupped, again. The neck is scratched with the razor, a tin cup is clapped on it, the air in the cup is exhausted by the barber sucking a tube, which enters the cup near the top. The patient bends back so that the tin cup may hang down.

The barber is also the dentist. He does not stop teeth, but with an old key-wrench (manufactured for backward countries in France or Germany) he will pull a tooth out. The Berber teeth are splendid, so he does not do much of this.—Branding I believe is fairly common. If a man complains of a pain in the kidney, he is "fired"—that is to say some smith will burn him with a piece of hot iron somewhere in the direction of the kidney. Rohlfs introduced caustic into Morocco—this they called "cold fire," in contradistinction to branding.

But when the Souk is full it is like any other market, more or less. It is when there is nobody there that you get at the root of its meaning. And a sinister shell it generally is, with gaping gums of built-up boulder-stones. These universally met-with, somewhat more organized Stonehenges—with their butcher-gallows nearby—are if anything more suggestive of the inner facts of the life of the Berber than are the enormous Kasbahs of the Mountain Dictators.

At the beginning of my account of the Kasbah I remarked that this outburst of Berber Art was probably the last that would occur. I think it is obvious that this must be so, for the French have penetrated the Atlas and organized their domination with a scientific thoroughness that the Maghzen had no means of doing. It is not more than a half dozen years since the French have been able really to make free of the High Atlas. But now the tourist may go almost anywhere in safety, and the *Syndicat d'Initiative* helps him comfortably to spots to which ten years ago he could not have gone without great risk.

But most important of all, the "Great Lords of the Atlas" are no longer the great personages they were in the time of the Tharauds, when they wrote of their "Grands Seigneurs de l'Atlas." They are still there, it is true. These great mountain dictators have transformed their allegiance from the Sultan to the French, or rather, with the Maghzen, passed (for a consideration of course) under French protection. What these "considerations" were we are not told, but they must have got (all of the principal ones) very substantial sums. Their bribes have for the most part been dissipated.

I have seen in Marrakech all these "Great Lords of the Atlas," except the Glaoui. The M'Touggi is an impressive chief. The Goundafi is a spectacled man, of somewhat mild appearance: you could easily imagine that you had his grandfather, the village schoolmaster of Tagontaft, there before you.—The Glaoui they say is still rich. His brother is the Pascha of Marrakech. Between them they have managed their affairs well. But not so the others: they, it appears, are chronically insolvent, and mortgaged up to the eyes or higher—they are scarcely any longer to be regarded as effective chiefs, much less dictators. They have nothing more that they can sell or pawn except their skins. No bank will advance them a Hassani dollar more. All that they are supposed to control has in fact passed into the hands of other people.

No more Kasbahs under these circumstances are built; nor ever will be again upon that scale, it is to be supposed. By way of these accommodating dictators the French have rapidly reached the mastery of almost the whole of the High Atlas. There will be no more *Amghars*, except such as may be from time to time appointed by the French. And all those political circumstances that brought the Atlas Dictator, and so the great mountain Kasbahs, into being, are now permanently transformed. The Kasbahs themselves, a century hence, will probably have vanished—in a business-like way, from a charge of military dynamite, or else from abandonment and neglect.

POSTSCRIPT

"POOR BRAVE LITTLE BARBARY"

The last stand of the Berber nation, in the Atlas mountains, has lately been occupying the attention of the world. [. . . .] It is not without significance that simultaneously Andorra and the Atlas are in the news. Both are being attacked by the French. An army of policemen has been sent into Andorra by the French government to make Andorra safe for international capital, and to break up the ancient republican system that has obtained there for nearly a millennium. And into the Atlas the same government has sent German mercenaries to make the Atlas safe, again for European capital. [. . . .] The poor, brave little Barbary that is being bullied into subjection by mercenaries is a European race, to look at not at all unlike Andorrans, or the blacker of the Welsh, and probably of a not dissimilar stock. [. . . .] When you consider that, although the Berbers occupy the largest area of any racial stock in Africa, nevertheless the Atlas or the Riff—the only part of Morocco entirely Berber—is not so large that it could not be called the "poor little Atlas": that they are Europeans like ourselves—if that is any recommendation—and that their resentment at being overrun is at least equal to that of the "brave little Belgians" of the War, it does, I think, reflect upon our logic in political matters that we are so complacent at the spectacle of the destruction of their liberty. And it, perhaps, is a little ironical that the French can only do it at all with the assistance of German troops.

BIBLIOGRAPHY

SOME OF THE BOOKS USED BY LEWIS

Henri Basset, *Essai sur la littérature des Berbères* (Algiers, 1920)

R. B. Cunninghame Graham, *Mogreb-el-Acksa: A Journey in Morocco* (London, 1898)

Vicomte Charles de Foucauld, *Reconnaissance au Maroc* (Paris, 1898)

Antoine de Saint-Exupéry, *Vol de nuit* (Paris, 1931)

E. F. Gautier, *Le Sahara* (Paris, 1928)
      Les Siècles obscurs du Maghreb (Paris, 1927)

Jan and Cora Gordon, *Star-dust in Hollywood* (London, 1930)

Stéphane Gsell, *Histoire ancienne de l'Afrique du Nord*, Vols I & II (Paris, 1928)

Hakluyt's Voyages

Georges Hardy, *Le Maroc* (Paris, 1930)
      Le Sahara (Paris, 1930)

Walter B. Harris, *Tafilet: The Narrative of a Journey of Exploration in the Atlas Mountains and the Oases of the North-West Sahara* (Edinburgh, 1895)

Joseph D. Hooker, John Ball and George Maw, *Marocco and the Great Atlas* (London, 1879)

Lieutenant-Colonel L. Justinard, *Tribus berbères: Les Aït Ba Amran* (Paris, 1930)

Joseph Kessel, *Vent de sable* (Paris, 1929)

Arthur Leared, *Marocco and the Moors,* introduction by Sir Richard Burton (London, 1891)

Budgett Meakin, *Life in Morocco* (London, 1905)
      The Moorish Empire (London, 1899)
      The Moors (London, 1902)

Lady Dorothy Mills, *The Road to Timbuktu* (London, 1924)

Robert Montagne, *Les Berbères et le Makhzen dans le Sud du Maroc* (Paris, 1930)

Plato, *Timaeus*
    Critias

Gerhard Rohlfs, *Adventures in Morocco* (London, 1874)

V. C. Scott O'Connor, *A Vision of Morocco: the Far West of Islam* (London, 1923)

Jérome et Jean Tharaud, *Marrakech ou les Seigneurs de l'Atlas* (Paris, 1920)

Joseph Thomson, *Travels in the Atlas and Southern Morocco* (London, 1889)

NOTES ON ILLUSTRATIONS

("M" refers to the descriptive catalogue contained in Walter Michel's
Wyndham Lewis: Paintings and Drawings, 1971)

Cover: "A Berber Stronghold in the Valley of the Sous," M707.

Frontispiece: "Berber Horseman." Pencil, pen and ink and watercolour, heightened with body colour. Private collection.

P.28 "Two Japanese Officers," M731. Private collection.

P.32 "The Queen of the High Table," M722.

P.48 "Design for 'Islamic Sensations'," M713. Private collection.

P.68 "Nouala." From reproduction for 1931 *Everyman* magazine
serialization of *Filibusters in Barbary*.

P.72 "A Hut of Petrol Tins," M716.

P.78 "The Tomb of Tachefin," M729.

P.118 "Berber Woman." Pencil and watercolour. Private collection.

P.144 "French Soldier in Morocco," M715.

P.159 "Portrait of a 'Blue Woman'," M719. Private collection.

P.198 "Desert Soukh," M712. Herbert F. Johnson Museum of Art,
Cornell University.

P.216 "A Kasbah in the Atlas," M717. Private collection.

P.224 "Desert Soukh," M711.

P.230 "Head of an Arab Horse." Detail. Chalk, pencil and watercolour.
Private collection.

The Sous

Heartland of
The Berbers

MEDITERRANEAN

SICILY

SPAIN

ALGERIA

Alicante

Oran
Tlemcen

Tangier
Tetouan
Larache
THE RIFF (Sp.)
Rabat
Casablanca
Mazagan
Fedhala
Safi
Mogador
Agadir

Ajdir
Oujda
Fez
Taza
Meknes
Figuig

MOROCCO

Marrakech
TAFILALET
THE SOUS

Cap Dra

CANARIES

Cap Juby

Villa
Cisneros

RIO DE ORO
(SPANISH SAHARA)

Saguia el Hamra
Smara

MAURETANIA

Port Etienne

Sidi bou Otman

Demnate

Marrakech

Telouet
Animiter

Ouarzazat

High Atlas

Jebel
Siroua

Anti Atlas

Irherm

Taroudant

Oued Sous

PLAIN OF
THE SOUS

Inezgane
Fount
Agadir

Dar
Lahouisine
Biougra

Assads
Aït Baha

Jebel
Lesk
Tafraout

Kerdous

Tazerwalt
area

Zaïa
Ilirla

Tiznit

Ifni
(Sp.)

Oued
Noun

N

**Morocco
and its
Environs
1931**

Printed January 1983 in Santa Barbara & Ann Arbor
for the Black Sparrow Press by Graham Mackintosh
& Edwards Brothers Inc. Design by Barbara Martin.
This edition is printed in paper wrappers; there
are 500 cloth trade copies; & 226 deluxe copies handbound
in boards by Earle Gray have been numbered & signed by
the Editor.

Wyndham Lewis (1882-1957) was a novelist, painter, essayist, poet, critic, polemicist and one of the truly dynamic forces in literature and art in the Twentieth Century. He was the founder of Vorticism, the only original movement in Twentieth Century English painting. The author of *Tarr* (1918), *The Lion and the Fox* (1927), *Time and Western Man* (1927), *The Apes of God* (1930), *The Revenge for Love* (1937), and *Self Condemned* (1954), Lewis was ranked highly by his important contemporaries: "the most fascinating personality of our time . . . the most distinguished living novelist" (T. S. Eliot), "the only English writer who can be compared to Dostoievsky" (Ezra Pound).

C. J. Fox was editor, with Walter Michel, of *Wyndham Lewis on Art* (Thames and Hudson, 1971) and, with Robert T. Chapman, of a collection of short fiction by Lewis, *Unlucky for Pringle* (Vision Press, 1973). He also edited *Enemy Salvoes* (Vision Press, 1975), a selection of Lewis's literary criticism. He is a former editor of the newsletter of the Wyndham Lewis Society and has published articles on David Jones, Karl Kraus and Robinson Jeffers, as well as reviewing for the magazine, *PN Review*. A Canadian, he worked as a correspondent in London, Paris and Brussels for the Canadian Press news agency and now is an editor in London with Reuters.